International Criminal Justice Series

Volume 12

Series Information

The *International Criminal Justice Series* aims to create a platform for publications in the whole field of international criminal justice. It, therefore, deals with issues relating, among others, to:

- the work of international criminal courts and tribunals;
- transitional justice approaches in different countries;
- international anti-corruption and anti-money laundering initiatives;
- the history of international criminal law.

The series concentrates on themes pertinent to developing countries. It is peer-reviewed and seeks to publish high-quality works emanating from excellent scholars, in particular from African countries.

Editorial Office

Prof. Dr. Gerhard Werle
Humboldt-Universität zu Berlin
Faculty of Law
Unter den Linden 6,
10099 Berlin, Germany
gerhard.werle@rewi.hu-berlin.de
moritz.vormbaum@rewi.hu-berlin.de

More information about this series at http://www.springer.com/series/13470

Verena Zoppei

Anti-Money Laundering Law: Socio-Legal Perspectives on the Effectiveness of German Practices

ASSER PRESS

Springer

Verena Zoppei
International Security Division
German Institute for International
and Security Affairs
Berlin
Germany

ISSN 2352-6718 ISSN 2352-6726 (electronic)
International Criminal Justice Series
ISBN 978-94-6265-179-1 ISBN 978-94-6265-180-7 (eBook)
DOI 10.1007/978-94-6265-180-7

Library of Congress Control Number: 2017937919

Published by T.M.C. ASSER PRESS, The Hague, The Netherlands www.asserpress.nl
Produced and distributed for T.M.C. ASSER PRESS by Springer-Verlag Berlin Heidelberg

Printed on acid-free paper

This T.M.C. ASSER PRESS imprint is published by Springer Nature
The registered company is Springer-Verlag GmbH Germany
The registered company address is: Heidelberger Platz 3, 14197 Berlin, Germany

Acknowledgements

Many valuable people have contributed to the discovery process that has allowed me to write this book. I would like to especially thank Prof. Fernandez, who motivated me with his enlightening and inspiring lectures on international law relating to money laundering, and who supported me strongly in the publication of this book.

I am also enormously thankful to Prof. Heinrich, whose supervision has been fundamental. I am grateful to have had the opportunity of discussing with him the challenging issues confronting German criminal law. I amply enjoyed our exchange of information, and I found particularly inspiring the discussions on doctrinal matters. I would like to thank Prof. Mancini for the supervision of the methodological part, and I appreciate highly the support she lent me in consultation with her and in dealing with practical challenges inherent in the undertaking research at the doctoral level.

I am very thankful to Prof. Werle for having given me the opportunity to take part in the LL.M. programme 'Transnational Criminal Justice and Crime Prevention: An International and African perspective' at the University of the Western Cape in Cape Town. The course afforded a chance to widen my perspective on international anti-money laundering law. I am also thankful for having had the opportunity of being part of his department and profiting from the exchange between experts, and among them especially Mark Pieth, and scholars from all over the world.

I am honoured to thank Prof. Dalla Chiesa, who, to me, is a wonderful example of an academic devoted to social causes, and whose profound sociological knowledge about mafia-related issues has influenced my reflections and improved the quality of my work.

This study has benefited hugely from Prof. Ferrari's theories on legal effectiveness. I am so glad to have had a chance to discuss personally my research with both him, with Prof. Pannarale, Prof. Sbraccia, and Prof. Campesi. I am also heavily indebted to Prof. Villegas, whom I met during the initial stages of my research and who inspired me to set the socio-legal, theoretical critical framework which guided me in approaching the topic of my research.

I had a chance to meet personally Andreas Frank, a *Don Quichotte*, as he defines himself, one of the most venerated money laundering law experts in Germany, whose disenchanted approach towards anti-money laundering policy and politics helped to inform my critical reflections.

I am grateful to Regine Schöneberg for having always stressed the importance of empirical research and for having appreciated my work and giving me the chance to engage with different scholars who have written on the topic of transnational organised crime.

I am grateful to have spent some time at the International Institute for the Sociology of Law of Oñati as a visiting scholar. I thank in particular Prof. Czarnota for his precious advice.

I am thankful to Lars Kroidl, who put me in contact with defence attorneys for the purpose of the empirical research; many thanks to Mr. Finger, who, besides accepting to be interviewed, gave me valuable input on new political developments relating to the anti-money laundering regime. Ambos Weibel, too, I thank for giving me the opportunity to divulge to the greater public some of the considerations triggered by the research. I am grateful for the insights that were shared with me by senior, a researcher of the South African Institute of Security Studies, Charles Goredema, and by Tax Justice Network's founder, John Christensen, whom I have met throughout the duration of my research. I am much indebted to Markus Henn and Markus Meinzer, with whom I had an interesting exchange of opinions on the German anti-money laundering regime. I am especially thankful to all the interviewees.

Many thanks to the Law and Society Institute of the Humboldt University for having affording me an opportunity to discuss my research project with other scholars. I am thankful to the anonymous reviewers of the European Review on Organised Crime and to the staff of the Standing Group on Organised Crime for having given me the opportunity to present some of the findings of my research. My gratitude goes out to Mr. Delalande and Prof. Killias for giving me the opportunity to hear different views on anti-money laundering legislation. I would like to thank the Caroline von Humboldt Excellence Initiative for having supported me financially.

Gratitude is owed to my fellow doctoral degree colleagues, in particular Marshet Seada, Matteo, Silvia, Irene, Carolina, Riccardo, Fiammetta, Marianna, Ana Carolina Oliveira, Cristina Martin Asensio, Barbara, Chantal, Marisa, and Giulia.

I am immensely thankful to the Association *Mafia? Nein Danke! e V.*, and particularly to Sarah, Sandro, Luigino, Giulia and Giulia, Vera, Marta, Gisella, Fabio, Laura, Florian, Gabriella, Bianca and Michael, and Luigi, who have always motivated me. I owe thanks to the authors Ombretta Ingrascì, Stefania Limiti, Claudio Fava, and Angela Iantosca, who inspired me with their mafia-related stories.

Last but not least, I am very grateful to my boyfriend, my family, and my friends.

Very special thanks I owe Till, who went through the most difficult moments that I experienced during my experience and patiently supported me, both practically, with his ideas, comments and translations, and spiritually, by reminding me not to take things too seriously. Without him, I would have not been able to accomplish such an ambitious project. I would like to thank my brother Federico, who has always reminded me that things can be seen from different perspectives.

A great many thanks I owe my parents Maria and Giancarlo for having infused me with the curiosity and the passion for learning. I am thankful to my grandparents Olga, Rosa and Saverio, and to my relatives Eva and Marco, Ute and Horst, Maria, Vincenzo and Angelo.

I am deeply thankful to my friends Lavinia, Chiara, Serena, Lorenza, Laura, Giulia, Anna, Carme and Carme, Valeria and Andrea, Camilla, Jenny and Docque, Mary and Daniele, Stefi, Antonella, Eva, Julieta, Leyre, Erich, John, Noela, Sofie and Yoni, Killian Firas, Niccolò, Isaia, Giorgia, Ioana, Vanessa, Mariagrazia, Andrea, Knuth, Thomas, Berta, Mario and Claudio; a special mention to Ilaria and Giulia who stood by me in the most stressful months of writing this book.

Contents

Abbreviations and Acronyms

BAFIN	Die Bundesanstalt für Finanzdienstleistungsaufsicht (German Federal Financial Supervisory Authority)
BCBS	Basel Committee on Banking Supervision
BGBl.	Das deutsche Bundesgesetzblatt (German Federal Law Gazette)
BGH	*Bundesgerichtshof* (German Federal Court)
BKA	*Bundeskriminalamt* (Federal Criminal Police Office)
BMF	*Bundesministerium der Finanz* (German Federal Ministry of Finance)
BMI	*Bundesministerium des Innens* (German Federal Ministry of Interior)
BMJV	*Bundesministerium der Justiz und für Verbraucherschutz* (German Federal Ministry of Justice and consumer protection)
BO	Beneficial Owner
BR-Drucks.	*Bundesrat Drucksache* (German federal parliamentarian records)
BT-Drucks.	*Bundestag Drucksache* (German federal parliamentarian records)
BverfG	*Bundesverfassungsgericht* (German Federal Constitutional Court)
CDU	Christlich Demokratische Union Deutschlands (Christian Democratic Union of Germany)
CoE	Council of Europe
CSU	Christlich-Soziale Union in Bayern e. V. (Christian Social Union in Bavaria)
DM	*Deutsche Mark* (German Mark)
EC	European Community
ECB	European Central Bank
EEC	European Economic Community

EU	European Union
FATF	Financial Action Task Force
FDP	Freie Demokratische Partei (Free Democratic Party)
FIU	Financial Intelligence Unit
G7/G8/G20	Group of 7/Group of 8/Group of 20
Gcc	German Criminal Code
GDP	Gross Domestic Product
GFG	*Gemeinsame Finanzermittlungs Gruppe* (Common financial investigative group)
GFI	Global Financial Integrity
GG	*Grundgesetz* (German Constitution)
GwG	*Geldwäschegesetz* (German Anti-Money Laundering Act)
IMF	International Monetary Fund
LKA	*Landeskriminalamt* (German State Criminal Police)
MEP	Members of the European Parliament
MER	Mutual Evaluation Report
ML	Money Laundering
MONEYVAL	Committee of Experts on the Evaluation of Anti-Money Laundering Measures and the Financing of Terrorism
MP	Member of the Parliament
NGO	Non-Governmental Organisation
OECD	Organisation for Economic Cooperation and Development
OJ	Official Journal of the European Union
Palermo Convention	United Nations Convention against Transnational Organised Crime
PEP	Politically Exposed Person
PKS	*Polizeiliche Kriminalstatistik* (German police statistic)
SPD	*Sozialdemokratische Partei* (German Social Democratic Party)
STR	Suspicious Transaction Report
TFEU	Treaty on the Functioning of the European Union
TI	Transparency International
TJN	Tax Justice Network
UK	United Kingdom
UN	United Nations
UNCAC	United Nations Convention Against Corruption
UNODC	United Nations Office on Drugs and Crime
US	United States
Vienna Convention	United Nations Convention Against Illicit Traffic in Narcotic Drugs and Psychotropic Substances
WB	World Bank
WEED	World Economy, Ecology & Development

Chapter 1
Introduction

> La politica, l'eterna madre dell'accadere umano,è rimasta inceppata nell'economia e nel mercato [...].[1]
>
> (Mujica 2014, p. 109).

In a time of excessive legislation, questioning the effectiveness of a law helps lawmakers in assessing whether the law fulfils the purpose for which it was enacted, and thus in drafting more effective reforms. This book focuses on the money laundering offence; yet it surveys also the rules governing the prevention of money laundering.

Against the background of events such as the Panama Papers, the FIFA scandal, the Lux leaks, the Swiss leaks, and the Bahama leaks, which brought to the fore the role played by offshore financial centres in complex international money laundering schemes, there has been a universal call for the formulation and implementation of effective anti-money laundering regulations. What is more, in recent times the world has witnessed prominent individuals, such as Russian Mikhail Borisovich Khodorkovsky and Boris Berezovsky, South African former African National Congress Youth League leader Julius Malema, Brazil's President Lula da Silva being collared for money laundering. It has, therefore become urgent to ascertain what the boundaries of anti-money laundering law are—what can they accomplish and what not in order to avoid an arbitrary use of the offence.

Money laundering is the process of imparting an appearance of legality to the proceeds of crime. When the ill-gotten gains intermingle with legitimate monies, it becomes almost impossible to distinguish the lawful from the unlawful. While the motives for engaging in the practice of making ill-gotten gains look legal have remained the same throughout the ages, the conduct was first criminalised under international law in 1988. Money laundering was criminalised specifically to prevent the proceeds of crime from infiltrating the lawful economy. Since then scholars have devoted themselves to this subject irregularly but continually. The scholarly debate peaked in the period following the 9/11 attacks in the US and again recently after the global 'leaks' came to light. A considerable part of the international

[1] Own translation: Politics, the eternal creator of human development, has got stuck in the economy and in the market.

V. Zoppei, *Anti-Money Laundering Law: Socio-Legal Perspectives on the Effectiveness of German Practices*, International Criminal Justice Series 12,
DOI 10.1007/978-94-6265-180-7_1

anti-money laundering legal framework addresses also the financing of terrorism; however, this book deals only marginally with the financing of terrorism, and focuses instead on money laundering as a phenomenon related to organised and economic crime. For over a quarter of a century the official rhetoric has been that money laundering was criminalised to prevent and combat organised and serious crime and to protect the soundness of the world's financial system. But scholars have been strongly critical of the anti-money laundering laws, contending that they have not achieved their goals. It is especially the vague definition of the crime of money laundering that been the subject of relentless scholarly attack.

While most assessments have measured the outcomes of the anti-money laundering policies against declared official purpose of the law, this book questions instead, the underlying motives for criminalising money laundering. The aim is to see whether lawmakers had ulterior motives, or as they say, hidden agendas, that could rationalise the existence of a policy despite its apparent ineffectiveness. In addition, whereas the literature has thus far sought to simplify the complexity of the matter by measuring effectiveness quantitatively, this study opts for qualitative method, using empirical investigations, thereby underlining the involvedness and multifaceted nature of the issue at hand. This methodological approach does not presume the rationality of those who make, implement, or enforce the law. This book, therefore, seeks to fathom the perceptions, expectations, and opinions of those actors in the law, who are referred to in the book as legal actors. The definition of effectiveness used in the book is indeed a socio-legal operational definition, which goes beyond considerations bearing on technical quality, deficiencies and the formal, potential adequacy of the 'law in books', and assesses instead the concrete impact of the 'law in action', and of the law 'inaction'. The book hence connects to the vibrant discussion on the concept of legal effectiveness. It does this by proposing a methodological definition, which is then applied to the empirical research. Thus, the study contributes to the existing body of scholarly research that analyses the effectiveness of criminal laws that are meant to tackle illicit financial flows or target white-collar criminality as well as economic and organised crime.

The genesis of the anti-money laundering legal regime and the subsequent most significant developments are traced at the international, European and domestic level. The implementation of the law is conducted by way of a case study of the money laundering offence in a national context. In particular, the book focuses on the money laundering offence of the German criminal code and on the preventive regulations adopted in Germany to the extent that the latter impact on the effectiveness of the criminal provision. I have chosen Germany as an arena of investigation because the country seems to be at the same time less vulnerable to organised crime than other neighbouring countries[2] but at the same time particularly prone to

[2] Yet, it seems that the country is getting more and more susceptible to organised crime and corruption. *See also* 'Dirty Money. The Rise of Organized Crime in Europe'. In Deutsche Welle, 15/11/2015, 19.15; Schnaust R, Korruption in Deutschland steigt unaufhörlich an. Neopresse, 12/11/2015.

money laundering. Especially since the publication of a report on the implementation of anti-money laundering standards in 2010, which stated that Germany had 'a higher risk profile for large scale money laundering than many other countries',[3] the media have continuingly reported the country as an ideal place or even a paradise for money launderers.[4] According to most recent studies, the amount of money laundering in Germany is estimated to be between 50 and 100 billion Euros per year.[5] In comparison: the federal budget for 2016 amounts to 316,9 billion Euros. Renowned banks such as Commerzbank, Deutsche Bank, and Hypovereinsbank have been the focus of recent scandals because of their involvement in money laundering schemes, investigated mostly by foreign law enforcement agencies.[6] The issue has been already satirised, for instance in 2016 by the German *Greenpeace* magazine (see Fig. 1.1).[7]

Against this situation, the legal framework for combating money laundering has been often criticised. In 2007 and 2010 the European Commission initiated two proceedings against the German government for its contravention of the European treaty by failing to transpose effectively into national law the European legal provisions regulating money laundering and terrorist financing.[8] In 2010 the IMF, the

[3] FATF 2010.

[4] The latest news at the time of writing is that Germany is second only to Luxembourg as country facing the risk money laundering risk, according to a report published by Eurodad; *See* Eurodad 2015. *See also* Crisp J, Deutschland belegt bei Geldwäsche Platz zwei hinter Luxemburg. Viel getan hat sich nach der Luxleaks-Steueraffäre nicht bei den EU-Ländern, so das Ergebnis einer Analyse des Netwerks Eurodad. Der Tagesspiegel, 04/11/2015; OECD: Deutschland ist Geldwäsche-Paradies. Deutsche Wirtschafts Nachrichten, 18/01/2013; Dick W, Germany, a safe haven for money laundering. Deutsche Welle, 30/10/2012; Rimpel K, Geldwäsche-Paradies Deutschland. Nummer acht unter den Steueroasen. Tz-online, 07/11/2013; Ramthum C, OECD: Deutschland versagt im Kampf gegen Geldwäsche. Wirtschaftswoche, 26/04/2014; 'Steueroase Deutschland ist Eldorado für Geldwäsche'. In Handelsblatt, 07/11/2013; Deutschland ein "Eldorado für Geldwäsche"? Deutsche Welle, 07/11/2013; Netzwerk Steuergerechtigkeit, Deutschland ist ein Eldorado für Geldwäsche. Frankfurter Allgemein, 07/11/2013. On the estimated amount of money laundering, *see* Grabitz M, Geldwäsche floriert in Deutschland. 50 Milliarden Euro illegale Zahlungen. General Anzeiger Bonn, 01/06/2015. The FATF/OECD and IMF estimated the amount of proceeds of crime that could be potentially laundered in the country to be between 43 and 57 billion Euros. FATF 2010, p. 24.

[5] *See* Unger et al. 2013, and Bussman 2015. For a critical study on these estimates, see Schneider 2016.

[6] Crisp J, Deutschland belegt bei Geldwäsche Platz zwei hinter Luxemburg. Viel getan hat sich nach der Luxleaks-Steueraffäre nicht bei den EU-Ländern, so das Ergebnis einer Analyse des Netwerks Eurodad. Der Tagesspiegel, 04/11/2015; Rosbasch J, Deutschlands Problem mit der Geldwäsche-Bekämpfung. Deutschlandfunk, 06/08/2015; Geldwäsche Affäre in Russland. Deutscher Bank drohen Milliarden Bußgelder. In Spiegelonline, 14/08/2015.

[7] Keine Anzeige. With the permission of www.greenpeace-magazin.de.

[8] On 14th October 2004, European Commission was addressed with a complaint against the German government with reference to a report published by the IMF (International Monetary Fund), the OECD (Organisation for Economic and Commercial Development), and the FATF (Financial Action Task Force) to argue that Germany was contravening the Second European Anti-Money Laundering Directive (Directive 2001/97/EC). Andreas Frank, an expert in the field of

Fig. 1.1 Keine Anzeige. With the permission of www.greenpeace-magazin.de. *Source* Greenpeace Magazine

OECD and the FATF were sharply critical of the fact that German legal system was not fully compliant with international anti-money laundering standards. In response to this wave of criticism, some important changes have been made.[9] With specific regard to criminal law, the legislature has amplified the scope of the money laundering offence and the sphere of criminal liability in order to improve the effectiveness of the existing legislation.[10] Yet the continual expansion process has raised legal challenges that could constitute an obstacle for the effective enforcement of the measure. In fact, at present Article 261 of the GCC continues to be subjected to a welter of attacks from abundant literature on this topic.

The structure of the book is as follows: Part I presents the theoretical socio-legal framework and provides an operational definition of the concept of effectiveness that informs this empirical study. The Part concludes with a description of the methodology of the qualitative research. The subsequent Parts are developed on the basis of a set of variables suggested in Part I. Part II traces the genesis of the money laundering offence at an international, European and domestic level. The Part, as a desktop study, analyses legislative intents, parliamentary debates and other outside contributions as declarations of intents and opinions. Part III is dedicated to the doctrinal debate on the money laundering offence as regulated in the GCC. The Part highlights, in particular, the controversial issues that have come out of the profuse body of scholarly writings with regard the anti-money laundering provisions. Parts IV and V present the empirical research. Part IV analyses the quantitative data of the implementation of the money laundering offence from a qualitative perspective. The last Part presents the results of the interviews.

(Footnote 8 continued)

anti-money laundering, filed the complaint, which was particularly focused on the lack of regulations in respect of casinos, which were not sanctioned pursuant to the German legal system in case they did not report a suspicious transaction. On 21 March 2007, the European Commission, on the basis of Frank's complaint, initiated a proceeding against Germany for violation of the EU treaty. On 16 July 2007 the Ministry of Justice declared that the legislative process to close the loopholes was in progress. The process concluded with the enactment of the 'law to fight money laundering and terrorist financing' (*Gesetz zur Bekämpfung der Geldwäsche und der Terrorismusfinanzierung, Geldwäschebekämpfungsergänzungsgesetz, GwBerkErgG*) on 13 August 2008, which discharged the complaint, according to the EU Commission. But Frank was not satisfied with the transposition of the Third Anti-Money Laundering Directive into German law and filed another complaint in 2009, after the Ministry of Finance declared that implementation at a state level of international standards against money laundering and terrorist financing was considered to be very critical. For more details on the proceeding, *see* Roth et al. 2007, pp. 287 ss.

[9] *See* the FATF 2014; IMF 2016.

[10] The main amendments to the money laundering offence recently approved are introduction of the elimination of the exemption of punishment for persons who participated in the predicate offence, and the introduction of the newly created offence of terrorist financing as a predicate offence for money laundering. For a more detailed overview, *see* Part II.

References

Bussman K (2015) Dark figure study on the prevalence of money laundering in Germany and the risks of money laundering in individual economic sectors. http://wcms.itz.uni-halle.de/download.php?down=41244&elem=2937177. Last accessed on 16 September 2016.

Eurodad (2015) Fifty Shades of Tax Dodging: the EU's role in supporting an unjust global tax system. http://www.eurodad.org/files/pdf/56378e84d0fac.pdf. Last accessed on 16 September 2016.

FATF (2010) Mutual Evaluation Report of Germany. http://www.fatf-gafi.org/media/fatf/documents/reports/mer/MER%20Germany%20full.pdf. Last accessed on 16 September 2016.

FATF (2014) 3rd Follow-up Report of Germany. http://www.fatf-gafi.org/media/fatf/documents/reports/mer/FUR-Germany-2014.pdf. Last accessed on 16 September 2016.

IMF (2016) Country Report No. 16/190. Germany, Financial sector assessment programme. https://www.imf.org/external/pubs/ft/scr/2016/cr16190.pdf. Last accessed on 16 September 2016.

Mujica J P (2014) La felicità al potere. EIR, Rome.

Roth J, Fromm R, Nübel R (2007) Anklage unerwünscht. Korruption und Willkür in der deutschen Justiz. Eichborn Verlag, Frankfurt am Main.

Schneider F (2016) Der Umfang der Geldwäsche in Deutschland und weltweit: Einige Fakten und eine kritische Auseinandersetzung mit der Dunkelfeldstudie von Kai Bussmann. Friedrich Naumann Stiftung. http://stiftung-marktwirtschaft.de/fileadmin/user_upload/Tagungsunterlagen/21_09_Bargeld/Schneider_FNS-Studie_Geldwaesche_2016.pdf. Last accessed on 16 December 2016.

Unger B, Addink H, Walker J, Ferwerda J, van den Broek M, Deleanu I (2013) ECOLEF final report. http://www2.econ.uu.nl/users/unger/ecolef_files/Final%20ECOLEF%20report%20(digital%20version).pdf. Last accessed on 16 September 2016.

Part I
Instructions for the Socio-Legal Research

[...] Quelle gride, ripubblicate e rinforzate di governo in governo, non servivano ad altro che ad attestare ampollosamente l'impotenza de' loro autori; o, se producevan qualche effetto immediato, era principalmente d'aggiunger molte vessazioni a quelle che i pacifici e i deboli già soffrivano dà perturbatori, e d'accrescer le violenze e l'astuzia di questi. L'impunità era organizzata, e aveva radici che le gride non toccavano, o non potevano smovere.[1]

Manzoni 1840, p. 21

[1] Own translation: 'Notwithstanding this, or, it may be, in consequence of this, these proclamations [grida], reiterated and reinforced from time to time, served only to proclaim in pompous language the impotence of those who issued them; or, if they produced any immediate effect, it was that of adding to the vexations which the peaceful and feeble suffered from the disturbers of society. Impunity was so organised that the proclamations were powerless'.

Chapter 2
The Socio-Legal Framework

Abstract This chapter proposes an operational definition of socio-legal effectiveness that is then applied for the empirical research. It first discusses different approaches to the definition of legal effectiveness provided not only by socio-legal studies, but also by other disciplines, such as administrative sciences, economic theories of law, and political sciences. Secondly, it outlines the preferred definition, and presents the variables chosen to assess empirically the effectiveness, according to the chosen definition, and the different methods used. Thirdly, based on the theoretical framework illustrated, it formulates a hypothesis on the effectiveness of the money laundering offence.

Keywords Legal effectiveness · Symbolic function of law · Law (in)action · Legal implementation · Law-making process · Discourse analysis · Criminal statistics · Semi-structured interviews · Qualitative research · Empirical research

Contents

Embarking on a study of the effectiveness of a law is a complex task, because the definition of legal effectiveness itself has been the subject of intense debate. Legal theorists, political scientists, political sociologists, administrative experts, and economists, have added their respective views to this debate. Legal effectiveness might depend too on the impact the law has on areas of human life outside the

V. Zoppei, *Anti-Money Laundering Law: Socio-Legal Perspectives on the Effectiveness of German Practices*, International Criminal Justice Series 12,
DOI 10.1007/978-94-6265-180-7_2

immediate legal sphere. Despite this complexity, it is critically essential, especially in the light of prodigious legislative enactments nowadays, to verify the effectiveness of a statute first, before introducing a new one. Even more importantly is to assess the usefulness of criminal laws at a time when policy-makers appear to be fashioning laws randomly that are ineffective, purely symbolic or even supportive of criminality.

In the literature, the term 'effectiveness' is at times substituted by expressions such as 'efficiency', 'validity', or efficacy'; this work adopts the term 'effectiveness', on the basis of *Friedman's* milestone 'The Legal System: A social science perspective'.[1] Commonly a rule can be defined as effective if it achieves the goals for which it was adopted. However, legal experts and the different categories of professionals involved in preventing and combating money laundering have different perspectives on how to define an effective legal act. In order to be able to acknowledge their diverse perceptions, this book conceives a definition of legal effectiveness that draws mostly upon socio-legal theories on legal effectiveness, but also upon some other disciplines, all of which provide the relevant elements for the interpreting the different perspectives.

One of the most common socio-legal definitions of effectiveness is the one that looks at compliance rates: A legal act shall be effective if the addressees comply with it, and ineffective when the addresses deviate from the prescribed conduct.[2] According to this approach, the effectiveness of a law is measured quantitatively. An example of this typology of definitions is the one provided by *Geiger* in his groundbreaking work *Vorstudien zu einer Soziologie des Rechts*. He expresses the concept through the mathematic formula '$e = (s \rightarrow bg) + [(s \rightarrow c\breve{g}) \rightarrow r]$', which shows that the coefficient (e) of effectiveness corresponds to the sum of the compliant behaviours (g) and of the deviant behaviour ($\breve{g}$) to which a sanction follows (r). Dividing the coefficient of effectiveness (e) by the number of cases in which the addresses are in typical situations (s), it equals the level of obligatory (v) of a legal act: '(v): $v = e/s$'.[3] The formula has been criticised because of the reduced

[1] The author defines effectiveness as the 'power to make an intended result occur, or the capacity to produce effects'. Friedman 1975, p. 45. Also Allott, in his popular book 'The limits of law' speaks of 'effectiveness of law' to indicate whether a particular provision fulfils its purposes. *See* Allott 1980, pp. 28 ss; 1981, p. 233. Often it is referred to the same sociological concept of effectiveness by using the word 'efficacy'. *See* for instance, 'Black's Law Dictionary', Garner 2014, pp. 628–629; and Villegas 2003. The term effectiveness is translated in different ways. Piovani, for example uses the term 'effectivity' (*effettività*) to refer to legal orders and effectiveness (*efficacia*) to mention legal acts; *see* Piovani 1953, pp. 5–8. Kelsen instead uses the word *Effektivität* (effectiveness) to refer to legal orders and *Wirksamkeit* to talk about single legal acts. *See* Kelsen 1952, pp. 2, 24.

[2] Generally there is the tendency to define the law's effectiveness by having in mind behavioral rules. These thoughts are not yet completely applicable to private law. For a detailed analysis of the differences existing between an effectiveness assessment of criminal law and of private law; *see* Rottleuthner 1983, pp. 85 ss.

[3] Geiger 1987, p. 182.

applicability and because of the incapability of taking into account other factors.[4] There are some critical issues that pose a challenge to *Geiger*'s formula. As regards to the obligatory relation, *Geiger* does not define a 'typical situation', thus making it difficult to apply the formula in those cases in which it is not easy to calculate the number of typical situations.[5] Taking the crime of murder as an example, for which the obedience consists in the abstention from killing, it is impossible to calculate how many times individuals have been in a 'typical situation' and have not committed a murder as a consequence of the deterrent effect of the criminal provision.[6] Where an act sanctions numerous deviant behaviours, its degree level of effectiveness increases, according to *Geiger*'s the formula. This might frustrate the deterrent potential and thus actually diminish its effectiveness.[7] At another level, *Geiger*'s formula has been questioned for not providing information on other variables that can influence the addressees' behaviour. Also, an evaluation of the effectiveness of the law can be influenced by the reasons for the deviant behaviour, to the extent, for example, that voluntarily disobedient conduct aimed at expressing rejection of a certain law differs from deviant behaviour caused by a mistake. There are also rules that are respected also, not because they are perceived as being right, but because there is no other alternative, or because it is better to have them than to have no rules at all.[8] In such cases, a high compliance rate might not mean that the rules are very effective. Moreover, the mathematical formula is unable to take into account cases in which a high deviance rate does not nullify the effectiveness of the law, or cases in which, on the contrary, a high compliance frustrates the goal of the law. On the one hand, 'frequent violations of a legal act are not evidence of the fact that act has not had any influence.'[9] On the other hand, full compliance with law might not lead to the intended goal,[10] and could even frustrate its purpose. The addresses could fall short of meeting the social aims of the law where they do not obey the content of a legal provision. In such a case, obedience actually causes unforeseen collateral effects.[11] In other words, partial non-compliance might lead to

[4] Geiger gives more indications on the other variables relevant to an assessment of legal effectiveness in its work; *see* Geiger 1987, pp. 182 ss; + 204 ss. Yet according to Rottleuthner its formula has not been very successful in the sociology of law. Rottleuthner 1983, p. 82. Blankenburg on the contrary believes that Geiger has specifically provided such a formula in order to show that most rules regulating daily life are violated without that such deviant behaviors are followed by a sanction and are thus ineffective. Blankenburg 1995, p. 3.

[5] Blankenburg 1995, p. 5.

[6] Rottleuthner 1983, p. 80.

[7] The same criticism could be raised against the philosophical definition of *effectuality*. An even more extreme criticism is brought forward by scholars who believe that laws are effective if they do not need to be enforced by legal authorities. Kelsen 1952, p. 20. *See also* Rehbinder and Schelsky 1972, p. 558.

[8] Friedman 1975, p. 45.

[9] Aubert 1965, p. 316.

[10] Blankenburg 1985, p. 209.

[11] Noll 1972, p. 261.

fulfilling the functions of a legal act better than full compliance.[12] Furthermore, some rules do not achieve their social goals only through compliance. *Rottleuthner* gives the example of rules that impose speed limits that are aimed at reducing or eliminating car accidents.[13] If all drivers respected the limits and thus complied with the rule but caused many more car accidents, those rules would not be effective because they would be unable to demonstrate their social function. In addition, compliance and deviance are controversial concepts. *Friedman* defines them as 'two poles of a *continuum*'.[14] Different people can interpret the same behaviour differently in different circumstances. In fact, the two concepts are attributes deriving from sequences of decisions-definitions that emerge in the course of the interaction.[15] 'Deviance and compliance do not exist; they are merely social definitions of what is compliant and what is deviant'.[16] Particularly in respect of criminal law, there might be different definitions of deviance for the same fact, depending on whether the perspective is from the point of view of the victims, the police, or the public prosecutors. None of them is the correct one, for only a view that would take into account all of them could come closer to the real fact.[17] Most studies on deviance and compliance have been looking at the causes of deviant behaviour or at the processes through which, and the conditions under which, a criminal sanction is applied to particular deviance categories. The dominant problem relating to criminalisation is whether criminalisation is a neutral process or whether it serves the interests of the powerful. In this context, the labelling theory has turned the traditional question around from 'Why do they deviate?' to 'Why do they label it as deviant?'[18] Besides being a socially relevant topic, the labelling of deviance has a marked political aspect, namely, the fact that policy-makers can have an interest in defining certain behaviour as deviant.[19] The labelling theory is used in

[12] Blankenburg 1985, p. 214.

[13] Rottleuthner 1983, p. 90.

[14] Friedman 1975, p. 47.

[15] Ferrari 1992, p. 143.

[16] Gallino 2012, p. 217. A definition given is 'the violation of a norm that would, if discovered, result in the punishment or condemnation of the violator'. Yet not all deviant behaviors result in the punishment or condemnation of the deviant. Ritzer and Ryan 2011, pp. 139–140.

[17] Blankenburg 1995, pp. 13 ss.

[18] The labelling perspective has been influenced by the thought of Tannenbaum who believed that the social definition of delinquency was attached to people, who would be more prone to take on a deviant role. In particular the author stated that 'the process of making the criminal, […], is a process of tagging, defining, identifying, segregating, describing, emphasizing, making conscious and self-conscious; […]'. *See* Tannenbaum 1938, p. 20. Moderate reactivists belonging to the functionalist school of thought, such as Becker and Erickson believed that the labelling process is crucial to understand deviance as a social phenomenon, by taking into consideration problems such as the selectivity issue, the role and consequences of stigmatization, the difference between known and secret deviants. *See* Becker 1963, pp. 3 ss; and Erickson 1962.

[19] Gallino gives the example of the strike, once perceived as a deviant act and nowadays as a fundamental right of workers. *See* Gallino 2012, p. 218.

this work to interpret the reasons behind the criminalisation or the non-criminalisation of certain behaviours.[20]

Given all these situations in which a calculation based on compliance and deviance rates does not correspond to the effectiveness of a law, it can be inferred that an evaluation of the effectiveness cannot be limited to a quantitative assessment. There is, furthermore, a methodological issue, namely, the following: The anti-money laundering laws are characterised by a high level of uncertainty with regard to whether they are obeyed or disobeyed, for the statistics are often inconsistent. Therefore, despite the quantitative approach provides relevant information on the criminal justice activity against money laundering, data on deviance and compliance shall be interpreted qualitatively, in order to take into account other variables.

Administrative sciences use the concept of efficiency as opposed to the one of effectiveness.[21] While effectiveness looks at the outcome of the application of the law, efficiency refers to the optimal relationship between the goals achieved and the means employed.[22] The concept of efficiency refers to the methods used to implement a law, particularly the executive mechanisms to enforce it. An executive mechanism is said to be efficient if it succeeds in fulfilling its purpose by employing rational means. A peculiar type of efficiency is the 'efficiency regardless of the purpose' (*zielunabhängige Effizienz*),[23] which refers to entire legal frameworks and not only to individual statutory provisions. According to this view, an apparatus is efficient if it functions optimally, notwithstanding the effects it achieves, because its purpose consists in its mere existence.[24] While not being exhaustive, any opinion on the efficiency of a law or of a legal structure provides information on the effectiveness too. Therefore, assessments on the efficiency of the anti-money laundering regime contribute to the wider socio-legal evaluation of effectiveness.[25]

From a political science point of view, the analysis on legal effectiveness belongs to the broader category of policy analysis.[26] Certain typologies of policy-analyses assume typically that legislative intent is capable of being made clear and known, that language itself is transparent, and that the policy-making process is rational and geared towards attaining stipulated goals. Yet, for the purpose of this research, other typologies of policy-analyses are taken in consideration.

---

[20] The work does not seek to explain the motives of deviance.

[21] According to the Burton's legal Thesaurus 'efficiency' is a synonym of ability, ableness, adeptness, capability, excellence, productiveness, but also efficacy, and effectiveness. *See* Burton 2007, p. 206.

[22] This definition of efficiency is taken in particular from Leisner. The scholar describes a specific type of efficiency, the '*Zweck-Mittel Effizienz*', which consists of the optima relation between the goal (*Zweck*) and the means (*Mittel*). *See* Leisner 1971, pp. 7 ss.

[23] Leisner 1971, pp. 7 ss; *see also* Paliero 1992, p. 494.

[24] Hierro 2010, p. 180; and Villegas 1994.

[25] Bettini 1983, p. 107.

[26] In this work policy to indicate the whole system of legislations adopted to prevent and repress money laundering is referred to.

Particularly, those directed at revealing and interpreting tensions between legislators, implementers, and other public role players, let alone the fact that ambiguity in policy can also be purposeful. Given that the main source of policy meanings is in the language, the methodology used by policy analysts is the discourse analysis.[27] This work focuses on the effectiveness of a single legal provision, which is the money laundering offence, yet, given the fact that the provision is part of a broader policy, its effectiveness cannot be detached from the impact of the whole policy. The genesis of the money laundering offence is also analysed in the context of the international, European and national discourses on the introduction of the anti-money laundering policy.

Finally, it might be useful to bring to mind the definition of effectiveness in the context economic legal analysis. In this field, legal efficiency is often measured on a rational cost-effectiveness basis, which compares the expenses with the results in economic terms.[28] A rational analysis of crime control processes assumes that different actors, from the lawmakers to the enforcers of the law, have a rational attitude, for instance, implementers respect the legislature's directives. In addition, economic analysis disregards the personal motives of law enforcement agents. Yet, the economic approach can offer interesting ideas, especially with regard to criminal law. In particular, according to an economic perspective, the criminal justice system shapes the legal response to a crime on the basis of a cost-benefit analysis.[29] A study conducted by German scholars has highlighted that the compliance rate with a certain criminal law will be inversely proportional to the costs of preliminary investigations.[30] The economic approach assumes that the goal of law enforcement

[27] Yanow 2014, p. 142. For a complete overview, *see also* Pal 1995, p. 185; and Swaffield 1998, p. 199.

[28] A cost-benefit analysis is 'a method of setting put the factors that need to be taken into account in making choices about major investments in public sector projects. The objective is to assign all costs and all benefits, social and economic, so that one can see clearly whether the benefits exceed the costs of a venture […]'. *See* Scott 2014, p. 130.

[29] With regards to criminal law, Amelung describes the efficiency as the optimal relation between the means adopted and the goals achieved through a cost-benefit analysis. According to the scholar, such analysis should take into account as costs also non-economic costs, such as social or individual costs and the collateral effects, which are those non-intended consequences. *See* Amelung 1980, pp. 30–31.

[30] In addition, law enforcement will try to collect as much information as possible during preliminary investigations if this proves to be more convenient. Prosecutors will prefer to indict for crimes that require the lowest degree of evidence. Prosecutors decide whether to indict a person on the basis of the potentiality that the information gathered proves the fact with the aim of conviction. In this regard, information revealed by the suspect in the appeal can be essential. Furthermore, public prosecutors will never try to close a proceeding if they possess enough evidence to indict the offender, in the opposite situation they will always accept the proposed offer of closing the proceedings. According to the economic approach, the discretion granted in these situations does not frustrate the effectiveness of the law, because law enforcement has the liberty to choose whether to continue or to close a proceeding, and therefore could also always choose to continue it. *See* Jost 1998, pp. 268 ss.

is the maximisation of compliance rates, and that agencies act in a rational way. The economic calculation can also be applied in the initial phase in order to decide whether to punish behaviour under criminal or administrative law, depending on expedience. Despite the diversities between the sociological and the economic approaches, this book takes into consideration the outcomes of some cost-benefit analyses undertaken by other researchers on the anti-money laundering regime in order to contribute to the general socio-legal assessment of its effectiveness.[31] In a cost-benefit analysis of criminal law, costs are also understood as the social costs of punishment and exclusion. If these are higher than the benefits, the law infringes the principle of proportionality.[32]

2.1 An Elastic Concept of Legal Effectiveness

All things considered, for the purposes of this study, I have adopted an elastic concept of legal effectiveness, which draws upon the definition given by *Ferrari* in his essay '*Le funzioni del diritto*', the functions of law.[33] Such elastic approach is meant to serve the empirical research and to interpret the perceived concepts of effectiveness emerging from the interviews. It is in fact an operational concept. This has the advantage of providing a measurable outcome, rather than a static one. By taking into account elements that influence the formulation, the application and the reception of the law across a certain lapse of time and against the backdrop of the diverse perceptions of the effectiveness, the assessment is revisable and modifiable. The elasticity thus permits the limits of a contingent and relative assessment to be overcome.

According to *Ferrari*'s definition, a statutory law is effective when 'there is correspondence between the political plan (*disegno politico*) and the effects of such law'.[34] The political plan is a wider concept than the purposes of the rule-makers and includes those intentions that are not explicitly expressed by the rule-makers. With this as its operational definition, the book assesses the effectiveness of the German anti-money laundering legislation, using the following variables: The expressed and latent intentions of lawmakers and of other actors that influence the law-making process (the political plan), the reception of such legislation by legal actors and legal role-players and the implementation, including all the conse-

[31] The economic approach is similar to the one proposed by the legal realism's method of reasoning. Legal realism determines the meaning of a legal act by weighting the costs, benefits, probable consequences, and underlying values and purposes of the law. In addition, it also considers whether the interpretative result will be fair and just. Black's Law Dictionary 2014, p. 1456.

[32] Baratta 1990, p. 94; Marinucci and Dolcini 2006, p. 8.

[33] Ferrari 1992, p. 148.

[34] Ibid.

quences attributable to the legislation (the effects). In addition, given that 'the impact of the law cannot be studied in isolation from the impact of other factors',[35] other external factors are taken into account. In particular, the analysis is indeed embedded in and strongly influenced by a particular historical-economic context.

2.1.1 The Political Plan

A political plan is always a compromise among different opinions rather than the expression of the unanimous will of the lawmakers. The legislature is a collective organ, comprised of different social groups that pursue their respective interests. Political parties are composed of various individuals that might have diverse expectations and might interpret signals and messages differently. The intentions of lawmakers may vary with time, so that the same provision can be interpreted differently in time, and if such differences are not translated into an amendment, the intent of the legislator cannot be predicted in relation to those provisions.[36] Laws are influenced not only be legislatures, but also by external factors, such as lobby groups, economic actors, and international institutions. The 'elastic' notion allows all actors that have an influence in the process of rule-making to be taken into account.[37]

This book focuses especially on the role of lawmakers as architects of the political plan and of its implementation, and as communicators of the legal message to its public. Yet, it is important to focus not only on formal decision-making processes, but also on non-decision-making processes that involve the mobilisation of the political agenda by powerful groups, taking decisions that prevent issues from becoming and emerging as the subject of formal decision-making.

The socio-legal concept of function is used to interpret critically the political plan. In order to assess the effectiveness of the money laundering offence not only on the basis of the official goals, a functional approach is adopted. By studying the functions attributed to the offence, and thus the interests brought forward by the different actors taking part in the law-making process, conflicting interests and diverging expectations emerge. A statute has direct and indirect functions. The first correspond to the prescribed behaviour and are thus fulfilled through compliance. The second are the purposes that lawmakers aim to achieve through compliance. The legislature might or might not declare the function of a law. The legislature might declare a fictitious intention to make the new law more acceptable for the

[35] Aubert 1965, p. 88.

[36] It has to be noted that the legislator is not the only actor that can interpret the law, in fact in common law systems the judiciary has the same duty. Reflections made with regard to the legislator can be applied *mutatis mutandis* for the Supreme Court. *See* Ferrari 1992, p. 135.

[37] Ferrari 1992, p. 133.

public, while the real function is kept latent.[38] Non-declared intents may be kept secret due to stylistic or opportunistic reasons, for example, to avoid a loss of popularity.[39] While intended functions may be inapplicable in practice, the law could be re-directed to attain a different aim. Moreover, the legislature can consider enacting a law that lacks a clearly-defined function in order to allow for contradictory and alternative applications. Sometimes declared intentions can be misleading, as *Friedman* observes, 'lawmakers may say one thing and mean another'.[40] In other words, where the intention is declared, this might not be the real will of the legislature. What lawmakers say is the manifest function, what lawmakers mean is the latent purpose of a law.

There is abundant literature that deals with the dichotomy between manifest and hidden functions of a law. It is especially sociologists with a functional approach who consider research of the latent intentions of the law to be essential, because it has allowed the revelation of patterns that go beyond the moral, naive judgements based on declared goals and obvious effects.[41] The concept of latent functions, as opposed to manifest functions, was introduced in the western sociology of law by *Merton*.[42] Yet, for purposes of this book, the term 'latent functions' is used with the meaning attributed by *Aubert*, who, includes in the category also those functions that are wanted but not expressed by rule-makers.[43] He states in particular that, if one wants to understand the reasons why a law that does not achieve the goals for which it was enacted continues to remain in force, it is necessary to look at that law's latent functions. In his study of a social policy regulating housewives' working conditions, *Aubert* observed that the policy was ineffective in pursuing the declared goals'.[44] The scholar came up with the hypothesis that parliament consciously formulated 'empty legislation'.[45] He concluded that the legislation, while appearing ineffective, had the latent function of reconciling internal conflicts amongst parliamentarians by providing the satisfaction that the enactment gave to the political parties supporting the cause of the policy, and the certainty of its ineffectiveness to those opposing the legislative novelty.[46] The concept of latent

[38] Ferrari 1992, p. 134.

[39] Villegas 1994.

[40] Friedman 1975, p. 55.

[41] Merton 1983, pp. 195, 197, 203.

[42] Merton takes as an example the indigenous propitiatory rituals, for instance, the rain dance or the fertility ritual, none of which results in rain or pregnancy, but have the latent goal of fostering the collectiveness of a community. *See* Merton 1983, pp. 173, + 191–193.

[43] Aubert 1965, p. 329.

[44] Aubert conducted an empirical study on the Norwegian housewives' legislation. *See* Aubert 1965, pp. 321 ss.

[45] From the empirical research conducted on the effective implementation and on the legislative process, Aubert highlighted diverse factors that influence the legislation's effectiveness, among others the historical context, the level of implementation, the level of knowledge and the opinions of the addresses about the provisions. *See* Aubert 1965, pp. 317 ss.

[46] Aubert 1965, p. 329.

functions is fundamental to this study. In order to analyse a law by using this concept, it suffices that, without those functions, it would be impossible to explain the law.[47] Researchers can observe latent functions by, on the one hand, reading the parliamentary debates and the *travaux préparatoires*, which 'constitute the privileged place of a study about the relations between social science and law',[48] on the other hand, by observing the real effects of the law in practice.

2.1.2 The Symbolic Function of Law

Laws whose latent functions prevail over the manifest ones are also defined as symbolic laws.[49] Only those laws whose symbolic dimension was intended by the legislature are actually considered symbolic laws.[50] There is abundant literature on the concept of 'symbolic legislations'.[51] The German Constitutional Court has recognised the existence of a typology of laws that have symbolic effectiveness, as 'permanent expressions of a socio-ethical, and thus legal evaluation of human actions'.[52] In 2006, the Federal High Court described the German Anti-corruption Law, '*Antikorruptionsgesetz*' as symbolic legislation, '*symbolische Gesetzgebung*'.[53] Criminal law has a strong symbolic component that explains its general-preventive function.[54] This symbolic dimension does not yet exhaust the purpose of criminal law, which is usually directed at an instrumental function of solving social conflicts through the protection of determined interests.[55] Constitutions often contain principles that are purely symbolic, the vague formulation of which might be filled with a different content, according to social

[47] Merton 1983, p. 201.

[48] Treves 2002, p. 234.

[49] Hassemer, NStZ, 1989, p. 556.

[50] In this sense, *see also* Funcke-Auffermann 2007, p. 53.

[51] The adjective 'symbolic' is used with slightly different meanings. For instance, Hegenbarth defines it as a corroboration of the normative claim, in opposition with the guarantee for enforcement; Ryffel considers the symbolic impact of law as latent; and according to Amelung such legislations aim at prestige rather than effectiveness; Neves defines a symbolic legislation as a text [...] that have a manifest relation with the substantial normative reality, yet they primarily serve the realization of political purposes. *See* Hegenbarth, ZRP, 1981, p. 202; Ryffel 1974, pp. 255 ss; Amelung, ZStW, 1980, p. 54; and Neves, IfS-Nachrichten 16, 1999, p. 9.

[52] BVerfG, final sentence, 25 February 1975, Neue Juristische Wochenschrift 1975, p. 580.

[53] BGH, LG Wuppertal, 9 May 2006, 5 StR 453/05.

[54] *See* for example Günther, who believes that punishment in penal law should be symbolical. *See* Günther 2002, p. 219.

[55] According to Hassemer, on one hand associating criminal law, with all the consequences connected as execution, incarceration, and all the other duties imposed on the suspects, to a symbolic dimension is rather odd, because the impact of penal law on people's life is all but not symbolic. Yet, the scholar argues that, on the other hand, it is obvious that penal laws have a symbolic '*Wirkung*'. *See* Hassemer, NStZ, 1989, pp. 553–554.

progress.[56] Principles such as human dignity, freedom and equality have been interpreted very differently over the course of history; they are thus rather symbolic in nature, yet they are accepted as expressions and confirmations of shared values. Hence, the symbolic effectiveness of the law can be a positive thing.[57] Indeed, the adjective 'symbolic' derives from the word 'symbol', which stems from the ancient Greek *sun-ballein*, which means 'to meet', and thus in this context can be referred to laws that connect the public with the legal system. Symbols used by the law can communicate cohesion in order to unify a society and legitimise institutions, or differentiation, to glorify or degrade a specific social group.[58]

Symbolic laws might be enacted for different reasons. Alibi laws are introduced to give the appearance that something has been done and that the polity is taking care of the regulated matter. These types of laws gain consensus through their mere existence: The effective content of the law is unimportant, for what counts in these situations is the appearance of justice.[59] In a cost-effectiveness analysis, such laws might represent a perfect solution for a legislature dealing with a complex phenomenon, subject to time pressure, and one that does not want to lose its popularity by attracting criticisms for increasing public expenditures.[60] A symbolic alibi-law will not require any implementation costs because it is ineffective. Moreover, it will be perceived by the public as an efficient solution, because those who do not have enough information to recognise the ineffectiveness of the laws will be satisfied by their mere adoption. In fact, these types of laws can serve propagandistic functions. Yet, if that satisfaction remains empty and the law does not have any instrumental effectiveness, individuals may eventually be deceived by the legislature. Compromise laws are directed at mediating conflicting opinions and interests within the parliament and are usually formulated vaguely in order to allow various interpretations that would then satisfy all parties. This typology is also known as '*gesetzgeberischer double talk*' (legislative double talk)[61] or trade-off laws.

Yet, when not all that the law promises becomes true, and if in fact, only a minimal part of the promises is maintained, the law is an empty promise that deceives its addressees.[62] The problem with symbolic laws arise when such laws, while seeming to be pure declarations of values, deceive citizens, making them think that the law is regulating a specific issue, while the laws actually have the purpose (and the latent effect) of maintaining the status quo—thanks to their ineffectiveness.

---

[56] Noll 1972, p. 262.

[57] *See* Bryde 1993, p. 16 ss.

[58] A symbol is most generally 'any act or thing that represents something else'. Scott 2014, p. 746.

[59] Ferrari 1997, p. 268.

[60] Newig 2007, p. 308. *See also* Moccia 1995, pp. 27, 97, and Newig 2003, p. 112.

[61] The term 'gesetzgeberischer double talk' is used also by Lucke in the work 'Das Geschlechterverhältnis im rechtspolitischen Diskurs. Gleichstellungsdiskussion und gesetzgeberischer "double talk",' 1991.

[62] The term 'promise' was used in a sociology of law conference held in Berlin in September 2015, 'the promises of law' ('Die Versprechungen des Rechts'). *See* LSI Berlin 2015.

Such laws legislations have a symbolic, manifest function, but at the same time an instrumental latent function, which is to keep the situation as it was before the law was enacted. While the declared goal will not be achieved, the latent one will have a practical impact on society. Hence, while giving the appearance of a legal change, *mutatis mutandis*, the status quo will not be modified. It is especially provisions whose declared goal is to protect weaker social groups by changing certain power relations that disadvantage them, that can cause real harm if they are merely symbolic. In fact, not only will the weak social groups remain without legal protection, but also social claims based on the law will be symbolically neutralised by the rule.[63] At the same time, those who did not want to change the *status quo* remain unaffected. These provisions deceive citizens that their social claims for justice are satisfied, but actually, they do not provide the effective legal protection needed by society. These laws create situations of actual impunity, covered by the appearance of symbolic punishment. Therefore, these mechanisms create victims and at the same time, they make privileged people de facto immune from the criminal justice system. Scholars have interpreted this impunity as a planned impunity, as a desired effect of the practice of decriminalising certain social groups in order for the perpetrators of such crime to avoid being punished. Against this background, *Cottino* interprets *Aubert*'s research outcomes even more critically. He believes that the housewives' law, which *Aubert* proved to be ineffective in improving housewives' working condition, but effective in solving a parliamentarian conflict, actually perpetuated power relations between 'workers' and 'bosses'. This was ultimately a defeat for the workers, according to *Cottino*. In fact, the law confirmed and even legitimised the *status quo*. The instrument of the ineffective piece of legislation belongs to a social control strategy. *Aubert* theorises the practice of 'decriminalisation', which envisages different ways of avoiding punishment through a blockage of the criminalisation process, which starts with the adoption of a law and ends with the action of law enforcement agencies. The adoption of a planned, ineffective norm is one of the possible ways of blocking such a process. If class struggle nowadays is conducted through laws, which are intended to entrench the position and the interests of the dominant class, while impeding the fight of the lower classes for their rights,[64] it can be argued that the money laundering offence has been designed as non-effective in order not to harm the interests of money launderers. Laws against white-collar crimes have always been, after all, very harsh on paper, but in practice have not been widely applied.[65] In fact, 'statistics unequivocally show that crime, as popularly conceived an officially measured, has a high incidence in the lower class and a low

[63] *See* Noll, ZschwR, 1981, pp. 347 ss; and Hassemer, NStZ, 1989, p. 554.

[64] Gallino 2012, p. 21. This assumption is based on a Marxist approach to law that conceives law as a superstructure of a capitalist society. In this context legal concepts and doctrines reinforce the position of the ruling class.

[65] Sutherland 1940. *See also* Blankenburg 1985, p. (205) 210. Yet, this can be also explained by saying that individuals belonging to privileged classes obtain a better education, hence tend to commit more sophisticated crimes that are harder to be detected or to be proved at court. Blankenburg 1995, p. 22.

incidence in the upper class'. It returns again to the difference between the law in action and law in the books.

In addition, those laws would be disproportional because they are not appropriate for achieving their declared outcomes. Even an attempt at implementing them would require a useless effort that might cause collateral damages and costs. Their de facto inapplicability could lead to a public loss of confidence in the legal order. As *Beccaria* observed in the 18th century, 'useless provisions, disregarded by people communicate their humiliation also to the healthiest rules'.[66] The concept of the symbolic dimension of the law is therefore necessary to reveal patterns of power underlying the law. The relationship between the symbolic dimension of law and the effectiveness of law still is a controversial topic. In reality, it is not possible to clearly distinguish such categories; in fact, often those attributes can be measures by using different measures for the same provision.[67]

2.1.3 The Integration of the Law in the Existing Criminal Justice System

On the assumption that the integration of a provision in the legal system can influence the effectiveness of a law, this study looks at the scholarly debate surrounding the money laundering offence and at the opinions of practitioners and privileged observers. Those who should enforce it, in order to avoid conflicts with other rules, might disregard a new rule that hardly integrates in an established legal framework. Oppositely, a well-accepted reform is more probable to become part of legal professionals' practice. In order to investigate the relationship between the level of acceptance of the law and its effectiveness, it is necessary to understand to what extent the legal community of scholars, experts and practitioners have integrated the piece of legislation in their theoretical frameworks or in their daily practice. Legal actors might consider a policy effective and adequate with respect to certain aspects, or to have met certain goals, but simultaneously very ineffective in other respects.

Many factors can affect the perceived legitimation of a legal novelty, for instance, the way that news is communicated to the public.[68] Yet, given that the

---

[66] Beccaria 1786, p. 129.

[67] Also Hagenbarth recognises that the law has a double nature, and that along with instrumental functions, provisions can also have a symbolic function. *See* Hagenbarth, ZRP, 1981, p. 201. According to Hassemer the question of the symbolic nature of a law cannot be answered with a yes or a no, but rather with a 'more or less'. Hassemer, NStZ, 1989, p. 555. *See also* Funcke-Auffermann 2007, p. 56.

[68] The Media delivers messages to the public and can amplify social needs and expectations of the justice system. It can create the necessary consensus among society, for instance, by reporting primarily and constantly about misbehaving immigrants in order to justify the enactment of specific criminal laws that target immigrants, for example. This happens by manipulating social perceptions about risk related to certain situations about which the public does is not sufficiently

analysed law is very complex, this study does not aim to assess the public's perception of legitimacy. Rather, it focuses on the opinions of legal scholars who have a profound understanding of the law. The acceptance of the law is also potentially influenced by political decisions. In fact, policy makers can influence the reception of laws, for example, by choosing a certain type of language. This makes it important to adopt a critical perspective. In the final analysis, issues concerning a vague or mistaken legal formulation might be ascribed to a political decision. In the case study analysed by *Aubert*, one of the variables that influenced the law's ineffectiveness was the lack of knowledge on the part of the addressees. *Aubert*, however, interpreted this issue as part of a political plan of enacting an ineffective piece of legislation by adopting complex legal vocabulary that was not appropriate for the addressees. In this sense, *Aubert* hypothesised that the legislature was not interested in letting housewives understand the content of the legal news. The use of complex language, while at first sight may seem like a guarantee of impartiality, precision and credibility, and thus legitimise the legislator's action, can be used to achieve latent functions. A 'bad formulation' may be a technical issue linked to the appropriateness of the legislation, but it can also be a part of a planned ineffectiveness. By recalling the symbolic dimension of law, the use of complex language can serve the symbolic function of legitimation while concealing other latent functions.

2.1.4 The Effects of the Implementation

By using the word 'effects' and not 'compliance' or 'deviance', the operational definition considers not only those consequences foreseen by lawmakers, but also those that were not planned, and the so-called 'collateral effects', as well as the costs of enforcement. Through the elastic definition, the conflicting dimension of law emerges in the implementation phase, when a piece of legislation can display *eu-functions* for certain addresses and *dys-functions* for others. The reference is here *Friedman*'s notion of impact, which encompasses all consequences somehow linkable to the application of the law.[69] *Friedman* includes in the notion of impact also those collateral effects that *Boudon* would define as '*effet pervers*', namely, those consequences that are unexpected and contrary to the will of the legislator.[70]

(Footnote 68 continued)

informed and thus not able evaluate automatically. However, this study does not critique the media although the topic concerning the media did crop up in the interviews. *See* Part V.

[69] According to Friedman's definition, a legal act is any act performed by a public institution. In this study, the term 'legal act' is equated with a legal provision in a statute. *See* Friedman 1975, p. 45.

[70] Boudon 1981, p. 24. The classical example are laws that criminalize abortion with the declared goal of safeguarding women's health, but which actually have had the opposite effect of increasing the risk to women's health by making them resort to illegal abortions.

The impact of a law can also be defined as all the consequences that would have not occurred had the law been not enacted. In fact, even though not all scholars agree on the fact that new laws create new customs, it cannot be denied that a new piece of legislation creates a different situation, despite the fact that it is often violated.[71] Legal effectiveness corresponds to the positive impact of a law, namely, to those consequences, which are in line with the intents of the rule-makers.[72]

'Non-enforcement is common in the law, perhaps as common as enforcement'.[73] Failed enforcement can be ascribed to the legislative process or to the enforcement structure without returning to the legislator. The question whether it is the first or the second can be answered on a case-by-case basis. Implementers of the law can influence policy-makers with respect to which policies might be more feasible to apply in relation, for example, to their competences. Political decisions can impact on implementation to the extent that the implementing authorities are provided with the requisite resources and instruments such as incentives, supervisory capacity, and information. For example, in federal states local authorities are given the necessary power, structure and resources in order to implement state legislation.

Research on the effectiveness of criminal law has to take into account the so-called 'dark number', namely the number of cases that do not surface through the workings of the criminal justice system. Especially in the field of organised crime and money laundering, the dark area is considered to be rather large. Besides undetected acts, the number of which could be registered in statistics compiled by the police, the organisational strategy of detecting some crimes is biased. Modern criminology has shown that the use of discretion operates as a filter for the imposition of punishing criminal acts. Research on the offences reported shows that criminal investigators can play an important role in labelling criminality. Also, after arrest and once prosecutions are instituted, prosecutors may categorize certain forms of conduct, and can prioritise certain cases over others. It has been proven that the action of the investigative authorities, namely, the police, might influence the implementation of a law, to the extent that, for example, investigative efforts can be directed towards the prosecution of certain conducts rather than others.[74] In addition, it bears noting that the successful prosecution of crimes often does not eliminate the further commission of crime but might simply transfer its manifestation to a different sector. This phenomenon, known as 'spill-over effect' or '*Verlagerungseffekt*' can frustrate the efforts to counteract crimes perpetrated with respect to a particular field of criminal law, or a region or state or group of states when one actor does not implement effective penalties, thus enabling crimes to be committed with impunity.

The imposition of sanctions is part of the enforcement of penal laws. The menace of punishment can foster the deterrent effect of criminal law.

---

[71] Aubert 1965, p. 89.

[72] Friedman 1975, p. 48.

[73] Friedman 1975, p. 94.

[74] Blankenburg 1995, pp. 10, 20.

Yet, deterrence can only be verified through behavioural research of potential offenders. This study infers the deterrent potential of the provision from interviewees' opinions and from criminal statistics on sanctions applied to offenders. Sanctions cannot be deterrent if they are not applied. What prevents a potential offender from violating the law is the perceived risk of the real sanction applicable and not the vague threat of being punished. The certainty of punishment is, therefore, of great importance, apart from it being one of the fundamental principles of penal law. In order to influence people's perception of the risk of sanctions, the criminal justice system can accentuate its role through surveillance methods. As much as police cars parked along a street have a deterrent effect, to the extent that drivers will believe that their driving is being monitored, other surveillance systems have a similar effect.

Another premise is necessary when assessing the effectiveness of criminal law: Effectiveness means assessing the right balance between the repressive claim and the necessity of respecting fundamental legal principles, and thus limiting the scope and use of criminal law. If on the one hand there is public interest in the prosecution of crime, on the other hand the effectiveness of criminal law cannot be guaranteed at any cost. When prosecuting crimes, a state needs not to violate other fundamental principles. It is thus necessary, while assessing the effectiveness of a criminal policy, to look at the attributed functions and thus at the law-making process.

Besides being part of a strategic plan, law enforcement may be the result of a distorted perception about the seriousness of crime. The implementers of the law are able to interpret criminal law provisions within the limits of the discretionary powers they enjoy and in so doing, they are able to influence the effectiveness of the criminal law. In this context it is important to bear in mind that certain offences are perceived to be less serious than others. White collar crimes and other economic crimes are notoriously perceived to be less serious than, for example, bodily injury or offences linked to organised crime. Economic crimes such as money laundering are characterised by a high level of technicality that hinders the public from fully understanding their seriousness. Moreover, they are usually perceived as 'victimless' offences that do not directly harm specific individuals or goods.

2.2 Assessing the Variables

The study is comprised of a combination of different methods, namely, a discourse analysis, an analysis of a study of the doctrinal debate, a qualitative analysis of quantitative data, and an empirical research conducted by way of semi-structured interviews. The following lines describe the methodology adopted to assess the variables identified as relevant for evaluating the effectiveness of the money laundering offence. The discourse analysis's aim is to reveal manifest purposes of the law that are communicated to the public and to unveil the latent intentions that have underpinned the foundation of the anti-money laundering initiatives and their subsequent developments. The discourse analysis is conducted by way evaluating primary documents such as official documents, recommendations and declarations of intents, UN-Resolutions and Conventions, official commentaries, statements and fact-sheets, European directives and decisions, explanatory and evaluation reports, action plans and official records of the German Parliament (*Drucksachen*). The historical and political context has also been inferred through secondary sources, such as books, articles, and the work done by NGOs. This is therefore a pure desktop study, based on primary sources such as legal and parliamentarian documents, and secondary sources, namely, legal scholarship. Research conducted on institutional documents has advantages and disadvantages. Among the positive aspects are the fact that it is possible to analyse a phenomenon in a diachronic way and, thanks to the availability of the literature, such research can be conducted with minimal financial cost. The drawbacks of especially formal documents, according to one scholar, is that the information at one's disposal is incomplete and has an official character.[75] It is, on the other hand, true that official documents often provide a distorted image of the reality, in accordance with the will of the authority that produced them. This is the technical perspective discussed above in relation to the issue of the manifest and latent purposes of a given law. It is however possible, to integrate and contextualise notions contained in the documents with other related sources. From official parliamentarian documents, for example, the manifest intents are inferred, while from the political discussions that preceded the approval of the final draft of the law, latent goals are deducted. The analysis of the law-making process is closely aligned to the theoretical assumptions spelt out above, and this will include looking at both the sociological, political and economic factors that play a role in obtaining a more balanced understanding of the issues at play here.

The qualitative interpretative analysis of quantitative secondary data makes use of criminal statistics published by the federal police, by the Ministry of Justice and Consumers Protection (BMJV), the Ministry of Finance (BMF) and by the Federal bureau for statistics. Moreover, data is inferred through reports compiled by transnational bodies such as the Financial Action Task Force (FATF). Secondary data is data that has been previously collected and tabulated by other sources. Due to the external origin, this type of data may not be 100% reliable, however, thanks to the qualitative approach, a critical perspective on the outcome of the statistics is maintained. The use of a qualitative technique to analyse quantitative data serves the goal of keeping a critical approach in evaluating criminal statistics on money laundering. Furthermore, the joint use of qualitative and quantitative generates a unique insight into the complexity of social phenomena, which would not be evident from an analysis of either type of data alone. Part IV looks into the deeper considerations relating to the collection of data. Given that the underlying hypothesis is that the offence of money laundering does not address the phenomenon of money laundering in its complexity, the official numbers are seen as being representative of the functioning of the criminal justice system and thus as only one of the factors constituting the variable of the implementation of the law.

[75] Corbetta 2003, p. 159.

Between January 2014 and July 2015 30 semi-structured interviews were conducted with individuals who have a key-role in the decision-making process for the amendment of anti-money laundering law, and with legal role-players that apply the law in their daily practice. Interviews make it possible to gain an understanding of the perceptions, opinions and practices otherwise not come across in purely textual research findings. In addition, the opinions and perceptions of practitioners offer a useful insight into law enforcement practices and thus on the effects of the 'law in action', on the background of the previous assumptions about the importance of revealing the latent functions and effects of law.

In particular, the experts interviewed were, a policy advisor for the German Parliament for the socialist party (SPD); a former and a current deputy director general respectively, heads of the economic, computer, corruption related and environmental crime divisions of the Ministry of Justice and Consumers Protection, the head of Division VII A 3, Payment systems; German SEPA Council; prevention of money laundering, terrorism financing and other forms of financial crime of the Ministry of Finance, two civil servants from the Division I 18, public security and order of the State department of Hessen, and a policy officer of the NGO WEED (World Economy, Ecology and Development). The legal role-players consisted of 11 lawyers, three police officers, two representatives of the Chamber of Public Accountants and four public prosecutors, the former head of Department Three of the detective branch of the police of the state of Berlin which deals with organised crime, and two chief superintendents of the Berlin State Detective branch of the police, leading the financial investigations group—Berlin LKA 311GFG—(*Gemeinsame Finanzermittlungs Gruppe*).[76] The sampling was confined geographically to Berlin.[77] A pilot-interview was conducted with a member of the NGO Tax Justice Network Germany, and one of the authors of the report '*Schattenfinanzentrum Deutschland. Deutschlands Rolle bei globaler Geldwäsche, Kapitalflucht und Steuervermeidung*'[78] (Shadow Financial Centre Germany: Germany's role in global money laundering, capital flight and tax evasion @own translation) published in November 2013 by WEED (*Weltwirtschaft, Ökologie & Entwicklung*), GPF (Global Policy Forum), Tax Justice Network Deutschland, and Misereor. The pilot interview proved particularly useful since the report he co-authored was one of publications that helped to public awareness then, and because it was the first report published by the non-governmental sector on the topic of about money laundering in Germany.

The sample of respondents to be interviewed was based on a selection of a subset of the whole population. The sampling design chosen was the so-called 'expert sampling'. Respondents were chosen in a non-random manner, based on

[76] The interview sample consists of a majority of male respondents. Yet, given that gender is not considered a relevant variable for the purpose of this research, this element is not taken into account.

[77] Two interviews with interviewees outside of greater Berlin were conducted by telephone.

[78] Henn et al. 2013.

their expertise in the area of anti-money laundering law. The advantage of this approach is that experts tend to be more familiar with the subject matter than non-experts, which lends more credibility to their opinions. Yet, the findings are still not generalizable to the overall population at large. Interviews were semi-structured along the flowing lines: A track of questions was set, but the order in which topics were addressed and the way of formulating questions was left open. A protocol was set on the basis of the study conducted on legal scholarship, the law-making process and the quantitative data collection. Some questions were set for all interviews, while others were designed to correspond to the group of experts to be interviewed. This semi-structured interview afford the interviewer the liberty to introduce fresh questions arising from the responses to the questions put, thus ensuring that all topics are covered and the necessary information is gleaned. All interviews except one were conducted face-to-face, either where the respondent's place of employment or at the interviewer's university workplace. As all interviewees were mother tongue German speakers, the interviews were conducted in German. This made it easier for the interviewees to respond confidently and eloquently, whilst at the same time allowing for spontaneity. The aim of a qualitative interview is indeed to provide a frame within which the respondents can express their own way of thinking in their own words.[79] Subject to the approval of the interviewees, interviews were recorded in order to keep records. Where they requested this, the interviewees were give a list of the questions prior to the interview. During the initial conversations, the nature and purpose of the project, how the collected data would be used, people involved and desired interviewees were communicated to the respondent. However, during the interview, respondents were left free to express their own opinions, without being influenced by the perspective of the interviewer. Also, if required, complete anonymity was assured. Yet, notwithstanding what methodology manuals suggest,[80] respondents were not left completely free to talk. The role of the interviewer was, on the contrary, an active one. This tactic was adopted because of the specificity of the sample and of the object of the research. The risk an interviewer runs when dealing with government officials and with public servants, is that they might be prone to avoid 'hot issues' and would prefer to talk without interruption about a topic more desirable to them. Since the goal was, instead, to stimulate conversation and specifically on problematic issues and bothersome questions, respondents were often interrupted or urged not to divert from the discussion. Despite being time-consuming and at risk of bias, the choice of using personal interviews was informed by the several advantages: the opportunity to clarify any issues raised by the respondent, the possibility of asking probing or follow-up questions, the improvement of response rates through persuasion, the inferring of information read from the body language, pauses, tone of voice, and the dynamics between respondents.[81] Given that the aim

---

[79] Corbetta 2003, p. 72.

[80] Corbetta 2003, p. 93.

[81] Bhattacherjee 2012, p. 78.

of the empirical research was to understand the opinions, perceptions, interpretations and the motives of the actions of the role-players who apply the law (legal actors), the interview was considered the best tool to assess the respondents' perspective on a particular issue, for purposes of obtaining a close understanding of their way of thinking. In addition, the information garnered from the interviews is supplemented with official declarations of intent and opinions issued by the respective organisations from which the interviewees came, as well as other official documents. Given that many topics that were touched were strongly political in nature, the author desisted from interposing her perspective. Therefore, Part V contains the actual words spoken by the interviewees in the direct conversations, all of which the author has translated into English.

2.3 Considerations

Against the background based on the socio-legal framework that sets the definition of legal effectiveness, and on the critical literature on the inadequacy of the international anti-money laundering system to eliminate the targeted activity, as set out in the introduction of this book, the hypothesis underlying the case study is the following: Article 261 of the GCC may be an example of a symbolic legal provision, whose latent purposes prevail over its declared purposes. In particular, it is hypothesised that the law satisfies all parties taking part in the law-making process, thanks to the actual ineffectiveness, which pleases those who were against the enactment of the provision. While the manifested purpose of tackling money laundering has in fact remained in the background, other latent goals might have been pursued. It is further hypothesised that the 'legal inaction' is part of a process of decriminalisation that intentionally grants impunity to a certain group of actors, in this case those laundering money, while giving the appearance that the practice is not accepted by law by labelling it as criminal.

References

Allott A N (1980) The limits of law. Butterworths, London.

Allott A N (1981) The effectiveness of laws. Valparaiso University Law Review 15 (2): 229–242.

Amelung K (1980) Strafrechtswissenschaft und Strafgesetzgebung. Zeitschrift für die gesamte Strafrechtswissenschaft (ZStW) 92 (1): 19–72.

Aubert V (1965) Alcune funzioni sociali della legislazione. Quaderni di sociologia 14: 313–338.

Baratta A (1990) Requisitos minimos del respeto de los derechos humanos en la ley penal. Introducción. In Aa. Vv. (ed.) Seminario Criminologia critica y sistema penal. Universidad Nacional Mayor de San Marcos, Lima, pp. 89–107.

Beccaria C (1786) Dei delitti e delle pene. Cazin, Paris.

Becker H S (1963) Outsiders. Studies in the sociology of deviance. The Free Press of Glencoe, New York.

Bettini R (1983) Il Circolo vizioso legislativo: efficacia del diritto ed efficienza degli apparati pubblici in Italia. Franco Angeli, Milan.

Bhattacherjee A (2012) Social Science Research: Principles, Methods, and Practices. Textbooks Collection. Book 3. http://scholarcommons.usf.edu/oa_textbooks/3. University of South Florida.

Boudon R (1981) Effetti perversi dell'azione sociale. Feltrinelli, Milan.

Blankenburg E (1985) Research concept for the study of implementation. Tidskrift för Rättssociologi 2 (3/4): 205–226.

Blankenburg E (1995) Mobilisierung des Rechts: Eine Einführung in die Rechtssoziologie. Springer-Verlag, Berlin/Heidelberg.

Bryde B O (1993) Die Effektivität von Rechts als Rechtsproblem. Vortrag gehalten vor der Juristischen Gesellschaft zu Berlin am 17. März 1993. De Gruyter, Berlin/New York.

Burton B (ed.) (2007) Burton's Legal Thesaurus, 4th edn. McGraw-Hill, New York.

Corbetta P (2003) La ricerca sociale: Metodologia e tecniche. III Le tecniche qualitative. Il Mulino, Bologna.

Erickson K T (1962) Notes on the Sociology of Deviance. In: Becker H S (ed.) The Other Side: Perspectives on Deviance. The Free Press, New York, pp. 9–21.

Ferrari V (1992) Le funzioni del diritto. Laterza, Bari.

Ferrari V (1997) Lineamenti di sociologia del diritto. Azione giuridica e sistema normativo. Laterza, Bari.

Friedman L M (1975) The Legal System: A Social Science Perspective. Russell Sage Foundation, New York.

Funcke-Auffermann N (2007) Symbolische Gesetzgebung im Lichte der positiven Generalprävention. Eine Untersuchung am Beispiel des „Gesetzes zur Änderung der Vorschrift über die Straftaten gegen die sexuelle Selbstimmung und zu Änderung anderer Vorschriften" vom 27. Dezember 2003. Duncker & Humblot, Berlin.

Gallino L (2012) La lotta di classe dopo la lotta di classe. Laterza, Rome/Bari.

Garner B A (ed.) (2014) Black's law dictionary, 10th edn. Thomson Reuters Opperman Drive.

Geiger T (1987) Vorstudien zu einer Soziologie des Rechts. Duncker und Humblot, Berlin.

Günther K (2002) Die Symbolisch-expressive Bedeutung der Strafe, Eine neue Stratheorie jenseits von Vergeltung und Prävention? In Prittwitz W et al. (ed.) Festschrift für Klaus Lüderssen. Nomos, Baden-Baden, pp. 205–220.

Hagenbarth R (1981) Symbolische und instrumentelle Funktionen moderner Gesetze. Zeitschrift für Rechtspolitik (ZRP) 14 (9): 201–204.

Hassemer W (1989) Symbolisches Strafrecht und Rechtsgüterschtutz. Neue Zeitschrift für Strafrecht (NStZ) 9: 553–559.

Henn M, Mewes S, Meinzer M (2013) Schattenfinanzzentrum Deutschland. Deutschlands Rolle bei globaler Geldwäsche, Kapitalflucht und Steuervermeidung. http://www2.weed-online.org/uploads/schattenfinanzzentrum_deutschland.pdf. Last accessed on 17 September 2016.

Hierro L (2010) La eficacia de las normas jurídicas. Fontamara, México.

Jost P J (1998) Effektivität von Recht aus ökonomischer Sicht. Duncker und Humblot, Berlin.

Kelsen H (1952) Lineamenti di dottrina pura del diritto. Einaudi, Turin.

Law and Society Berlin (LSI Berlin) Die Versprechungen des Rechts. http://easychair.org/smart-program/Berlin2015/program.html. Last accessed 17 September 2016.

Leisner W (1971) Effizienz als Rechtsprinzip. Mohr Siebeck, Tübingen.

Marinucci G, Dolcini E (2006) Manuale di diritto penale. Parte generale. Giuffrè Editore, Milan.

Merton R K (1983) Teoria e struttura sociale 1. Teoria sociologica e ricerca empirica. Il Mulino, Bologna.

Moccia S (1995) La perenne emergenza. Tendenze autoritarie nel sistema penale. Edizioni scientifiche italiane, Naples.

Neves M (1999) Von der symbolischen Gesetzgebung zur symbolischen Konstitutionalisierung: Ein Überblick. Institut für Staatswissenschaft, Neubiberg.

Newig J (2003) Symbolische Umweltgesetzgebung. Duncker & Humblot, Berlin.

Newig J (2007) Symbolic environmental legislation and societal self-deception. Environmental Politics 16 (2): 276–296.
Noll P (1972) Gründe für die soziale Unwirksamkeit von Gesetzen. In Rehbinder M, Schelsky H (eds.) Zur Effektivität des Rechts. Jahrbuch für Rechtssoziologie und Rechtstheorie 3. Bartelsmann Verlagsgruppe, Düsseldorf, pp. 259–269.
Noll P (1981) Symbolische Gesetzgebung. Zeitschrift für Schweizerisches Recht (ZschwR): 347–364.
Pal L (1995) Competing Paradigms in Policy Discourse. Policy Sciences 18 (2): 185–207.
Paliero CE (1992) Il principio di effettività del diritto penale. Rivista italiana di diritto e procedura penale: 430–478.
Piovani P (1953) Il significato del principio di effettività. Giuffrè, Milan.
Rehbinder M, Schelsky H (1972) Zur Effektivität des Rechts. Jahrbuch für Rechtssoziologie und Rechtstheorie 3. Bertelsmann Universitätsverlag, Düsseldorf, pp. 555–564.
Ritzer G, Ryan J M (eds.) (2011) The concise encyclopedia of sociology. Wiley-Blackwell, West Sussex.
Rottleuthner H (1983) Teoria del diritto e sociologia del diritto. Il Mulino, Bologna.
Ryffel H (1974) Rechtssoziologie. Eine systematische Orientierung. Luchterhand, Neuwied-Berlin.
Scott J (ed.) (2014) A dictionary of Sociology, 4th edn. Oxford University Press, Oxford.
Sutherland E H (1940) White-Collar Criminality. American Sociological Review 5 (1):1–12.
Swaffield S (1998) Contextual Meanings in Policy Discourse. Policy Sciences 31 (3):199–224.
Tannenbaum F (1938) Crime and the community. Ginn, Boston.
Treves R (2002) Sociolgia del diritto. Origine, ricerche, problemi. Einaudi, Turin.
Villegas M (1994) La eficacia simbólica del derecho. Ediciones Uniandes, Bogotá.
Villegas M (2003) Symbolic Power Without Violence? Critical Comments on Legal Consciousness Studies. International Journal for the Semiotics of Law 16 (4): 363–393.
Yanow D (2014) Interpretive Analysis and Comparative Research. In Engeli I, Rothmayr C (eds.) Comparative policy studies: Conceptual and methodological challenges. Palgrave Macmillan, New York, pp. 131–59.

Part II
The Genesis of the Anti-Money Laundering Regime: Tracing Statements of Legislative Purposes

It is vital to place the debate in its historical context if we are to understand how we got to the present ludicrous state of affairs!

Bosworth-Davies 2006, p. 346

Chapter 3
The International Law-Making Process

Abstract This part describes the genesis of the money-laundering offence and the subsequent developments. An historical look at how the legislative process has developed from the beginning to the present day is taken. The aim is not only to describe events anecdotally, but to comment on the developments as well. Given that the offence was introduced in the German Penal Code in fulfilment of international duties, the book traces firstly the international law-making process. The chapter specifically sheds light on which motives triggered the introduction of the offence as a transnational crime. Among European Member States, it has been mostly the European Directives that have further triggered the development of anti-money-laundering laws. Therefore, the book focuses on the European legal framework, and on the motives that drove European policymakers to adopt the current laws. The emphasis will be on the ever-new functions that lawmakers, at both the international and national level, have ascribed to the anti-money laundering regime, in order to reveal its ultimate latent or symbolic functions. In fact, the aim of this study is to investigate whether intents, other than those expressed officially, have driven the creation and the consequent development of the money-laundering offence.

Keywords Money-laundering offence · United Nations Convention Against Illicit Traffic in Narcotic Drugs and Psychotropic Substances · FATF · European Anti-money Laundering Directives · Anti-money laundering regime

Contents

V. Zoppei, *Anti-Money Laundering Law: Socio-Legal Perspectives on the Effectiveness of German Practices*, International Criminal Justice Series 12,
DOI 10.1007/978-94-6265-180-7_3

Although nowadays it is not uncommon to view money laundering either as a crime typically linked to organised crime, or as a phenomenon related to the banking sector, 30 years ago it was not criminalised at all. While prior to 1988, only few national legislatures criminalised the laundering of the proceeds of crime in their respective criminal codes, the genesis of the offence of money laundering in the international arena[1] is considered to have occurred in 1988 with adoption of the United Nations Convention Against Illicit Traffic in Narcotic Drugs and Psychotropic Substances (Vienna Convention).[2] Whereas the UN treaty marks the creation of the crime of money laundering at the international level, the Financial Action Task Force's (FATF) 'Forty Recommendations' that were issued shortly thereafter in 1990 introduced the preventive approach to combating money laundering by emphasising the role of private entities.[3] These two aspects, the repressive and the preventive one, still characterise the current anti-money laundering policy. The money-laundering offence has been amended often with the purpose of increasing the effectiveness of the fight against money laundering. In particular, given that money laundering is a derivative crime, the scope of the offence has been expanded mainly by adding ever-new emergency-driven provisions in the list of the designated predicate offences. In order to understand the continuous expansion of the reach of the money-laundering offence, the book refers to the parallel development of the preventive regime.

---

[1] The offence is not considered as one of the core crimes under international criminal law that are listed in the enabling statute of international criminal courts. Yet, it is regarded as a serious crime by the African Union for the jurisdiction of the African Court of Justice and Human and People's Rights. *See* African Union 2014, Article 28 A(1) 9 (International jurisdiction of the court).

[2] The money laundering offence, in the threefold definition that has remained in force so far, was conceived in the Vienna Convention of 1988 under Article 3(1) b i and ii and c. Although this instrument does not use the term 'money laundering', the conducts described have been defined as money laundering in the following UNCAC of 2000 and in the Palermo Convention of 2003. *See* United Nations Convention Against Illicit Traffic in Narcotic Drugs and Psychotropic Substances, opened for signature on 20 December 1988, 1582 UNTS 95 (entered into force 11 November 1990) [hereinafter Vienna Convention]; United Nations Convention Against Transnational Organized Crime, opened for signature on 15 November 2000, 2225 UNTS 209 (entered into force 19 September 2003) [hereinafter Palermo Convention], and United Nations Convention against Corruption, opened for signature on 9 December 2003, 2349 UNTS 41 (entered into force 14 December 2005) [hereinafter UNCAC].

[3] *See* FATF 1990.

3.1 Tracing the International Law-Making Process

From the very beginning, the money-laundering offence was drafted broadly to allow it to be interpreted in such a way as to satisfy the various wills and interests of the actors that took part in the law-making process. Very different, indeed, were the motives that triggered the respective legislatures to introduce the offence of money laundering. For example, Italy criminalised money laundering in 1978 to tackle armed robbery and crimes cognate to organised crime, such as extortion and kidnapping for the purposes of extortion.[4] The UK was concerned with Irish terrorism, but because of influence by the US, it initially developed money-laundering control as part of an anti-drug trafficking policy.[5] The Australian government sought to tackle tax evasion when it enacted its anti-money laundering law. The Australian anti-money laundering law was introduced specifically by the Proceeds of Crime Act of 1987, which aimed to prevent individuals from hiding assets that might be subject to confiscation.[6] Likewise, in the US, money-laundering control was introduced initially to combat tax evasion using international banks: The US Bank Secrecy Act of 1970 was aimed primarily at preventing the use of foreign banks to launder criminal proceeds or to conceal money from American fiscal authorities.[7] Thus, the focus of the US legislature was 'black money' (monies deriving from tax evasion) and not 'dirty money' (monies deriving from other serious crimes, such as crimes linked to organised crime).[8] Yet, the first 'Money Laundering Control Act' passed in 1986 was part of the 'Anti-Drug Abuse Act'.[9] France's President *Mitterand* sought to outlaw the abuse of offshore jurisdictions for the purpose of evading taxes while taking part in the negotiations for the FATF Recommendations.[10] Switzerland, on the other hand, where money deriving from tax evasion was not perceived as harmful

[4] Italian law decreto legge 591/1978, which, under Article 3, introduced Article 648 *bis* of the Italian criminal code; despite the conduct not being labelled money laundering, the law criminalised acts of laundering proceeds of crime.

[5] Levi and Reuter 2006, p. 305.

[6] FATF 2005, p. 27.

[7] The law 'Financial Record-keeping and Reporting of Currency and Foreign Transactions Act'—known as Bank Secrecy Act—sets regulations requiring various reports and record-keeping of financial institutions and individuals United States Code, Title 31, Subtitle IV, Chapter 53, Subchapter II (*alias* 31 U.S.C. 5311 et seq.).

[8] Arzt 1997, p. 37.

[9] US Public Law, an act to strengthen Federal efforts to encourage foreign cooperation in eradicating illicit drug crops and in halting international drug traffic, to improve enforcement of Federal drug laws and enhance interdiction of illicit drug shipments, to provide strong Federal leadership in establishing effective drug abuse prevention and education programs, to expand Federal support for drug abuse treatment and rehabilitation efforts, and for other purposes; pp. 99–570.

[10] Pieth 2004, p. 8.

as money deriving from other serious crimes such as drug trafficking, accepted to join the FATF decision-making process on condition that tax offences were not listed as predicate offences for money laundering.[11] Put differently, Switzerland was interested in fighting money laundering without relinquishing its status as an international financial centre.[12] The private sector, too, took the initiative to combat the laundering of proceeds of crime, the motives being, once again, different. After Swiss banks became involved in 'dubious practices', for example the Chiasso banking scandal of 1977, the Swiss banking sector became worried about public confidence in the banking system. Therefore, to impart to their clients an image of integrity, the banks began becoming involved in the prevention of money laundering. In addition, the adoption of self-regulations would have allowed the private sector to avoid the imposition of external regulations. In 1977, the Swiss Bankers Association adopted a code of conduct that contained rules on internal risk management, which were to become the core principles of the preventive anti-money laundering law.[13] Furthermore, in 1974, a total of 10 leading banking supervisors founded the Basel Committee on Banking Supervision (BCBS) which in 1988 adopted a text in which for the first time 'bank supervisors agreed internationally, in such prominent way'[14] that '[b]anks and other financial institutions may be unwittingly used as intermediaries for the transfer or deposit of funds derived from criminal activity'.[15] They referred also to the use of the financial system to make payments and transfers of funds to hide the source and beneficial ownership of money as 'money laundering'. As the previous Recommendation of the Council of Europe had already stressed, the Basel Committee's Statement of Principles of 1988, too, recognised the significant role of the preventive strategy in the field of anti-money laundering and encouraged banks to ensure that the banking sector would not be 'associated with criminals or be used as a channel for money-laundering'.[16] In this context, according to the Statement of Principles, the primary function was 'to maintain the overall financial stability and soundness of banks rather than to ensure that individual transactions conducted by bank customers are legitimate. Nevertheless, [...] supervisors cannot be indifferent to the use made of banks by criminals'.[17] Thus, while adopting anti-money laundering declarations, banks committed themselves mainly to the protection of the financial and the banking sector.

---

[11] Ibid.

[12] Pieth 1993, p. 101.

[13] Levi and Reuter 2006, p. 305; Pieth 2004, pp. 7–8.

[14] Pieth 2004, p. 7.

[15] BCBS 1988, para I.

[16] Ibid.

[17] Ibid. para 6.

3.1.1 The Genesis of the Money-Laundering Offence in the Vienna Convention

Given the different and contrasting expectations, a consensus had to be found on a topic upon which all parties could agree.[18] In this context, the need to wage the 'war on drugs' accommodated all parties under the strong influence of the US.[19] The 'war on drugs' held more success than the commitment to combat terrorism and political extremism, or the desire to curb tax evasion. The Vienna Convention emphasised the universal agreement on the necessity of tackling the scourge of drug trafficking and drug consumption. According to the Commentary on the United Nations Convention against Illicit Traffic in Narcotic Drugs and Psychotropic Substances (hereinafter the Commentary on the Vienna Convention), there was already a worldwide consensus on the threats posed by the magnitude of the drug problem since the beginning of the 20th century.[20] This was attested to by several international initiatives that were launched to control the use of drugs, and by the various multilateral conventions that were adopted with regard to the regulation of drugs, for instance, the 'Single Convention on Narcotic Drugs' of 1961, and the Protocol Amending the Single Convention on Narcotic Drugs and the Convention on Psychotropic Substances' of 1971.[21] The UN was even called upon to declare drug trafficking a crime against humanity.[22] This proposal, despite having been included in the preliminary elaboration of the draft, was not attached in the final version because of strong governmental opposition from many countries. In the aftermath of the Vietnam War, and in the wake of the US's interest in tackling the 'drug problem', the 15th Conference of the European Ministers of Justice of 1986 also 'discussed the need to combat drug abuse (…), for example, by freezing and confiscating the proceeds from drug trafficking'.[23] A consensus was, thus, found

[18] In fact, only western countries were represented in this preliminary phase of the anti-money laundering policy-making process. But the expansion of the anti-money laundering system would be justified afterwards in view of the harm money laundering caused to developing economies. *See* Alldridge 2008, pp. 446 ss.

[19] For a complete overview on the war on drugs, s*ee* Duke and Gross 1993.

[20] Commentary on the UN Convention against Illicit Traffic in Narcotic Drugs and Psychotropic Substances, 1998 [hereinafter Commentary on the Vienna Convention].

[21] The main purpose of the first two treaties was to codify internationally applicable control measures in order to ensure the availability of narcotic drugs and psychotropic substances for medical and scientific purposes, and to prevent their diversion into illicit channels. The Convention on Psychotropic Substances of 1971 established an international control system for psychotropic substances. *See* http://ec.europa.eu/world/agreements/prepareCraeteTreatiesWorkspace/treatiesGeneralData.do?redirect=true&treatyld=526 Last accessed on 16 October 2012.

[22] *See* UN Resolution A/RES/40/121 that recalled the Quito Declaration against Traffic in Narcotic Drugs of 11 August 1984, and the New York Declaration against Drug Trafficking and the Illicit Use of Drugs of 1 October 1984 in which drug trafficking was considered a crime against humanity.

[23] Council of Europe 1990b, p. 1.

also at European level on the topic of drug trafficking. At the UN Conference that preceded the Convention, the legitimation for resorting to criminal law was based on of the extreme danger that illicit trafficking and consumption of narcotics posed to national security and public health. The Convention was adopted at the United Nations Conference for the Adoption of a Convention against Illicit Traffic in Narcotic Drugs and Psychotropic Substances, held in Vienna from 25 November to 20 December 1988. The treaty was signed on 19 December 1988 and entered into force on 11 November 1990. The Vienna Convention set the basis for the criminalisation of money laundering within the context of the fight against drug trafficking.

Given the declared consensus expressed for the UN treaty by the signatory parties on the necessity of stopping drug-related criminality, the criminalisation of money laundering acquired the appearance of an instrument universally recognised as useful to wage the 'war on drugs'. Yet, the urgency of tackling drugs was more of concern to the US, which indeed introduced the 'Money Laundering Control Act' explicitly as part of the federal 'war on drugs',[24] and regarded it since then as a significant component of the US fight against drug trafficking and drug consumption.[25] The drafters of the Commentary of 1998 stated that the Convention's definition of money laundering owed much to the then US formulation of the offence; however, the provisions were formulated in such a way to be acceptable to and compatible with most number legal systems.[26] In fact, the offence was designed broadly to allow different interpretations that would accommodated the various parties.

The definition provided in the UN treaty under Article 3(1) b and c has nevertheless been accepted globally. In particular, the offence was designed in a three-fold definition, which criminalised different conducts: (i) The conversion or transfer of property, knowing that such property is derived from any offence or offences established in accordance with subparagraph (a) of this paragraph, or from an act of participation in such offence or offences, for the purpose of concealing or disguising the illicit origin of the property or of assisting any person who is involved in the commission of such an offence or offences to evade the legal consequences of his actions; (ii) The concealment or disguise of the true nature, source, location, disposition, movement, rights with respect to, or ownership of property, knowing that such property is derived from an offence or offences established in accordance with subparagraph (a) of this paragraph or from an act of participation in such an offence or offences'.[27] Subparagraph (c) requires states to criminalise, 'subject to its constitutional principles and the basic concepts of its legal system: (i) The acquisition, possession or use of property, knowing, at the

[24] Levi and Reuter 2006, p. 296.

[25] This issue will represent an important point of criticism in the opinion of some interviewees. *See* Chap. 7.

[26] Commentary on the Vienna Convention, above n. 20, p. 10.

[27] Article 3(1) b of the Vienna Convention, above n. 2.

time of receipt, (ii) That such property was derived from an offence or offences established in accordance with subparagraph (a) of this paragraph or from an act of participation in such offence or offences'.[28]

Accordingly, the criminalised conducts are the following: (a) Conversion or transfer of property for the purposes of disguising the illicit origin of it. (b) Knowingly assisting in disguising the source of proceeds of crime. This means persons ranging from family members to friends who allow criminal proceeds to be laundered through the opening of bank accounts or the purchasing of immovable property in their names, to gatekeepers such as accountants, lawyers and financial advisers who are aware of the actual source of their client's income. (c) A further conduct included is the concealment of the true nature, source, location, disposition or ownership of or rights with respect to property with knowledge that the property is the proceeds of crime. This would cover situations where, for instance, anonymous shell companies are founded with the ultimate goal of hiding the true ownership of the sums of money invested in such company. The elements of the crime determining the *actus reus* are the commission of a predicate offence and the presence of the proceeds of crime. The *mens rea* required is the intent to conceal the proceeds and the knowledge of unlawfulness of the illegitimate origin. In the UN Conventions, the law requires that predicate offences must be established, but there is no requirement of a previous conviction. Thus, according to the wording of the UN treaty, the commission of the antecedent crime does not need to be proven beyond a reasonable doubt.

The UN treaty shaped the money-laundering offence as a derivative crime, whose existence is linked to a predicate offence. Having built the provision on the fact that the handled objects derive from another offence, the wording of Article 3, para 1, and subparagraph (b) and (c) has allowed lawmakers to fill the definition of the offence by taking into account continuously unfurling emergencies. In particular, the expansion of the scope of the money-laundering offence can be triggered in different ways, through an automatic process, in cases in which national legislatures adopt an 'all-crimes approach', every time a new offence is introduced in the penal code, this will automatically belong to the catalogue of the predicate offences; or through a specific process, in cases in which national legislatures set a limited catalogue of predicate offences, the introduction of new offences needs to be provided explicitly by new provisions that modify the money-laundering offence. Finally, given that predicate offences can be committed abroad, there can be an indirect expansion because of the criminalisation of new conducts in foreign jurisdictions. The result has been that anti-money laundering laws have assumed, for example, the additional functions of combating non-drug related organised crime, the financing of terrorism, the funding of the proliferation of weapons of mass destruction, tax evasion, and other types of conduct arising out of the recent financial crisis, as it will be showed in the next paragraphs.

---

[28] Article 3(1) c of the Vienna Convention, above n. 2.

While allowing different interpretations, a certain degree of harmonisation among national jurisdictions ought to have served the co-operation among Member States. Given the transnational dimension of the phenomenon of money laundering, the Convention aimed at providing a common minimum standard for the implementation of the criminalisation of money laundering. One of the purposes of the Convention, set in Article 2, was in fact to address more effectively the international illicit traffic in narcotic drugs and psychotropic substances through the promotion of co-operation among states. The then UN Secretary-General, Kofi Annan, stated: 'If crime crosses borders, so must law enforcement'.[29] Hence, improving the effectiveness of domestic criminal justice systems in relation to drug trafficking was considered a precondition for such enhanced international cooperation.[30]

3.1.2 The Money-Laundering Offence: A Tool to Tackle Organised Crime

The criminalisation of the practice was legitimised based on the so-called 'follow the money' strategy.[31] In particular, the UN treaty motivated the criminalisation of

[29] Palermo Convention, above n. 2, para iii.

[30] Commentary on the Vienna Convention, p. 48, above n. 20.

[31] Stessens 2000, p. 86. The 'follow the money' strategy and the rationale linked to the confiscation of criminal assets that justified anti-money laundering law as a tool to fight organised crime have been criticised. First, following the money might not always bring investigators to the criminals, since cash that is further invested in criminal markets is not subject to anti-money laundering checks, because it remains out of the reach of anti-money laundering control. In addition, the confiscation of assets, due to its strong potential, should not only be attached to money laundering cases. In fact, Alldridge argues that once there is enough evidence to prove the serious predicate offence, states could impose a duty to proceed with assets forfeiture to the main offence, without needing the money laundering conviction. Alldridge 2008, p. 450. Yet, confiscation of assets is, according to Italian scholars and practitioners, together with the subsequent assignment of such assets to the State which then devotes them to social purposes, has a particularly symbolic effect in territories where organised criminal groups exercise territorial control. Such a system gives credibility to the state that can re-establish public power over private illegal control. A good-practice example is the work of the Italian association, Libera Terra, which manage several confiscated properties and farms and produce organic products in a sustainable and socially responsible way. Yet such a system is not perfect: issues rise, especially with regard to confiscated firms, which, after being seized, run a high risk of going bankrupt and thus cause unemployment. Such firms, indeed, could compete on the market, thanks to the illicit managing and the illicit funding. Furthermore, financial institutions, customers and commissioners may not want to prolong their relations with the new managed company, which, therefore, is economically isolated in an often already socially adverse context. Solutions are being currently discussed in relation to the possibility of placing side by side the judicial administrator to the entrepreneur already during the seizure phase; allocating part of the confiscated sums to the reintegration in the market of such firms; training judicial administrators with entrepreneurship skills. The European Economic and Social Committee awarded the association with a prize for civil society in 2009. The EU Directive 2014/42/EU of the European Parliament and of the Council of 3 April 2014 on

money laundering to defeat drug abuse and drug trafficking by depriving drug traffickers of their ill-gotten gains in order to eliminate the incentive for engaging in these crimes.[32] The fifth and sixth paragraphs of the Preamble of the Vienna Convention stress the magnitude and the danger of the economic profit deriving from drug trafficking and highlight the necessity to eliminate the incentive for criminal activities, by depriving criminals of such illicit gains. These paragraphs should be read, according to the Commentary, as the introduction to Article 3, as it relates to the offence of money laundering.[33] Given the huge amount of drugs sold in the late 1980s, estimated to have been worth around 124 billion,[34] the solution identified in the Preamble of the UN treaty was to eliminate 'the root causes of the drug abuse problem, namely, the enormous profits derived from illicit traffic'. One of the principal elements of an effective strategy to combat drug trafficking was considered to be to undermine organised crime's financial power by providing law enforcement agencies with the necessary tools.[35] In this context, the offence of money laundering emerged as one of those necessary tools. The money-laundering offence was thus introduced in the UN treaty as a tool to counteract drug trafficking effectively by making it less attractive, due to the risk of confiscation of criminal proceeds. In this way, the forfeiture of criminal assets, besides its repressive function, acquired the purpose of criminal deterrence. In particular, the introduction of a duty to confiscate and to co-operate internationally to implement forfeiture orders was justified as the only way to deprive offenders of their ill-gotten gains, given the fact that money laundering was a victimless crime, especially in those situations where confiscation might otherwise not be possible.[36] The imprisonment of even top-ranking criminals was not effective, because while public sectors devote more criminal justice system resources to incarcerating increasing numbers of

(Footnote 31 continued)

the freezing and confiscation of instrumentalities and proceeds of crime in the European Union introduced the social reuse of confiscated property under Article 10. OJ, L 127, 29/04/2014.

[32] In the Preamble the drafters expressed their concern with the 'magnitude of and rising trend in the illicit production of, demand for and traffic in narcotic drugs and psychotropic substances, which pose a serious threat to the health and welfare of human beings and adversely affect the economic, cultural and political foundations of society'. *See* Preamble of the Vienna Convention, above n. 2. According to the Commentary on the Vienna Convention, many threats were recognised as being linked to illegal drug traffic besides the health and well-being of individuals, such as the spreading of corruption, criminal conspiracy and the subversion of public order, threats for sovereignty and security, disruption of the economy and the society. *See* Commentary on the Vienna Convention above n. 20. In addition to social and health concerns, the Preamble highlighted the 'links between illicit traffic and other related organized criminal activities which undermine the legitimate economies and threaten the stability, security and sovereignty of States'. *See* the Preamble of the Vienna Convention, above n. 2.

[33] Commentary on the Vienna Convention, p. 18, above n. 20.

[34] IMF 2001.

[35] Commentary on the Vienna Convention, p. 65, above n. 20.

[36] Stessens 2000, pp. 4, 85.

organised crime members, criminals would expand their rings of violence and of corruption to higher levels of the public sectors in order to protect themselves from punishment. Specifically in the context of the 'war on drugs,' the prosecution of dealers and consumers did not yield much success. In fact, it was observed that even when 'oligarchs of crime' were serving terms of imprisonment, they could continue to manage the criminal networks and to profit from their crimes.[37] This strategy, which was initially related to the proceeds of drug trafficking, was subsequently adapted to tackle any other type of organised criminal activity; in fact, it was considered also advantageous in terms of the source of funding for law enforcement activity.[38] Criminals, while enjoying the proceeds of crime, by purchasing items, services and properties, come into the legitimate economy. This integration of criminal money into the lawful economy, which is called the 'integration phase' of the money-laundering process, has been considered the weakest part of the money-laundering process, organised crime's Achilles heel. Since most high-level criminals usually stay aloof from the commission of crimes, while enjoying the financial profits, the offence of money laundering could serve the purpose of gathering evidence against top-ranking criminals by tracking the movement of money. By following the 'paper trail', law enforcement agencies should be able to trace the illicit money and thus find the criminal network acting behind the 'foot soldiers' engaged in the frontline of illicit activities. Thus, the criminalisation of money laundering as set in the Vienna Convention, by allowing the confiscation of the proceeds of crime under Article 5(1) should have served the purposes of attacking criminal organisations' economic power, and of facilitating investigations into criminal networks, thanks to the possibility of following the paper trail.

3.1.3 The FATF Recommendations

Concurrently with the adoption of criminal instruments to counteract the phenomenon of money laundering, the necessity of a preventive regime emerged in the debate of the G7 and other industrialised countries. This led to the creation of the Financial Action Task Force in 1989. The FATF is a body that aims to set

[37] In support of this philosophy, a study conducted between 2000 and 2007 on 107 countries about the most effective policies to counteract organised crime, showed that criminal groups react to higher expected punishments by re-assigning resources to expanding the scope and scale of violence and of corruption to higher levels of the public sectors in order to protect themselves from prosecution. As a result, when the expected punishment increases, but financial assets remain relatively untouched, there is a parallel paradoxical growth of organised crime, too. 'This constitutes the paradox of criminal sanctions where more frequent and stiffer punishments applied to physical persons lead to higher levels of organized crime and to higher levels of corruption'. *See* Buscaglia 2008, pp. 2, 11.

[38] Nadelmann 1986, pp. 33–34.

international standards to promote the Vienna Convention.[39] In 1990, the FATF issued 40 Recommendations, which went beyond the scope of the UN treaty, by leaving it up to each country to decide whether to extend the offence of money laundering to proceeds generated by any serious offence.[40] The standards are the 'result of a patchwork of elements thrown together in complex negotiations by various contributing parties'.[41] Because the negotiations took place behind closed doors, the exact circumstances that brought about the approval of such Recommendations remain unclear.[42] The FATF Recommendations have been particularly relevant in the evolution of the international anti-money laundering regime, because they introduced the preventive approach and they managed to trigger compliance on almost a global level.[43] The FATF's declared goal to protect the soundness of the global financial system from the infiltration of proceeds of crime or other illicit financial flows (e.g. terrorists' funds) into the legitimate economy.[44] In order to stop ill-gotten gains from entering the lawful economy, the Recommendations required the commitment of the private sector. Particularly financial institutions and other businesses and professions at risk of being abused by launderers, should embark on specific due diligence procedures to detect

[39] The FATF is an 'inter-governmental body that develops and promotes policies to protect the global financial system against money laundering [...]'. Currently the FATF consists of 36 member countries, eight associate members, the so-called FATF-Styled Regional Bodies, and 26 observers. The FATF is housed within the Organisation for Economic Cooperation and Development (OECD), in Paris. The group had in the beginning an 'ad hoc' mandate that has been extended to the point that the FATF is currently a permanent body with a much broader competence.

[40] FATF 1990. The FATF standards are a broad framework for preventing and combating money laundering. These standards lay down the criteria for criminalising particular types of conduct as conduct falling within the meaning of money laundering. In addition, they provide a framework that governments can implement to recover the proceeds of money laundering offences (assets recovery), and they set out how countries can go about preventing the misuse of financial institutions and non-financial designated businesses and professions (e.g. law firms) for money laundering purposes. The standards are made up of the Recommendations themselves as well as the Interpretive Notes to each Recommendation and the applicable definitions in the Glossary.

[41] Pieth 2004, p. 9.

[42] Pieth 2004, p. 8.

[43] The Recommendations are a source of soft law, which means that governments are not legally bound to implement these measures. Yet, given the fact that soft law can be very influential, to the point that it can be very forceful, just like hard law, the FATF wields tremendous political binding power. In fact, the implementation of the Recommendations is rigorously assessed through Mutual Evaluation processes, and through the assessments conducted by the International Monetary Fund (IMF) and the World Bank (WB). In this regard, it is important to bear in mind that, when assessing compliance with FATF standards, 'the word *should* has the same meaning as *must*'. The FATF's persuasiveness stems from the fact that it has the enormous ability to influence whether or not a country can be seen as a viable business partner or an investment destination. The FATF, thanks to its informal structure and procedures and to its flexible mandate, manages to impose compliance with the ever-updated standards in an easier way that a UN treaty-based organisation, bound to formal decision-making procedures and to a legal mandate, could do.

[44] FATF 1990.

money-laundering activities. The FATF standards imposed a set of duties, such as the identification of customers' identity, the collecting of information, the reporting of suspicious transactions, which were supposed to, on one the one hand, prevent the circulation of dirty money, and on the other hand, support law enforcement with access to information to use in money-laundering investigations.

3.1.4 Expanding the Definition of the Money-Laundering Offence

On the assumption that the polluting capacity of money derived not only from the proceeds of drug trafficking, but also from other crimes, international and national legislatures amplified the reach of the money-laundering offence by endorsing the UN treaty. Since, as shown before, the 'war on drugs' was a priority mainly of the US, other legislatures took advantage of the flexibility of the money-laundering offence definition contained in the Vienna Convention, and expanded its scope to include proceeds of crimes other than drug-related offences. The focus was then on the risks posed by the laundering of proceeds of any crime and its adverse effect on the legitimate economy. Lawmakers justified the necessity of 'spreading the gospel'[45] with the argument that this was necessary to protect the lawful economy from being infiltrated by capital of criminal provenance. The ultimate goal, so the argument went, was to prevent the financial system from being destabilised. Moreover, the anti-money laundering discourse pointed to the fact that the laundering of proceeds of any crime was causing harm to society since it fostered the commission of further crimes. According to the Commentary on the Vienna Convention, the trend of extending the scope of the money-laundering offence by way of expanding the list of predicate offences was promoted by the Council of Europe with the Convention of 1990, the FATF and by some national legal systems.[46] The underlying motive for such a development was the difficulty encountered by law enforcement in 'proving that particular proceeds are attributable to drug trafficking activities, especially when the persons in question are involved in a broad range of criminal activities'.[47]

A common tactic to enlarge anti-money laundering law has been to identify 'soft targets', that is conducts, the criminalisation of which few would object, and then expand the reach of the offence. The catalogue of predicate offences for money laundering was expanded, so that the money-laundering offence became detached

---

[45] The expression is used by Pieth. *See* Pieth 2004, p. 12.

[46] The idea of expanding the definition of money laundering beyond its traditional link with proceeds of drug-related criminality was not a complete novelty. In fact, some national laws did not link the offence of money laundering to drug-trafficking, as the case Article 305 of the Swiss penal code enacted in 1990, which considers any crime as a possible predicate crime for money laundering. Gilmore 1992, p. XV.

[47] Commentary on the Vienna Convention, above n. 20.

from its original declared function of combating drug traffickers. This expansion resulted in a corresponding expansion of acts criminalised by national laws. While this development has been welcomed positively because of the refusal of many countries to pursue the 'war on drugs', it has also raised questions relating to the adequacy of the measure to tackle the new phenomena. In fact, often the grounds given to legitimise such developments did not satisfy many scholars.[48]

3.2 The EU's Motivation for Criminalising Money Laundering

What initially triggered the Council of Europe to adopt anti-money laundering measures was the need to respond to extremist terrorism in Europe. In particular, it was an attempt to counter the threat posed by the *Rote Armee Fraktion* and the *Brigate Rosse*, in Germany and Italy, respectively.[49] In the early 1980s the Council of Europe started looking with suspicion at illicit transfers of funds with a criminal origin that were used frequently by terrorist and political extremist groups to perpetrate further crimes. And because of the 'public anxiety' about 'acts of criminal violence, such as hold-ups and kidnappings', in 1980 the Committee of Ministers of the European Community adopted Recommendation 10 to 'define an overall policy' to tackle the serious problems generated by the laundering of funds with criminal origin. Aiming at preventing the spread of further criminal acts by terrorist organisations that injected illicit funds into the economic system, the Committee called upon banks to participate in a common effort with law enforcement agencies to prevent and to repress such acts.[50] However, Member States, that were probably not yet ready to endorse such rules in their respective national legal orders, did not implement the Recommendation.[51]

Two years after the Vienna Convention, in 1990, the Council of Europe adopted the Convention on Laundering, Search, Seizure and Confiscation of the Proceeds from Crime (Strasbourg Convention), which did not limit the scope of the money-laundering offence to drug-related proceeds of crime. The Convention was meant to pursue common policy to protect society from serious crime.[52] Having noted that Member States had very different and often inadequate national laws to counteract organised crime, the drafters of the Strasbourg Convention sought to lay

---

[48] *See* among others, Arzt et al. 2015, § 29, mn. 8; Dionyssopoulou 1999, pp. 118 ss; Mitsilegas 2003, pp. 14 ss; and Moccia 1995, pp. 730 ss.

[49] Pieth 2004, p. 4.

[50] Committee of Ministers of the European Community 1980.

[51] Nilsson 1991, p. 423.

[52] *See* the Preamble of the Council of Europe 'Convention on Laundering, Search, Seizure and Confiscation of the Proceeds from Crime', CETS 141, (1990a) [hereinafter Strasbourg Convention].

down the minimum standards for facilitating international co-operation as regards investigative assistance, search, seizure and confiscation-measures, which were considered essential for the suppression of money laundering.

The then European Economic Community (EEC) committed itself to the international fight against drugs and money laundering by ratifying the Vienna Convention, despite lacking competence in criminal matters.[53] The EEC justified such initiative based on its competence in commercial policy.[54] Subsequently the EU legislature incorporated anti-money laundering law as part of an economic preventive policy through the adoption of four Directives finalised to protect the financial system. Indeed, the first three EU Directives in the field of money-laundering law have been, generated within the Directorate General 'Internal Market and Financial Services'.[55] In 1991, in order to synchronise the EU's anti-money laundering policy with the FATF's 40 Recommendations, the European legislature adopted the First Anti-Money Laundering Directive.[56] Since the Community did not have an express competence in criminal law, the European legislature's approach was more a preventive, than a repressive one. In fact, Article 2, which requires Member States to prohibit money laundering, was initially rejected by the German parliament, due to the lack of competence in criminal matters of the ECC.[57] The wording 'prohibition' was used to avoid requiring an explicit criminalisation of such conducts since that would plainly fall outside the ECC's competence. However, the imposition of such criminalisation was included in a statement annexed by the end of 1992.[58] Like the Strasbourg Convention, the Directive, despite taking the definition of money laundering from the Vienna Convention, acknowledged that money laundering 'occurs also in relation to other criminal activities'[59] and therefore did not limit the scope of its application to drug offences. Although the legislature acknowledged in the preamble that money laundering 'must be combated mainly by penal means and within the framework of international co-operation',[60] and highlighted the link between organised crime and

[53] For an overview on the complete debate about the Community competence, *see* Mitsilegas 2003, pp. 62 ss; and 2014, pp. 155 ss.

[54] Council of the European Communities (1990) Decision of 22 October 1990 concerning the conclusion, on behalf of the EEC, of the UN Vienna Convention. OJ L 326, 24.11.1990, pp. 56–57.

[55] In particular the first three Directives (91/308/EEC; 2001/97/EC; 2005/60/EC) are categorised under the following subjects: Internal Market; free movement of capital and approximation of laws and are put under the Directories Taxation and Prevention of Tax Avoidance and Tax Evasion (09.50.00.00), and the Directory Economic and monetary policy and free movement of capital (10.40.00.00).

[56] Council Directive 91/308/EEC of 10 June 1991 on prevention of the use of the financial system for the purpose of money laundering, OJ L 166, 28/06/1991, pp. 0077–0083.

[57] BR-Drucks 288/1/90, p. 2.

[58] Mitsilegas 2014, p. 155.

[59] Preamble, Directive 91/308/EEC, above n. 56.

[60] Ibid.

drug trafficking, the Directive, as a matter of fact, focused on the preventive strategy. In order to legitimise such approach, the drafters resorted in the preamble to the 'emotionally charged concept of public trust',[61] underlining that 'when credit and financial institutions are used to launder proceeds from criminal activities [...], the soundness and stability of the institution concerned and confidence in the financial system as a whole could be seriously jeopardised'.[62] In this way, money laundering was described as a threat to individuals, institutions and to the whole financial system. The European Community declared its particular concern about money launderers taking special advantage of the freedom of capital movement and of the freedom of supplying financial services in the single market.[63] This justified the necessity of providing a preventive policy, besides the repressive one set out in the Strasbourg Convention, aimed at requesting the participation of private actors in defence of the free market. It was, indeed, signalled that 'preventing the financial system from being used for money laundering is a task which cannot be carried out by the authorities responsible for combating this phenomenon without the cooperation of credit and financial institutions and their supervisory authorities'.[64] For the first time, through the adoption of such Directive, the goals of penal deterrence were coupled, at least in the declared legislative intents, with the intention of protecting the cleanliness and integrity of the financial system, in the light of moves towards the creation of a single financial market. In addition, a further, less manifest function emerges. By looking at text of the first Directive, it is clear that the common criminal policy was introduced by the EC in order to prevent that 'Member States, for the purpose of protecting their financial systems, [...] adopt measures which could be inconsistent with completion of the single market'. In other words, the community was particularly afraid that Member States would have adopted restrictive measures to impede the entrance of illicit financial flows, which would have hampered the creation of the internal free market in which the free movement of capital must be guaranteed.

The subsequent developments in the EU anti-money laundering regime were triggered, as already mentioned, by the FATF's continuous updating of the standards enunciated in its Recommendations. The adoption of the Second Directive was considered a particularly 'top priority',[65]given the fact that the Recommendations were revised in 1996. Moreover, the EU was under pressure from the international community to find solutions to the global problem of serious and organised crime. The Second Directive, adopted in 2001, contributed to the further expansion of the scope of anti-money laundering law by recognising the

[61] Mitsilegas 2003, p. 63.

[62] Preamble, Directive 91/308/EEC, above n. 56.

[63] Ibid.

[64] Directive 91/308/EEC, above 56. In addition, the wording of the title stressed the need to protect the integrity of the financial system: 'Council Directive on prevention of the use of the financial system for the purpose of money laundering'.

[65] Debate of the European Parliament, 3/7/2000 and 4/4/2001.

'trend in recent years towards a much wider definition of money laundering based on a broader range of predicate or underlying offences'.[66] The EU legislature underlined the special necessity of ensuring the inclusion of a wider range of predicate offences in order to facilitate the reporting of suspicious transactions.[67] The Civil Liberties Committee rejected the proposal to extend the definition of predicate offence to include any serious offence because it was considered too broad, but the European Parliament plenary session reinstated the wording.[68] The final text, under Article 1(E) included in the list, apart from drug trafficking as defined in the First Directive, also activities of criminal organisations, fraud, corruption, and any other offence that may 'generate substantial proceeds' and is punishable by a severe custodial sentence according to the domestic criminal law. In addition, disagreement arose with regard to the degree of the exemption granted to the legal profession: While the Parliament advocated for a broader exemption, the Council and the Commission agreed to exclude the legal profession from the duty to report except under certain circumstances, and not, for example, when giving legal advice.[69] In order to comply with international standards and thus to extend the scope of the framework to cover terrorist financing, a key political priority in the post 9/11 world, and to update the regulations in the field of customers identification, the European legislature adopted in 2005 the Third Money Laundering Directive.[70] The Directive updated the existing framework to be in harmony with the FATF's revised Recommendations of 2003, which endorsed nine new standards in the field of terrorist financing.

3.2.1 *The Fourth EU Anti-Money Laundering Directive*

On 20 May 2015, the European Parliament and the Council adopted the fourth Anti-Money Laundering Directive on the prevention of the use of the financial system for the purpose of money laundering and terrorist financing in order to update the European legal framework to the new FATF Recommendations released in 2012.[71] The Directive is the result of a long debate that started in 2013 with the

---

[66] Directive 2001/97/EC of the European Parliament and of the Council of 4 December 2001 amending Council Directive 91/308/EEC on prevention of the use of the financial system for the purpose of money laundering, OJ L 344, 28.12.2001, pp. 76–82.

[67] *See* the Preface of Directive 2001/97/EC (7) above n. 67.

[68] Mitsilegas 2003, p. 96.

[69] Article 6(3) of the Directive 2001/97/EC, above n. 67.

[70] Directive 2005/60/EC of the European Parliament and of the Council of 26 October 2005 on the prevention of the use of the financial system for the purpose of money laundering and terrorist financing, OJ L 309, 25.11.2005, pp. 15–36.

[71] OJ L 141, 5.6.2015, pp. 73–117.

publication of a Proposal from the European Commission.[72] The final text is a compromise between conflicting concerns and interests, some of which emerge from the study of the law-making process. The main novelties introduced by the proposal were the inclusion of tax crimes in the list of predicate offences, a greater focus on the risk-based approach, and the obligation for Member States to conduct national risk assessments. In addition, the proposal defined more precisely certain concepts, such as PEPs and BOs, the simplified due diligence and the expansion of the scope of the obligated reporting institutions.[73] The Proposal was then submitted to the Council and the Parliament for amendments, and it was addressed to the European Data Protection Supervisor, the European Central Bank (ECB), and the European Investment Bank for consultation.[74] The opinions expressed by the three stakeholders are particularly relevant because they highlighted different perspectives and interests surrounding the proposed anti-money laundering Directive. The ECB welcomed the proposal but contested the fact that, due to the freedom of Member States to further lower or increase thresholds imposed by EU Directives, according to Article 114 of the Treaty,[75] stricter measures could have been applied to obliged entities. The Bank warned that 'any such measures should be carefully weighed against the expected public benefits'.[76] Furthermore, the ECB stressed the importance of ensuring the 'continued smooth functioning of payment systems in Europe and warned that certain burdens imposed on obliged entities 'could lead to significant difficulties and delays in processing payments between the banks and other entities providing payment services. This, in turn, would potentially have a severe impact on the banks' liquidity planning and ultimately on the smooth functioning of the financial markets'.[77] The European Data Protection Supervisor opposed the inclusion of fighting tax evasion among the purposes of the data processing contained in the Proposal, based on the purpose limitation principle pursuant to Article 7(e) of the Directive 95/46/EC.[78] In addition, the authority recommended that

[72] Proposal for a Directive of the European Parliament and of the Council on the prevention of the use of the financial system for the purpose of money laundering and terrorist financing (2013/0025/COD).

[73] A critical overview on the novelties introduced by the Commission Proposal can be found in Unger et al. 2014, pp. 43–44.

[74] Opinion of the European Central Bank of 17 May 2013 on a proposal for a directive on the prevention of the use of the financial system for the purpose of money laundering and terrorist financing and on a proposal for a regulation on information accompanying transfers of funds. OJ C 166, 12.6.2013, pp. 2–5.

[75] Consolidated version of the Treaty on the Functioning of the European Union [hereinafter TFEU], OJ C 326, 26.10.2012, pp. 47–390.

[76] OJ C 166, 12.6.2013, p. 4.

[77] OJ C 166, 12.6.2013, p. 5.

[78] Executive summary of the Opinion of the European Data Protection Supervisor on a proposal for a Directive of the European Parliament and of the Council on the prevention of the use of the financial system for the purpose of money laundering and terrorist financing, and a proposal for a Regulation of the European Parliament and of the Council on information on the payer accompanying transfers of funds, OJ C 32, 4.2.2014, pp. 9–12.

the Commission 'respect the proportionality principle when limiting data subjects' rights and, as a consequence, add a specific provision to specify the conditions under which the data subjects' rights may be limited'.[79] The European Economic and Social Committee recognised the necessity to balance data protection and the fight against money laundering.[80] In particular, the Committee advocated that the obligation set out in Article 39 of the proposed Directive to destroy documents and information collected after a period of five or ten years from the time of the end of the business relationship, should not apply in specific cases, such as criminal proceedings, bankruptcies or successions, in order not to counteract the general interest.[81] The Committee, thus, recognised that the general interest prevails over the interest of data protection in specific cases of serious economic crimes.

In March 2013, the European Parliament voted[82] on the Economic Affairs and the Justice and Home Affairs Committees' amendments, which inserted an important change, namely, the introduction of a European public register of ultimate owners of trusts and companies under Article 29 of the proposed text. The outcome of the European Parliament's vote was considered a big step forward in the fight against tax evasion, according to the Civil Liberties Committee rapporteur *Sargentini* (Greens/European Free Alliance, the Netherlands). The European-wide register of Beneficial Owners (BOs) 'will help to lift the veil of secrecy from offshore accountants and greatly aid the fight against money laundering and blatant tax evasion', added the other Economic and Monetary Affairs Committee rapporteur *Krišjānis Kariņš* (European People's Party, Latvia).[83] The introduction of more transparency in the financial sector was welcomed by most members of the Parliament as a benefit in the fight against tax evasion and money laundering. Yet, according to the official opinion expressed by a commercial litigation associate at the law firm 'Stephenson Harwood', which is specialised in corporate crime and financial services regulation, the provision would have triggered the emergence of more complex corporate structures, making due diligence correspondingly more complex, time consuming and expensive. 'As such, it is arguable and conceivable that the additional compliance burden that a public register may create will—somewhat ironically—come to outweigh any benefit associated with transparency'.[84] Again, the different opinions expressed reveal the complexity of the issue and the conflicting interests at play.

---

[79] Opinion of the European Data Protection Supervisor, 2013, p. 23.

[80] Opinion of the European Economic and Social Committee on the 'Proposal for a regulation of the European Parliament and of the Council on information accompanying transfers of funds' COM (2013) 44 final—2013/0024 (COD) and on the 'Proposal for a directive of the European Parliament and of the Council on the prevention of the use of the financial system for the purpose of money laundering and terrorist financing', OJ C 271, 19.9.2013, pp. 31–35.

[81] OJ C 271, 19.9.2013, p. 34.

[82] The legislative resolution on the amended text was passed by 643 votes to 30 with 12 abstentions; see European Parliament 2014a.

[83] European Parliament 2014b.

[84] Ward 2014, p. 3.

The Parliament tried to focus the Directive on the fight against tax havens and illicit financial flows.[85] In particular, when the Commission used the term 'dirty money', which in the common understanding of the term refers to money typically deriving from organised criminal activities, the Parliament substituted it with 'massive flows of illicit money', which encompasses also monies deriving from fiscal crimes, and listed facilitators such as 'secretive corporate structures operating in and through secrecy jurisdictions, often also referred to as tax havens'. As regards the duties imposed on the private sector to comply with due diligence, the Parliament warned that 'the preventive approach should be targeted and proportional, and should not result in the establishment of a comprehensive system for controlling the entire population'.[86] Moreover, Recital 2 stated that 'any requirement imposed on obligated entities to fight money laundering and terrorist financing should, therefore, be justified and proportionate'.[87] The MPs recognised the potential clash of interests between the goals of the Directive to tackle tax evasion and the interests of the private sector involved in the prevention of money laundering, and therefore added under Recital 9 that '[a]greeing on a definition of tax crimes is an important step in detecting those crimes [tax evasion, fraud, money laundering], as too is public the disclosure of certain financial information by large companies operating in the Union on a country-by-country basis. It is also important to ensure that obliged entities and legal professionals, as defined by Member States, do not seek to frustrate the intent of this Directive or to facilitate or to engage in aggressive tax planning'. The text was then passed to the Council and the Commission for further opinions and agreement, and then it was passed to the newly elected Parliament in May 2014. The members of the Parliament finally approved the text on 20 May 2015; the final Directive was adopted on the same day and signed by the Presidents of the Parliament and of the Council. The Directive entered into 24 days after its publication in the Official Journal of the European Union.[88]

In the final text, most of the significant changes introduced by the Parliament in 2013 were endorsed. For the first time a central European register had been created in which beneficial owners ought to be listed. The Directive uses the term 'flows of illicit money' instead of 'dirty money' and keeps mentioning its harm to international development. While not mentioning the risk that the policy would become a tool to control the entire population, the new Directive mentions that 'the objectives of protecting society from crime and protecting the stability and integrity of the

[85] European Parliament legislative resolution of 11 March 2014 on the proposal for a directive of the European Parliament and of the Council on the prevention of the use of the financial system for the purpose of money laundering and terrorist financing (COM (2013) 0045).

[86] Ibid. Recital 1.

[87] Ibid. Recital 2.

[88] Directive EU/2015/849 above n. 71.

Union's financial system should be balanced against the need to create a regulatory environment that allows companies to grow their businesses without incurring disproportionate compliance costs'.[89] The Fourth Directive introduces tax crimes within the scope of the money-laundering offence and thus allows the exchange of tax-related information among Financial Intelligence Units (FIUs). In this regard, the Directive utilises the term tax crimes and not tax offences as proposed previously by the Parliament. While not imposing a definition of tax crimes at the European level, the legislation requires that Member States 'should allow, to the greatest extent possible under their national law, the exchange of information or the provision of assistance between EU Financial Intelligence Units (FIUs)'.[90] Due to all these novelties, the final text of the Directive is considered a tool to counteract tax evasion.

The final text contains a further significant element, which was already present in the Commission's Proposal, namely, the legitimacy of the Union taking action in the field of money laundering, in accordance with the principle of subsidiarity set out in Article 5 TFEU.[91] In particular, the Union shall adopt common measures to tackle money laundering 'since the objective of this Directive [...] cannot be sufficiently achieved by the Member States, as individual measures adopted by Member States to protect their financial systems could be inconsistent with the functioning of the internal market [...]'.[92] Again, the European legislator needed to strike balance between the purpose of avoiding that perpetrators could abuse the freedom of movement of capital within the Union and the possibility that Member States could enact anti-money laundering policies inconsistent with the free movement of capital. In fact, the Directive, while imposing limitations on the market through the control of transactions, the criminalisation of gatekeepers, and the recording of users' data, it is endorsed as an instrument to foster the creation of the single market. Given the fact that the internal market is based on the principle of the free movement of capital and that the anti-money laundering legislation imposes, as a matter of fact, restrictions on the movement of capital, there is a clash of interests.

In February 2016, in the aftermath of the events in Paris, EU Institutions and national Governments decided to take further urgent action. The European

---

[89] Council Directive EU/2015/849 of the European Parliament and of the Council of 20 May 2015 on the prevention of the use of the financial system for the purposes of money laundering or terrorist financing, OJ L 141, 5.6.2015, pp. 73–117.

[90] Directive EU/2015/849 above n. 71.

[91] Article 5 of the TFEU, above n. 75, states: '1. The Member States shall coordinate their economic policies within the Union. To this end, the Council shall adopt measures, in particular broad guidelines for these policies. Specific provisions shall apply to those Member States whose currency is the euro. 2. The Union shall take measures to ensure coordination of the employment policies of the Member States, in particular by defining guidelines for these policies. 3. The Union may take initiatives to ensure coordination of Member States' social policies'. OJ C 326, 26.10.2012, pp. 47–390.

[92] Directive EU/2015/849 above n. 71.

Commission adopted an 'Action Plan to strengthen the fight against terrorist financing', which included also important steps to be taken in the field of money-laundering prevention.[93] On 5th July 2016, the Commission adopted a new Proposal to update the Fourth Anti-Money Laundering Directive of May 2015, which was supposed to be transposed by Member States by July 2017.[94] The Commission proposal was based on an extensive assessment of the impact of certain anti-money laundering measures by the Member States.[95] The goal of such assessment was to identify effective and suitable policy options aiming especially at ensuring a better cooperation among FIUs. The Commission proposal introduced important changes with specific regard to anonymous payment methods, such as virtual currency exchange platforms or pre-paid cards; enhanced information access and cooperation between EU FIUs, the introduction of centralised bank and payment account registers or electronic data retrieval systems for Members, and harmonised and enhanced due diligence measures for high-risk third countries.[96] In addition, the Proposal anticipate the date to the 1 January 2017 at the latest, by when Member States shall bring into force the laws, regulations and administrative provisions necessary to comply with the Directive.[97] The proposed changes seem to represent a concrete step in improving the effectiveness of the EU's efforts to combat the laundering of money from criminal activities and to counter the financing of terrorist activities. The necessary consensus among Member States and other stakeholders to introduce such rules has been found around the perceived grown of the terrorist threat in Europe, and by the consciousness about the gaps in the transparency of financial transactions around the world revealed by the investigations known as 'Panama Papers'. While Member States are busy implementing the Fourth Anti-Money Laundering Directive, the Council of the European Union is in the process of amending the Fourth Directive. The urgency of drafting a fifth directive is connected to the "recent terrorist attacks [that] have brought to light emerging new trends, in particular regarding the way terrorist groups finance and

[93] European Commission (2016b) Communication from the Commission to the European Parliament and the council on an Action Plan for strengthening the fight against terrorist financing. COM (2016) 50/2.

[94] European Commission (2016c) Proposal for a Directive of the European Parliament and of the Council amending Directive (EU) 2015/849 on the prevention of the use of the financial system for the purposes of money laundering or terrorist financing and amending Directive 2009/101/EC. 2016/0208 (COD).

[95] European Commission (2016d) Working Document Impact Assessment accompanying the document Proposal for a Directive of the European Parliament and the Council. http://eur-lex.europa.eu/legal-content/EN/TXT/PDF/?uri=CELEX:52016SC0223&from=EN. Last accessed on 22 December 2016.

[96] The EU list of high-risk countries, complementing the Fourth Anti-Money Laundering Directive, was adopted on 14 July 2016. See European Commission (2016a).

[97] European Commission (2016c), above n. 95.

conduct their operations".[98] In particular, the Council sees the need of improving the existing preventive framework to tackle the use of modern technology services and alternative financial systems that benefit from exemptions that are no longer justified.[99] Two of the most controversial issues debated at the time of publication is the question of the access to the national and European register containing beneficial ownership information and the shareholding threshold that defines a beneficial ownership. The proposal of the European Council dating 19 December 2016 requires that persons or organisations that want to access such register, should demonstrate a legitimate interest in accessing such information.[100] The Committee on Economic and Monetary Affairs and the Committee on Civil Liberties, Justice and Home Affairs instead supports the granting of access without any restriction at least to competent authorities and FIUs, and to obliged entities,[101] while civil society advocates for public access to the registers without restriction. In addition, while the actual text of the Directive states that a "shareholding of 25% plus one share or an ownership interest of more than 25% in the customer held by a natural person shall be an indication of direct ownership", there are proposals that would rather see a much lower threshold (5%) to define direct ownership.[102] There has been a clear acceleration in the legislative process at European level to improve the legal framework concerning the prevention of money laundering. A risk that emerges by observing the process is that once again too many (and perhaps too high) expectations are posed on such regulations. In fact, very different motives have been identified by the European legislator as the core incentives for the adoption of recent amendments: the terrorist attacks in Europe and the publication of the Panama Papers. If enhancing transparency in the financial and in the economic sector is surely a reasonable instrument to prevent the abuse of the financial and the economic sectors for the purpose of terrorist financing and of tax evasion, not all solutions can be indiscriminately adapted to both phenomena. In addition, legislations adopted under urgent circumstances to respond to public opinion needs have proved to be often not effective in the long-term. In particular, the adoption of policies that overlap with each other may create a fragmented patchwork that can be hardly implemented at national level.

---

[98] Council of the European Union (2016) Proposal for a Directive of the European Parliament and of the Council amending Directive (EU) 2015/849 on the prevention of the use of the financial system for the purposes of money laundering or terrorist financing and amending Directive 2009/101/EC. COM (2016) 450 final.

[99] Ibid.

[100] Ibid.

[101] Committee on Development for the Committee on Economic and Monetary Affairs and the Committee on Civil Liberties, Justice and Home Affairs (2016) Opinion on the proposal for a directive of the European Parliament and of the Council amending Directive (EU) 2015/849 on the prevention of the use of the financial system for the purposes of money laundering or terrorist financing and amending Directive 2009/101/EC (COM (2016)0450—C8-0265/2016—2016/0208 (COD)).

[102] See for instance Ibid.

3.2.2 New Developments: Organised Crime, Terrorism, Corruption and Economic Infringements of the Law

The years following the introduction of the anti-money laundering regime were marked by a shift in the policy agenda from the 'war on drugs' to the fight against transnational organised crime and, by a quite large consensus, in favour of the extension of the offence of money laundering to tackle further crimes.[103] In June 1997, the European Council, while approving an Action Plan on Organised Crime, recognised that the major driving force behind organised crime was the pursuit of financial gain.[104] The Action Plan called for a rigorous implementation of the existing international instruments in the field of anti-money laundering that can, in turn, require adjustments in national procedures and specialised training for law enforcement and judicial authorities.[105] The Council stressed the significance of the harmonisation and widening of the scope of the money-laundering offence in order to combat money laundering effectively.[106] In 2000, the UN adopted the Convention against Transnational Organised Crime (Palermo Convention). In the Foreword, Kofi Annan underlined the ability of the so-called 'uncivil society' to take advantage of 'the open borders, free markets and technological advances […]' and identified globalisation and organised crime, by underlying that 'the enemies of progress and human rights seek to exploit the openness and opportunities of globalization for their purposes'.[107] The Convention, which was 'the most impressive contribution of a UN multilateral treaty towards the globalisation of criminal law',[108] broadly criminalised money laundering. In fact, the treaty was expected to be 'an effective tool and the necessary legal framework for international cooperation in combating, *inter alia*, such criminal activities as money laundering'.[109] The wording referred to the property derived from any offence established in accordance with Subparagraph (a) of the paragraph, namely with the drug-related offences described under Article 3,1, (a) of the Vienna Convention, was substituted in the Palermo Convention by 'proceeds of crime', which referred to 'any property derived from or obtained, directly or indirectly, through the commission of an offence'.[110] According to Article 6, para 2(b) of this Convention, states are required to include as predicate offences all serious crimes punishable with up to four years' imprisonment,[111] and offences associated with organised crime, such as Article 5,

[103] Mitsilegas 2003, p. 87.

[104] Paragraph 26(e) of the European Council Action Plan on Organised Crime, OJ C 251, 15/08/1997, pp. 0001–0016.

[105] Paragraph 6(g) OJ C 251, 15/08/1997, pp. 1–18.

[106] Paragraph 26 OJ C 251, 15/08/199, pp. 1–18.

[107] Foreword, iii of the Palermo Convention, above n. 2.

[108] Mitsilegas 2014, p. 157.

[109] UN General Assembly 2001.

[110] Article 2(e) of the Palermo Convention, above n. 2; and Article 2(e) UNCAC, above n. 2.

[111] Article 2 of the Palermo Convention, above n. 2.

the participation in an organised criminal group, Article 8 corruption, and Article 23, the obstruction of justice. The Palermo Convention went beyond the Vienna Convention and regulated the private sector, by setting up a supervisory regime for designated bodies particularly susceptible to money laundering. In particular, Article 7, paras 1(b) and 2 called for exchange of information, establishment of a financial intelligence unit and the implementation of measure to detect the movement of cash. The European Community adopted instruments of signature and conclusion of the Palermo Convention based on its competence with regard to 'progressively establishing the internal market'.[112] In particular, the EC explicitly linked the adoption of measures to combat money laundering with the purpose of establishing an area 'without frontiers in which the free movement of goods and services is ensured'. Once again, the European legislature, while further adopting anti-money laundering laws, expressed the intention of supporting the internal free market.

After the 9/11 events in America, the anti-money laundering principles were extended to the financing of terrorism against the background of the idea that in order to crack down terrorists, pursuing the money trail and confiscating assets were two fundamental tools. Since then, the securitisation discourse that referred to organised crime threats was partially overcome by the rhetoric of the fight against terrorism generated in the post-September 11 period.[113] The EU diverted the attention to terrorism, too, and in 2005 amended the Second Directive and included the financing of terrorism in the scope of the anti-money laundering regime.[114] 'From that date on the anti-money laundering Directive was widely considered as part of the fight against terrorism'.[115] In addition, the Council of Europe committed itself to the fight against terrorism and in 2005 updated the Strasbourg Convention of 1990 by including terrorism and the financing of terrorism among the predicate offences whose proceeds should be subject to forfeiture.[116] The Convention justified the amendment by recalling the 'threats to international peace and security caused by terrorist'.

Against the background of the observation that methods of stashing away undue monetary advantages are the same ones used by organised criminals to conceal proceeds of other serious crimes, anti-money laundering law emerged as a tool to curb corruption, too. Several international and transnational documents expressed, in fact, the necessity of tackling the two phenomena together. On the one side,

[112] Council of the European Union (2004) Decision of 29 April 2004 on the conclusion, on the behalf of the European Community, of the United Nations Convention against Transnational Organised Crime (2004), Annex II Declaration of competence in accordance to Article 36(3) of the Convention. 2004/579/EC. OJ L 261, 6.8.2004, pp. 69–115.

[113] *See* FATF 2001.

[114] Directive 2005/60/EC above n. 71, Foreword (3).

[115] European Parliament 2001, p. 7.

[116] Council of Europe 'Convention on Laundering, Search, Seizure and Confiscation of the Proceeds of Crime and on the Financing of Terrorism' CETS 198 (2005) [hereinafter Warsaw Convention].

instruments to tackle corruption included money laundering as an offence constituting corruption, and on the other side, anti-money laundering regulations started being used to prevent and repress corruption too, by expanding the scope of the money-laundering offence. The UN Convention against Corruption, adopted in Merida in 2003 (UNCAC), listed the offence of money laundering as one of the eight offences constituting corruption.[117] The definition of money laundering adopted in UNCAC is adopted by the previous Palermo Convention and thus is not limited to drug offences. UNCAC is said to have a great potential for tackling illicit financial flows[118] with specific respect to the legal framework set for the confiscation of assets and for asset recovery mechanisms and international co-operation for such purposes.[119] In addition, the Council of Europe Criminal law Convention on Corruption of 2002, under Article 13, required signatory parties to criminalise the laundering of proceeds from corruption offences.[120] In 2003, the FATF introduced corruption and bribery in the list of designated categories of offences that states should include as predicate offences for money laundering. This further widening of the competence of the FATF has been justified because 'the G20 called upon the FATF to address the problem of corruption in the framework of its work on combating money laundering and terrorist financing', against the background that 'corruption and money laundering are intrinsically linked,' because 'corruption offences, such as bribery or theft of public funds, are generally committed for the purpose of obtaining private gain', while 'money laundering is the process of concealing illicit gains that were generated from criminal activity'.[121] More specifically, the FATF described corruption as a phenomenon negatively affecting on transnational crimes, poverty, disease, and political instability and on the economy, recalling the fact that empirical evidence suggested that the negative effects of corruption are stronger than any possible positive effects.[122]

The interest of tackling tax evasion through the anti-money laundering regime was manifested already in the initial phase of the anti-money laundering law-making process and re-emerged in a more mature phase of the policy, but there was no consensus on this.[123] Given the acceleration of economic globalisation,

[117] Article 23 of UNCAC, above n. 2.

[118] Christensen 2007, p. 11; and Chene 2011, p. 3.

[119] Article 51 of UNCAC, above n. 2.

[120] Council of Europe (1999) Criminal law Convention on Corruption (ETS No. 173).

[121] *See* FATF 2013.

[122] FATF 2011, p. 9.

[123] There are some practical hindrances that need to be highlighted with regard to making tax evasion a predicate offence to money laundering: If the suspected offence is committed abroad, it must be a criminal offence in that country too, and this imposes on domestic prosecution services the burden of collecting information on foreign laws regulating tax matters. In addition, tax authorities might discover the tax evasion only after some years, and this might undermine the system of reporting of suspicious transactions by financial institutions, if they cannot access information about the lawfulness of the transaction under tax law. Compelling disclosure on fiscal management, on the face of it, may seem a breach of the individual's right to privacy and of the

which multiplied the opportunities for economic crime in Europe, a new consciousness emerged that perpetrators of serious crime can be also firms. 'Following the multi-billion Euro financial fraud and misconduct schemes such as *Enron*, *WorldCom*, and *Tyco Internationa*l [...] the *Parmalat* scandal at the end of 2003 [...]demonstrated the importance of avoiding a frame of mind in which one looks only towards the organised crime underworld for serious economic crime threats'.[124] In particular, in the wake of the growing awareness about the negative effects of offshore jurisdictions and tax evasion, questions relating to money laundering and tax matters have come to be linked, since money laundering was considered an effective measure to counteract tax offences, too.[125] This further amplified the scope of anti-money laundering policy in the direction of the protection of the financial system. The debate on the urgency of tackling large-scale tax evasion through anti-money laundering policy was prompted by the Organisation for Economic Co-operation and Development (OECD), the UN, the International Monetary Fund (IMF), the G20, the FATF and other regional organisations. In 1998, the UN Office for Drug Control and Crime Prevention (UNODC) presented the results of its report called *Financial Havens, Banking Secrecy and Money-laundering*. The report concluded, among other things, that 'one of the key remaining facilitators of crime has been the tax avoidance/evasion exemption in the laundering regulations of many countries'.[126] The UNODC warned about the fact that the secrecy veil on tax matters would hamper the combating of money laundering by leaving open the opportunity of evading conviction by representing transactions as tax-related.[127] The G7 Finance Ministers, in May of the same year, encouraged the tackling of tax-related crimes through the international anti-money laundering system.[128] A dialogue between the FATF and the OECD came into being to examine ways of improving co-operation between tax and anti-money laundering authorities, and as a result, workshops for experts were organised to

(Footnote 123 continued)

confidentiality principle. In addition, if even the proceeds of crime are considered subject to taxation, there is the danger that law enforcement will treat proceeds of drug trafficking, for example, as tax evasion, and choose to charge drug dealers with money laundering, just by proving the undeclared income. *See* Alldridge 2001, p. 35. The underlying claim seems to be that tax evasion liability can serve as a useful fall back for authorities who are unable to acquire sufficient evidence to secure a conviction for the main crime, as in the famous case of *Al Capone,* who was finally convicted for tax evasion by American authorities, because of their incapability of bringing charges of organised criminal activities against him.

124 Council of Europe 2005, p. 9.

125 Alldridge 2001, p. 350. For the analogies between tax evaders and money launderers, *See* Christensen 2013, p. 35 ss. *See* Sharman 2011, p. 99 regards critically the FATF's approach to regulating offshore centres; also Alldridge disapproves of the approach of classifying both money laundering and tax evasion as offshore. *See* Alldridge 2008, p. 447.

126 Blum et al. 1988, p. 51.

127 The link with tax matters was often used as a ground to refuse co-operation and information disclosure for purposes of anti-money laundering.

128 OECD 2012.

share expertise in both fields.[129] In 1999, the G8 expressed deep concern about the growth in illicit international financial transactions, including money laundering, as well as wide-scale tax evasion, emphasizing how the two phenomena were related to each other.[130] Since 2000, IMF made the fight against money laundering a priority of its agenda to 'protect the integrity of markets and of the global financial framework'.[131]At the IMF meeting in Washington, in April 2000, the UK's Chancellor of the Exchequer called for a strong response to offshore tax havens and to financial crimes, and raised the need to link money laundering to tax matters.[132] In 2003, the FATF Recommendations were revised, and Recommendation 1 left it open to states to choose between the 'thresholds' or the 'all offences' approach. Tax related offences were not explicitly included, however, the interpretative note to Recommendation 13 (Reporting of suspicious transactions and compliance) stated that 'suspicious transactions should be reported by financial institutions regardless of whether they are also thought to involve tax matters'. Serious tax crimes were finally listed within the range of designated categories of offences that each state should at a minimum include in the FATF revised standards published on 16 February 2012. The rhetoric of the protection of the global financial system is used also in the European discourse on money laundering control. Already the Third Directive of 2005 highlighted the damages caused by massive flows of money to the stability of the financial sector and to the single market, and it stressed that 'the soundness, integrity and stability of credit and financial institutions and confidence in the financial system as a whole could be seriously jeopardised by the efforts of criminals and their associates either to disguise the origin of criminal proceeds or to channel lawful or unlawful money for terrorist purposes'.[133] The Fourth Anti-Money Laundering Directive includes tax crimes in the scope of the offence, and the Commission Proposal for amending the Directive adds further rules to impede tax avoidance or evasion through offshore jurisdictions, used as locations of intermediary entities that distance the real owner from the assets owned. With this regard, the Proposal seeks to prevent the large-scale concealment of funds, by ensuring enhanced corporate transparency through the disclosure of beneficial owners of companies or other legal arrangements.[134]

[129] Ibid.

[130] G7 1999, p. 6.

[131] *See* IMF 2016.

[132] Alldridge 2001, p. 350.

[133] *See* the Preface of Directive 2005/60/EC above n. 70.

[134] European Commission, Proposal for a Directive of the European Parliament and of the Council Amending Directive (EU) 2015/849 above n. 89, and amending Directive 2009/101/EC of the European Parliament and of the Council of 16 September 2009 on coordination of safeguards which, for the protection of the interests of members and third parties, are required by Member States of companies within the meaning of the second paragraph of Article 48 of the Treaty, with a view to making such safeguards equivalent, 2016/0208 (COD).

Whether the use of anti-money laundering law for the purpose of protecting the soundness of the global financial system represents a recent shift of paradigm or it has always been part of its double nature is debatable. As a matter of fact, the current discourse about anti-money laundering reflects the supremacy of this rationale over the necessity of tackling drug consumption or organised crime. The IMF, for example, on its website expresses the concern 'about the possible consequences money laundering, terrorist financing, and related crimes have on the integrity and stability of the financial sector and the broader economy' and further adds that 'these activities can undermine the integrity and stability of financial institutions and systems, discourage foreign investment, and distort international capital flows'.[135] They may have negative consequences for a country's financial stability and macroeconomic performance, resulting in welfare losses, draining resources from more productive economic activities, and even have destabilizing spill over effects on the economies of other countries'.[136] IMF Deputy Managing Director has declared '[a]ction to prevent and combat money laundering and terrorist financing [...] responds not only to a moral imperative, but also to an economic need'.[137]

3.3 Considerations

The process that has led to the formulation of the international and European current anti-money laundering criminal legal framework reveals that very different justifications were given for the criminalisation of money laundering at different stages. Often the declared functions did not correspond to the real goals of the actors taking part in the law-making process. In the beginning, for instance, the introduction of the offence of money laundering was presented to the public as a tool to counteract drug trafficking, and the resort to criminal law was justified on the background of the seriousness of the drug issue. The rhetoric connected to the seriousness of the drug issue was, therefore, the manifest function of the new criminalisation of money laundering. However, other latent goals, for instance, the desire of financial institutions to clean their reputation and gain customs confidentiality or the interest of some governments to curb tax evasion existed already present during this initial phase. Yet, given that no agreement could be found on the other aspects, the offence was legitimised as an instrument to wage the 'war on drugs'. On the other hand, the international 'war on drugs', in the critical interpretation of scholars, was used by the US to impose its criminal policies at global

[135] *See* IMF 2016. Also Tanzi strongly supported the argument of the negative impact of money laundering on the economy. *See* Tanzi 1997, p. 97.

[136] IMF 2016.

[137] Ibid.

level,[138] to the point that *Nadelmann* defines the process of universalisation of these policies as 'the Americanization of international law enforcement'.[139] In order to justify this strategy and to legitimise additional budgets and legal measures in front of the public, the US created a 'new moral panic', namely a phenomenon that needed to be addressed with special urgent measures.[140] Practically, this had the consequence that countries around the world had to actively contribute to the defeat of the common enemy, identified with drug producers, traffickers and abusers, by implementing the policies set under the US influence, the criminalisation of money laundering being one of them. Bearing in mind hidden agendas that brought to the criminalisation of money laundering is crucial to assess critically the effectiveness of the offence.

Some of the interests expressed more or less manifestly from the actors taking part in the initial phase of the creation of the anti-money laundering regime were strongly conflicting with each other. One representative example is the question whether to use the policy also to tackle large-scale tax evasion or to leave proceeds deriving from fiscal crimes outside of the regime. Despite the FATF eventually included tax crimes as predicate offences for money laundering, a worldwide consensus on such reform might actually not exist. This could potentially hinder international cooperation for the purpose of combating money laundering.

Another controversial issue concerns the fact that national states have adopted anti-money laundering measures under the pressure of the FATF. Besides being a 'rich countries club',[141] because it has been founded and is still led by most industrialised countries,[142] the FATF is criticised for being deliberately

---

[138] Aas 2013, p. 131. This mechanism, which has been defined as the doctrine of 'manifest destiny' is used by the US to protect its own interests, while using the rhetoric of a common war against an enemy threatening the whole world. Without using physical influence, as in the case of military invasion, the US has exercised its imperialistic strategy by taking advantage of its economic supremacy and by using the weapon of financial coercion. *See also* Andreas 2015, p. 49; and Bosworth-Davies 2006, p. 347.

[139] Nadelmann 1993, p. 469.

[140] Bosworth-Davies 2006, p. 349; and Naylor 2002. 'Drugs, like terrorism today, obtained the position of a suitable enemy. By stressing the necessity of a global effort to prevent the danger of the drug issue, the US has imposed 'global governance' built around the framework established by the UN and other international initiatives. *See also* Aas 2013, pp. 130–131. On an even more critical note, the crime-control policy model of the 'war on drugs' has been interpreted as an example of the 'blurred line between crime control and warfare, both in discursive and practical terms'. Aas 2013, p. 130. A known example is the American 'Plan Colombia', a US military intervention launched in the 90s of the last century in South-American, with the official goal of contrasting drug cartels, which was actually directed at controlling economically, politically and military an area rich of natural resources. Becucci and Massari 2003, p. 63.

[141] *See* Mitsilegas 2014, p. 174.

[142] Alldridge 2008, p. 443; Bosworth-Davies 2006, p. 358; Levi and Reuter 2006, p. 304; and Pieth 2004, pp. 8, 9. More specifically, from the definition of the social problem to the shaping of the policies and of the methods of monitoring compliance and punishing non-compliance the FATF owes a lot to the US. *See* Machado 2012, p. 361.

unrepresentative, and for lacking transparency and accountability.[143] The influence of the FATF Recommendations over the development of the European legal framework has been tremendous; in fact, main changes adopted by the directives have been justified as necessary adaptations to the FATF's updated regime. Despite EU Member States are member of the FATF, the uncritical transposition of the Recommendations into European law has been criticised by scholars because it does not allow European lawmakers to tailor legal measures to the Union's specific needs and patterns.[144] On the other hand, it has been emphasised that the EU's growing autonomy in the development of a global paradigm of crime governance may lead to more effective protection of human rights and fundamental principles.[145]

The analysis shows also that the criminal legal framework adopted to tackle money laundering has been used to address ever-new challenges, and this expansion process has been coupled by with a rhetoric that scholars have defined as the securitisation rhetoric.[146] One of the issues with which money laundering has been mostly associated, especially in the initial phase of the money-laundering control discourse, is organised crime. After the fall of the Berlin wall, when there was no longer a looming threat of war, new risks for society appeared on the political horizon, and organised crime was perceived as constituting a general threat to security and human life.[147] In the early 1990s, for example, a US Senator labelled organised crime as 'the new communism, the new monolithic threat'.[148] However, the notion of international governance over organised crime and the idea that there was a duty and a mechanism to impose minimum standards at global level to combat transnational criminal activities that developed at the end of the 1990s is not universally accepted.[149] In this context, money laundering has been considered 'more than any other, the crime that reflects and energises globalization [...]'.[150] The discourse around it pictures money laundering as 'one of the great moral panics of our day', which threatens the very existence of the state.[151] Yet, the idea that organised crime and money laundering represent the dark side of globalisation has also been contested. In addition, while in the beginning the emphasis was confined to the utility of the money-laundering offence for the purposes of confiscation, the link between anti-money laundering policy and confiscation has become less and

[143] Alldridge 2008, p. 443; Bosworth-Davies 2006, p. 358; and Pieth 2004, p. 22. Since the beginning, indeed, the body stated explicitly that, 'the FATF membership should not be further widened, in order to preserve the efficiency of the Task Force'. *See* FATF 1991, p. 19.

[144] *See* in particular Mitsilegas 2014, pp. 175 ss; and Unger et al. 2013, pp. 221 ss.

[145] Mitsilegas 2014, p. 198.

[146] *See* among others, Calvanese and Bianchetti 2003, p. 123; and Mitsilegas 2003, pp. 1 ss.

[147] Williams and Savona 1996, p. 129.

[148] The quote is taken from Bosworth-Davies. *See* Bosworth-Davies 2006, p. 349.

[149] Levi and Reuter 2006, p. 309. According to Pieth, the fact that organised crime poses the threat that western culture has always portrayed has been taken for granted. *See* Pieth 2004, p. 5.

[150] Alldridge 2008, p. 438.

[151] Alldridge 2008, p. 437.

less evident, especially since the monopoly of the fight against money laundering has been officially transferred from law enforcement to the private sector and thus leading to the switch from a forbidding to a preventive approach.[152]

With regard to the financing of terrorism, the logic behind the application of the anti-money laundering discourse and standards to the new threat of terrorism has been 'skewed'.[153] By simply defining the financing of terrorism as a variation of money laundering and failing to provide a specific framework for tackling terrorists, policy makers missed the opportunity to give a definition of 'terrorist'. This has raised a series of problems because in practice financial institutions have to follow concrete lists of names supplied by secret services, law enforcement agencies and supervisors.[154] Moreover, the extension of the scope of the anti-money-laundering offence to include the financing of terrorism has been criticised from a technical perspective, because funds available for terrorists have often an illicit origin and are used for (so labelled) illicit purposes. From a political point of view, according to *Pieth*, coupling anti-money laundering regulations with the 'war on terror' is dangerous because it makes the first to be perceived as an instrument of oppression, whereas the latter is instead regarded as an emancipatory tool.[155] Many scholars have contested the expansion of the catalogue of predicate offences to include the financing of terrorism as a diversion of the function of anti-money laundering law. The anti-money laundering regime endorsed the philosophy of the 'war on terror' without conducting a thorough debate about the suitability of the regime for tackling terrorism. Such a development was justified publicly, by using once again the rhetoric of securitisation, which essentially boils down to stressing the necessity to adopt special measures in order to protect the security of the people from terroristic attacks.

Corruption has been studied mainly from the demand side, which is to say the side of the corruptor. An example is the passive corruption of African political leaders and senior public officials. The Transparency International Corruption Perceptions Index classifies many African states as very corrupt countries and the industrialised world, such as Switzerland, as least corrupt.[156] Pointing fingers at petty officials and ruling kleptomaniacs has resulted in insufficient attention being paid to the largely western financial enablers that facilitate the laundering of the proceeds of corruption through offshore financial centres.[157] Global Financial

[152] At a European level, for example, the First Directive requiring a certain level of harmonisation in the context of confiscation of criminal assets was adopted only in 2014. Directive 2014/42/UE above n. 31.

[153] Pieth 2004, p. 34.

[154] Ibid.

[155] Pieth 2004, p. 35.

[156] Transparency International 2015.

[157] Christensen 2011, p. 186.

Integrity estimated that approximately US$ 858 to US$ 1 trillion flows annually from poorer countries as proceeds of corruption, state looting and tax evasion,[158] the main destinations being offshore jurisdictions in the western world. To make real efforts to stop illicit flows, it is necessary to tackle the abuse of banks and offshore jurisdictions.[159] Yet the anti-money laundering regime, being a product of western countries and thus of destinations jurisdictions, does not seem to be the best tool to effect this shift.

By following the developments of money-laundering control policy, the analysis focuses in the last part on the most recent function manifestly attributed to the anti-money laundering legal framework, that is, in short, the protection of the soundness of the financial system. Especially in times of financial insecurity, the tendency of toughening the laws against economic crimes increases. Having previously deregulated the financial system to enhance the free market, legislatures resort to criminal law to control illegality in the economy.[160] Due to domestic budgetary pressure, initiatives to tackle the abuse of the Internal Market accelerated. The European Community, for example, introduced community rules in the field of money laundering which were aimed at protecting the creation of the Internal Market. Since the beginning, the European legislature tackled the phenomenon of money laundering primarily as an economic matter: Despite mentioning the link with organised crime and the danger to society, the European discourse on money laundering has mostly been related to other threats, such as the destabilisation of the market, the abuse of the free movement of capital, and the disintegration of the internal economy. But why was the EU so keen on imposing a common standard for the criminalisation of money laundering, without the competence to make criminal laws? The introduction of a common money-laundering control policy served a latent function, namely to create a 'Single Market', by way of avoiding that Member States adopt measures inconsistent with the completion of the Internal Market when enacting laws to protect their own national economies from money laundering.[161] This was done by avoiding that domestic regulations implemented for protecting national economies from the infiltration of ill-gotten capital could have hampered the freedom of movement of capital within the European borders. The tension emerges also in the wording of the EU Money Laundering Directives. The lack of Community action against money laundering could lead Member States

[158] Global Financial Integrity 2008, p. 12.

[159] Eva Joly, French magistrate famous for her crusade against corruption, advocated for a shift of the corruption discourse to phase two, in which the role of bankers, lawyers and offshore financial centres in enabling corrupt practices comes under far sharper scrutiny. *See* Christensen 2011, p. 193.

[160] Levi and Reuter, for example, consider the regulatory provisions, which impose public control over the financial sector, as exceptional within the context of de-regulation. *See* Levi and Reuter 2006, p. 309.

[161] Gilmore 1992, p. xvi.

to adopt anti-money laundering measures to protect their respective economies but which could be inconsistent with attempts to attain the completion of the single market.[162] There are thus conflicting interests between the demand for regulation to avoid the infiltration of illicit capital, and the demand for deregulation to boost the free market. The European legislature, however, did not state this intention openly; it instead, justified the imposition of anti-money laundering rules by pointing to the threats posed by money laundering to the financial system and thus to society. Viewed critically, the criminalisation of money laundering turns out to be more of a political tool aimed at achieving uniform standards of governance within the EU, while being presented to the public as an essential intervention to guarantee security and well-being. Once again, in this way, the declared goals of the lawmakers did not correspond with the real intentions. It is especially in the interest of research on the effectiveness of the law to expose the unexpressed purposes of the law in order evaluate its outcomes more critically.

References

Aas K F (2013) Globalization and Crime. Sage Publications, London.

African Union (2014) Protocol on amendments to the Protocol on the Statute of the African Court of Justice and Human Rights of June 2014. http://www.iccnow.org/documents/African_Court_Protocol_-_July_2014.pdf. Last accessed on 11 September 2016.

Alldridge P (2001) Are Tax Offences Predicate Offences for Money-Laundering Offences? Journal of Money Laundering Control 4 (4): 350–359.

Alldridge P (2008) Money Laundering and Globalization. Journal of Law and Society 35 (4): 437–463.

Andreas P (2015) Illicit Globalisation Myths and Misconceptions. In: Mitsilegas V et al. (eds) Globalisation, Criminal Law and Criminal Justice: Theoretical, Comparative and Transnational Perspectives. Hart, Oxford.

Arzt G (1997) Das mißglückte Strafgesetz. Am Beispiel der Geldwäschegesetzgebung. In: Diedrichsen U, Dreier R (eds) Das missglückte Gesetz, 8. Symposium der Kommission "Die Funktion des Gesetzes in Geschichte und Gegenwart". Wandenhoeck & Ruprecht, Göttingen, pp. 17–38.

Arzt G et al. (eds) (2015) Strafrecht Besonderer Teil 3. Gieseking Verlag, Bielefeld.

BCBS (1988) Prevention of criminal use of the banking system for the purpose of money-laundering. http://www.bis.org/publ/bcbsc137.pdf. Last accessed on 11 September 2016.

Becucci S, Massari M (2003) Globalizzazione e criminalità. Laterza, Bari.

Blum J A et al. (1988) Financial Havens, Banking Secrecy and Money-laundering. UNODC Global Programme against Money Laundering. http://amnet.org.il/joomla/attachments/UN-FINANCIAL20HAVENS64%20laundering.pdf. Last accessed on 16 September 2016.

Bosworth-Davies R (2006) Money laundering: towards an alternative interpretation. Journal of Money Laundering Control 9 (4): 346–364.

[162] Directive EU/2015/849, above n. 71.

Buscaglia E (2008) The Paradox of Expected Punishment: Legal and Economic Factors Determining Success and Failure in the Fight against Organized Crime. Review of Law & Economics 3: 1–25.

Calvanese E, Bianchetti R (2003) Messaggi mediatici, funzioni della pena e senso di sicurezza dei cittadini. Sociologia del diritto 3: 99–138.

Chene M (2011) The potential of UNCAC to combat illicit financial flows. U4 Expert Answers 17. http://www.u4.no/publications/the-potential-ofuncac-to-combat-illicit-financial-flows-2/. Last accessed on 16 September 2016.

Christensen J (2007) The long and winding road: tackling capital flight and tax evasion. http://www.tni.org/sites/www.tni.org/archives/crimedocs/christensen.pdf. Last accessed on 16 September 2016.

Christensen J (2011) The looting continues: tax evasion and corruption. Critical Perspectives on International Business 7 (2): 177–196.

Christensen J (2013) 'What Do a Tax Evader and a Money Launderer have in Common? The Role of Secrecy in the Financial Sector'. In: Heinrich-Böll-Stiftung, Schönenberg R (eds) Transnational Organized Crime. Analyses of a Global Challenge to Democracy Transcript Verlag, Berlin, pp. 35–39.

Committee of Ministers of the European Community (1980) Recommendation No. R (80) 10 of the Committee of Ministers to Member States on measures against the transfer and the safekeeping of funds of criminal origin. https://rm.coe.int/CoERMPublicCommonSearchServices/DisplayDCTMContent?documentId=09000016804f6231. Last accessed on 16 September 2016.

Committee on Development for the Committee on Economic and Monetary Affairs and the Committee on Civil Liberties, Justice and Home Affairs (2016) Opinion on the proposal for a directive of the European Parliament and of the Council amending Directive (EU) 2015/849 on the prevention of the use of the financial system for the purposes of money laundering or terrorist financing and amending Directive 2009/101/EC (COM(2016)0450 – C8-0265/2016 – 2016/0208(COD)). http://www.europarl.europa.eu/sides/getDoc.do?pubRef=-%2f%2fEP%2f%2fNONSGML%2bCOMPARL%2bPE-594.116%2b02%2bDOC%2bPDF%2bV0%2f%2fEN. Last accessed on 22 December 2016.

Council of Europe (1990b) Explanatory Report to the Convention on Laundering, Search, Seizure and Confiscation of the Proceeds from Crime. https://rm.coe.int/CoERMPublicCommonSearchServices/DisplayDCTMContent?documentId=09000016800cb5de. Last accessed on 16 September 2016.

Council of Europe (2005) Organised Crime Situation Report. http://www.coe.int/t/dghl/cooperation/economiccrime/organisedcrime/Report2005E.pdf. Council of the European Union. Last accessed on 16 September 2016.

Council of the European Union (2016) Proposal for a Directive of the European Parliament and of the Council amending Directive (EU) 2015/849 on the prevention of the use of the financial system for the purposes of money laundering or terrorist financing and amending Directive 2009/101/EC. COM(2016) 450 final. http://data.consilium.europa.eu/doc/document/ST-15605-2016-INIT/en/pdf. Last accessed on 22 December 2016.

Duke S B, Gross A C (1993) America's longest war: Rethinking our tragic crusade against drugs. Tarcher, Putnam, New York.

Dionyssopoulou A (1999) Der Tatbestand der Geldwäsche: eine Analyse der dogmatischen Grundlagen des § 261 StGB. Frankfurter kriminalwissenschaftliche Studien 66. Lang, Frankfurt am Main.

European Commission (2016a) Annex to the Commission delegated regulation supplementing Directive (EU) 2015/849 by identifying high-risk third countries with strategic deficiencies. Brussels. C(2016) 4180 final. https://ec.europa.eu/transparency/regdoc/rep/3/2016/EN/3-2016-4180-EN-F1-1-ANNEX-1.PDF. Last accessed on 16 September 2016.

European Commission (2016b) Communication from the Commission to the European Parliament and the council on an Action Plan for strengthening the fight against terrorist financing. COM (2016) 50/2. http://ec.europa.eu/justice/criminal/files/com_2016_50_en.pdf. Last accessed on 22 December 2016.

European Commission (2016c) Proposal for a Directive of the European Parliament and of the Council amending Directive (EU) 2015/849 on the prevention of the use of the financial system for the purposes of money laundering or terrorist financing and amending Directive 2009/101/EC. 2016/0208 (COD).

European Commission (2016d) Working Document Impact Assessment accompanying the document Proposal for a Directive of the European Parliament and the Council. http://eur-lex.europa.eu/legal-content/EN/TXT/PDF/?uri=CELEX:52016SC0223&from=EN. Last accessed on 22 December 2016.

European Parliament (2001) Report on the Joint Text approved by the Conciliation Committee for a European Parliament and Council Directive amending Council Directive 91/308/EEC of 10 June 1991 in prevention of the use of the financial system for the purpose of money laundering A5 0380/2001. http://www.europarl.europa.eu/sides/getDoc.do?pubRef=-//EP//NONSGML+REPORT+A5-2001-0380+0+DOC+PDF+V0//EN. Last accessed on 13 September 2015.

European Parliament (2014a) Parliament toughens up anti-money laundering rules, Press release - Justice and home affairs/ Economic and monetary affairs. http://www.europarl.europa.eu/news/en/news-room/content/20140307ipr38110/html/Parliament-toughens-up-anti-money-laundering-rules. Last accessed on 13 September 2015.

European Parliament (2014b) Money laundering: MEPs vote to end anonymity of owners of companies and trusts. Press release - Economic and monetary affairs. http://www.europarl.europa.eu/news/en/news-room/content/20140210IPR35562/html/Money-laundering-MEPs-vote-to-end-anonymity-of-owners-of-companies-and-trusts. Last accessed on 13 September 2015.

FATF (1990) The Forty Recommendations of the Financial Action Task Force on Money Laundering. http://www.fatf-gafi.org/media/fatf/documents/recommendations/pdfs/FATF%20Recommendations%201990.pdf. Last accessed on 16 September 2016.

FATF (1991) Report 1990–1991. http://www.fatf-gafi.org/media/fatf/documents/reports/1990%201991%20ENG.pdf. Last accessed on 27 September 2015.

FATF (2001) IX Special Recommendations on terrorist financing, 2001. http://www.fatf-gafi.org/media/fatf/documents/reports/FATF%20Standards%20-%20IX%20Special%20Recommendations%20and%20IN%20rc.pdf. Last accessed on 27 September 2015.

FATF (2005) Mutual Evaluation Report of Australia. http://www.fatfgafi.org/media/fatf/documents/reports/mer/MER%20Australia%20full.pdf. Last accessed on 16 September 2016.

FATF (2011) Laundering the proceeds of corruption. http://www.fatf-gafi.org/media/fatf/documents/reports/Laundering%20the%20Proceeds%20of%20Corruption.pdf. Last accessed on 27 September 2015.

FATF (2013) The use of the FATF Recommendations to combat corruption. http://www.fatf-gafi.org/media/fatf/documents/recommendations/BPP-Use-of-FATF-Recs-Corruption.pdf. Last accessed on 16 September 2016.

Gilmore W C (1992) International efforts to combat money laundering. Grotius Publications, Cambridge.

Global Financial Integrity (2008) Illicit financial flows from developing countries: 2002–2006. www.gfintegrity.org/storage/gfip/executive%20-%20final%20version%201-5-09.pdf. Last accessed on 16 September 2016.

G7 (1999) Statement of G7 Finance Ministers and Central Bank Governors. http://www.g8.utoronto.ca/finance/fm992509state.htm. Last accessed on 16 September 2016.

IMF (2001) Financial System Abuse, Financial Crime and Money Laundering-Background Paper. https://www.imf.org/external/np/ml/2001/eng/021201.htm. Last accessed on 16 September 2016.

IMF (2016) Factsheet The IMF and the Fight against Money Laundering and the Financing of Terrorism. http://www.imf.org/external/np/exr/facts/aml.htm. Last accessed on 16 September 2016.

Levi M and Reuter P (2006) Money Laundering. Crime and Justice 34 (1): 289–375.

Machado M (2012) Similar in their differences: Transnational legal process addressing money laundering in Brazil and Argentina. Law & Social Inquiry 37 (2): 330–366.

Mitsilegas V (2003) Money Laundering Counter-measures in the European Union: A new paradigm of security governance versus fundamental legal principles. Kluwer Law International, The Hague.

Mitsilegas V (2014) The European Union and the Global Governance of Crime. In: Mitsilegas V et al. (eds) Globalisation, Criminal Law and Criminal Justice: Theoretical, Comparative and Transnational Perspectives. Hart, London, pp. 153–198.

Moccia S (1995) Impiego di Capitali illeciti e riciclaggio: la risposta del sistema penale italiano. Rivista italiana di diritto e procedura penale: 728–739.

Nadelmann E A (1986) Latinoamérica: Economía Política Del Comercio De Cocaína. Texto y Contexto. Sept-Dic 9: 27–49.

Nadelmann E A (1993) Cops Across Borders: The Internationalization of U.S. Criminal Law Enforcement. Pennsylvania State University Press, Park.

Naylor T (2002) Wages of Crime. Black Markets, Illegal Finance, And The Underworld Economy. Cornell University Press, Ithaca.

Nilsson H G (1991) The Council of Europe Laundering Convention: A Recent Example of Developing International Criminal Law. Criminal Law Forum 2 (3): 419–441.

OECD (2012) Tax and crime. www.oecd.org/ctp/taxcrimes. Last accessed on 16 September 2016.

Pieth M (1993) "Symbolische Gesetzgebung" gegen Geldwäscherei und organisiertes Verbrechen? Vortrag am 17. Deutschen Strafverteidigertag, Münster, 7. - 9.5.1993. In: Strafverteidiger-vereinigungen, Organisationsbüro der Strafverteidigervereinigungen (ed) Rechtsstaatliche Antworten auf neue Kriminalitätsformen. Der Andere Buchladen, Cologne, pp. 99–106.

Pieth M (2004) International standards against money laundering. In: Pieth M, Aiolfi G (eds) A Comparative Guide to Anti-Money Laundering: A Critical Analysis of Systems in Singapore, Switzerland, the UK and the USA. Edward Elgar, Cheltenham, pp 3–61.

Sharman J C (2011) The money laundry: Regulating criminal finance in the global economy. Cornell University Press, New York.

Stessens G (2000) Money Laundering: A New International Law Enforcement Model. University Press, Cambridge.

Tanzi V (1997) Macroeconomic Implications of Money Laundering. In: Savona E U (ed) Responding to Money Laundering, International Perspectives. Harwood Academic Publisher, Malaysia.

Transparency International (2015) Corruption Perception Index. http://www.transparency.org/cpi2015. Last accessed on 16 September 2016.

UN General Assembly (2001) Resolution United Nations Convention against Transnational Organized Crime A/RES/55/25. https://www.unodc.org/pdf/crime/a_res_55/res5525e.pdf. Last accessed on 16 September 2016.

Unger B, Addink H, Walker J, Ferwerda J, van den Broek M, Deleanu I (2013) ECOLEF final report. http://www2.econ.uu.nl/users/unger/ecolef_files/Final%20ECOLEF%20report%20(digital%20version).pdf. Last accessed on 16 September 2016.

Unger B, Ferwerda J, van den Broek M, Deleanu I (2014) The Economic And Legal Effectiveness Of The European Union's Anti-Money Laundering Policy. Edward Elgar Publishing Limited, Cheltenham.

Ward A (2014) Why we might not benefit from naming beneficial owners. Compliance Monitor 6 (3): 1–10.

Williams P, Savona E (1996) The United Nations and transnational organized crime. Frank Cass, London.

Chapter 4
The German Law-Making Process: Tracing Legislative Intents

Abstract This chapter analyses the German legislative process and the specific national legislature's motivations for the criminalisation of money laundering and for widening of the reach of the offence. It focuses on the parliamentarian debate that resulted in the introduction of Article 261 in the German Criminal Code (GCC), and on the main issues that raised along the legislative process, also with regard to the approval and the changing of the preventive regime.

Keywords Article 261 of the German Criminal Code · German anti-money laundering legislation · Act on the Suppression of Illegal Drug Trafficking and other Manifestations of Organized Crime

Contents

Germany signed the UN Convention against Illicit Traffic in Narcotic Drugs and Psychotropic Substances on 19 January 1989.[1] Therefore, it was bound to adopt the necessary legal and administrative measures to implement the UN treaty at a domestic level.[2] Germany, moreover, was bound by the Council Directive

[1] The German Democratic Republic had signed and ratified the Convention on 21 June 1989 and 21 February 1990, respectively. The Convention was ratified by unified Germany on 30 November 1993.
[2] BT-Drucks 12/3533, p. 12.

V. Zoppei, *Anti-Money Laundering Law: Socio-Legal Perspectives on the Effectiveness of German Practices*, International Criminal Justice Series 12,
DOI 10.1007/978-94-6265-180-7_4

91/308/EEC of 1991, Article 2 of which required states to prohibit money laundering.[3] In particular, Article 3 of the Vienna Convention imposes a duty to criminalise the laundering of proceeds of drug trafficking. Germany fulfilled this obligation by introducing Article 261 in the GCC, under Act on the Suppression of Illegal Drug Trafficking and other Manifestations of Organized Crime (*Gesetz zur Bekämpfung des illegalen Rauschgifthandels und andereren Erscheinungsformen der Organisierten Kriminalität*, OrgKG), which entered into force on 22 September 1992.[4] Already in 1988, the German government established a working group on money laundering, with the purpose of combating the laundering of proceeds of drug trafficking through the banking sector, in collaboration with the US government.[5] The debate that preceded the approval of the law shows that the German parliament was especially worried about the drug situation in West Germany between the late 1980s and the early 1990s.[6] Therefore, the government decided to issue a *nationaler Rauschgiftbekämpfungsplan*, a domestic policy to combat the trafficking in narcotics. Furthermore, the *Bundestag* (Federal Parliament) was concerned about the huge annual turnover generated through trafficking in narcotics in Germany, which was estimated in 1991 to be between two to four billion DM.[7] Such immense amounts of money were partly reinvested in drug trafficking and other criminal activities, and partly reintegrated in the lawful economy to make legitimate profit.[8] Germany was considered a particularly propitious destination for investing the proceeds stemming from organised crime because of its strong economy, stable currency, predictable legal system, solid public infrastructure, and geographical position.[9] The dirty money was integrated into the legitimate economy through the setting up of business with a high and regular cash turnover, such as restaurants, bars, cinemas, casinos and greengrocers.[10] Ill-gotten capital was invested too to fund or purchase companies. This was considered particularly harmful as it gave rise to unfair competition between business established lawfully with clean money and businesses with a criminal provenance.[11] Both the economy and the financial system were thus exploited for purposes of money laundering. Nevertheless, the main motive that triggered the legislature to criminalise money laundering was the necessity of tackling drug-related organised crime. In fact, the legislature defined money laundering as a phenomenon related to organised crime:

[3] Yet whether the federal state was bound under international law directly by the Vienna Convention or by the EC Directive is controversial. *See* Helmers 2009, p. 509.

[4] BGBI I 1992, 1302.

[5] Remmers 1998, p. 28.

[6] In 1992, for example, 2096 people died from abuse of drugs, with an estimated 150 000 addicted to drugs. These disturbing figures, and the harm it did to the fabric of society, necessitated the state to intensify its war on drugs. In BT-Drucks 11/5525, pp. 2 ss.

[7] BT-Drucks 12/989, p. 20.

[8] Aepfelbach and Fülbier 1994, p. 2.

[9] BT-Drucks 12/2720, p. 2.

[10] Aepfelbach and Fülbier 1994, pp. 4–5.

[11] Aepfelbach and Fülbier 1994, p. 2.

The main concern then was the 'infiltration of properties deriving from organised crime in the legitimate financial and economic circle for the purpose of disguising them'.[12] The connection between organised crime and money laundering was because criminal organisations were said to pursue the highest profit possible, so that money laundering was considered a consequence of organised criminal activities.[13] In this context, the German government recognised the importance of the 'follow the money' strategy and the possibility of tracking the paper trail (*Papierspur*) as a source of information for investigators.[14] The declared purpose of the new provision was, according to an official statement of Parliament, to confiscate organised crime's ill-gotten gains in order to hinder the proceeds of crime from becoming the 'operating capital' (*Betriebskapital*) with which to commit further crimes.[15] In other words, the threat of incurring criminal liability under Article 261(1) and (2) of the GCC should deter potential criminals from making illegal profits and should make the commission of further crimes unprofitable. Consequently, it would not be worth it to violate the law.[16] The legislature therefore pursued two goals with the introduction of Article 261 of the GCC. The first was a more effective exposing of organised crime structures, particularly drug trafficking, and the second was the elimination of the economic incentive for organised crime to violate the law through confiscation of ill-gotten gains and thus the isolation of offenders from their contexts.[17]

4.1 The Parliamentarian Debate

The first proposals for the introduction of specific norms directed at fighting the illegal traffic of psychotropic substances were drafted in 1990 by the government of Bayern and Baden-Württemberg.[18] On the basis of those drafts, Parliament drew up a draft law that was contested because it provided for very broad investigative instruments and it increased the punishments for some offences.[19] Financial institutions, professional associations and political institutions were particularly critical

[12] 'Die Einschleusung von Vermögengegenständen aus Organisierter Kriminalität in den legal Finanz- und Wirtschaftskreislauf zum Zweck der Tarnung'. *See* BT-Drucks 12/989, p. 26; BT-Drucks 13/8651, p. 9; similar BT-Drucks 12/3533, p. 11.

[13] GwG-Nestler 2014, § 261, mn 3.

[14] BT-Drucks 12/989, p. 26; BT-Drucks 12/3533, p. 12.

[15] BT-Drucks 12/2720, p. 2.

[16] Nestler 2010, GwG-Herzog, § 261, mn 12, 13.

[17] In the second purpose, the legislature included later also the fight against terrorism. *See* NK-Altenhain 2013, § 261, mn. 7.

[18] BR-Drucks 74/90; BR-Drucks 83/90.

[19] BT-Drucks 11/7663.

of the way the money-laundering offence was worded.[20] In the draft law of July 1991, Parliament explained the motives underlying the adoption of the law by stressing the fact that crime rate was alarming not only because of the increase in the incidence of drug-related delinquency, but also and especially because of the new organised way of acting and because of the transnational dimension of the phenomenon.[21] The debate that preceded the approval of the final text showed the complexity of the topic and the conflicting interests.[22] In particular, the opponents

[20] BT-Drucks 11/7663, pp. 49 ss; BT-Drucks 11/663; and BT-Drucks 11/5513. *See also* Caesar ZRP 1991, p. 242; Aepfelbach and Fülbier 1994, pp. 13–14; and Remmers 1998, p. 29.

[21] BT-Drucks 12/989, p. 20.

[22] The states of Baden-Württemberg and Bayern proposed a new draft law that elicited a lively debate among the representatives of the different states. The debate is reported in an official document of the *Bundesrat*. *See* Bundesrat 1991, pp. 139–151. The two Bundesländer Baden-Württemberg and Bayern stressed the urgency of introducing the proposed legal novelties in order to preserve the security of the citizens. The Baden-Württemberg Minister of the Interior, Schlee, of the Christian Democratic Union (CDU) stressed that the recent growth of organised crime and drug criminality was alarming, with the percentage of victims of drug abuse having increased by 50% between 1989 and 1990. In addition, he pointed to the need to protect victims of theft stemming from organised crime, especially the elderly who were vulnerable to burglaries. Given the severe danger that organised crime posed to society, he argued that state action was necessary to safeguard the safety of the people and for purposes of implementing a social policy. Schlee maintained that new laws, such as those pertaining to the crime of money laundering, were required to remove the financial incentive to commit further crimes. In his opinion, organised crime required more urgent attention than the issue of terrorism and the law relating to refugees. He said that terrorism could be dealt with by way of tackling organised crime, as the two were linked. Stoiber of the Christian Social Union (CSU) of Bavaria supported the argument by pointing to what was happening in the US and Italy at the time. He said that in Italy, organised crime had contaminated the society, undermined the integrity of the state, had resulted in an increase in taxes, and threatened the personal security of every citizen. He said that businesses run by the Mafia in the US made up 1.1% of the GDP of the US. He went on to say that, the German media was devoting little attention to the fact that white collar crime in the form of money laundering manifested itself silently in European financial centres. Finally, he described the draft law as a compromise, but still as a fundamental sign of engagement against organised crime that could not be ignored. Other political parties responded to these arguments, emphasising that these emergencies could be dealt with subject to upholding the fundamental principles underpinning the criminal justice system. Walter, a Social Democratic deputy from Saarland, opposed the introduction of the draft law by saying that the new provisions would give law enforcement agencies too wide a discretion in dealing with organised crime, thus infringing the rule of law. Kröning, Social Democratic Party deputy from Bremen, highlighted the conflict between safeguarding security and upholding the rule of law. While acknowledging the necessity of taking measures to combat organised crime, he argued that such measures should not violate constitutional principles. He warned that because the new instruments relied on the expertise of law enforcement agencies, which was lacking at the time, the effectiveness of the measures could be undermined. However, given the fact that a compromise was needed, and that Parliament had spent the last three quarters of the year dealing with other issues, he proposed that an agreement be reached in line with the compromise put forward by the parliamentary legal committee. Hohmann-Denhardt, a Social Democratic Party deputy from Hesse, welcomed the draft law subject to secret criminal procedural investigative instruments being limited. He contended that there could not be any compromise on the rule of law. Trittin, a representative of the Alliance90/The Greens Party from Lower Saxony, who was comfortable with the draft law despite the complexity of the issue, but refused to endorse

participants could be easily divided into two camps, with the one consisting of politicians, law enforcement forces, public prosecutors and judges, who advocated for the adoption of almost all legal novelties, and the consisting of attorneys and scholars, who, queried the constitutional legitimation and the efficiency of the new instruments.[23] The parliamentary debate leading up to the criminalisation of money laundering and the enacting of related laws shows that the discussions were deeply embedded in the political-historical context. Given that Germany had just been reunified after a period of two dictatorial regimes, the debates left no doubt that the lawmakers were keenly aware of their responsibility to create a new legal system against the backdrop of Germany's history. In order to balance the very different legal cultures, divergent compromises were necessary. The introduction of a new crime was a particularly delicate matter in view of the discriminatory and arbitrary use of criminal labels by previous dictatorial regimes. Therefore, deputies were not prepared to sacrifice fundamental rights just for the sake of prosecuting criminals. The legislation can be seen as an attempt to balance the need to adopt more effective measures to tackle crime and the need to respect the rule of law and to create a 'militant democracy'. Yet, given the external pressure coming from the FATF, the EU and the media, the text of the law was less of a compromise than it was of a need to ratify 'internationally' accepted standards.[24]

Controversial opinions were raised on the issue of *mens rea* as well and on the interest protected by the new criminal provision. Certain political parties, such as the SPD, supported the broadest criminal liability to ensure the effective prosecution of money laundering. Other parties, like the CDU, were worried that a

(Footnote 22 continued)

the new investigative rules, took the same approach. The Minister of Justice Kinkel of the Free Democratic Party (FDP) confirmed the complexity of the thematic issues raised by the Bill and recalled that the complexity of the issues cropped up also in the coalition agreement. Yet he underlined the importance of introducing the money-laundering offence in order to allow the confiscation of proceeds of crime thereby making the commission of offences less attractive. The Minister addressed the House by recalling the murder of Rohwedder by the Rote Armee Fraktion (*Rohwedder* was the president of the governmental agency charged with the task of privatising East German enterprises, the 'Treuhandstalt' (trust agency), who was killed on 1 April 1991 by the Rote Armee Fraktion) and the threat posed by terrorism. Yet he argued that a constitutional state based on the rule of law (*Rechtstaat)* should not violate the rule of law when defending itself from terrorist attacks. In fact, he undertook that, together with Schäuble, the then Minister of Internal Affairs, they were building a 'militant democracy' and therefore wanted to avoid exercising control over the citizens or groups of them. The Minister of Justice welcomed the introduction of the secret investigations and the Rasterfahndung (computer-based research of suspects), but said that the assembly should not arouse wrong public reactions. In conclusion, the Minister pleaded for the reaching of a compromise on the draft law, given the difficulty of the situation and the lack of other solutions. The exact result of the vote can be found in Bundesrat 1991, p. 151. The new text was then drafted and proposed to the Parliament; *see* BR-Drucks 219/91.

[23] Sotiriadis 2010, p. 173.

[24] In particular, Arzt observes that the German government was under pressure of the US government, which wanted to collect information on financial transactions. *See* Arzt 1997, p. 27. *See also* Sotiriadis 2010, p. 174.

broadening of liability would have encumbered the economy. Diverse were also the functions attributed to the criminalisation of money laundering. The ranged from the fight against organised crime, to the elimination of the incentives for committing any crime, or the need to safeguard the economy from being infiltrated by dirty money that, in turn, would distort free market competition. Parliament discussed this draft law, together with a proposal of the Social Democratic Party (SPD),[25] and after a public hearing of the parliamentary legal affairs committee in January 1992, the final text was adopted.[26]

---

[25] BT-Drucks 12/731.

[26] The current offence reads as follow: *(1) Whosoever hides an object which is a proceed of an unlawful act listed in the 2nd sentence below, conceals its origin or obstructs or endangers the investigation of its origin, its being found, its confiscation, its deprivation or its being officially secured shall be liable to imprisonment from 3 months to 5 years. Unlawful acts within the meaning of the 1st sentence shall be 1. felonies; 2. misdemeanours under (a) Section 332(1), also in conjunction with subsection (3), and Section 334; (b) Section 29(1) 1st sentence No 1 of the Drugs Act and Section 19(1) No 1 of the Drug Precursors (Control) Act; 3. misdemeanours under Section 373 and under Section 374(2) of the Fiscal Code, and also in conjunction with Section 12 (1) of the Common Market Organisations and Direct Payments (Implementation) Act; 4. misdemeanours (a) under Section 152a, Section 181a, Section 232(1) and (2), Section 233(1) and (2), Section 233a, Section 242, Section 246, Section 253, Section 259, Sections 263–264, Section 266, Section 267, Section 269, Section 271, Section 284, Section 326(1), (2) and (4), Section 328(1), (2) and (4) and Section 348; (b) under Section 96 of the Residence Act and Section 84 of the Asylum Procedure Act and Section 370 of the Fiscal Code, Section 38(1)–(3) and (5) of the Securities Trading Act as well as Sections 143, 143a and 144 of the Act on the Protection of Trade Marks and other Symbols, 106–108b of the Act on Copyright and Related Rights, 25 of the Utility Models Act, 51 and 65 of the Design Act, 142 of the Patent Act, 10 of the Semiconductor Protection Act and 39 of the Plant Variety Rights (Protection) Act. which were committed on a commercial basis or by a member of a gang whose purpose is the continued commission of such offences; and 5. misdemeanours under Section 89a and under Section 129 and Section 129a(3) and (5), all of which also in conjunction with Section 129b(1), as well as misdemeanours committed by a member of a criminal or terrorist organisation (Section 129 and Section 129a, all of which also in conjunction with Section 129b(1)). The 1st sentence shall apply in cases of tax evasion committed on a commercial basis or as a gang under Section 370 of the Fiscal Code, to expenditure saved by virtue of the tax evasion, of unlawfully acquired tax repayments and allowances, and in cases under the 2nd sentence no 3 the 1st sentence shall also apply to an object in relation to which fiscal charges have been evaded. (2) Whosoever 1. procures an object indicated in subsection (1) above for himself or a third person; or 2. keeps an object indicated in subsection (1) above in his custody or uses it for himself or a third person if he knew the origin of the object at the time of obtaining possession of it shall incur the same penalty. (3) The attempt shall be punishable. (4) In especially serious cases the penalty shall be imprisonment from 6 months to 10 years. An especially serious case typically occurs if the offender acts on a commercial basis or as a member of a gang whose purpose is the continued commission of money laundering. (5) Whosoever, in cases under subsections (1) or (2) above is, through gross negligence, unaware of the fact that the object is a proceed from an unlawful act named in subsection (1) above shall be liable to imprisonment of not more than two years or a fine. (6) The act shall not be punishable under subsection (2) above if a third person previously acquired the object without having thereby committed an offence. (7) Objects to which the offence relates may be subject to a deprivation order. Section 74a shall apply. Section 73d shall apply if the offender acts on a commercial basis or as a member of a gang whose purpose is the continued commission of money laundering. (8) Objects which are proceeds from an offence listed in subsection*

The law OrgKG (Act to combat illicit drug trafficking and other manifestations of organized crime) entered into force in 1992 and bound the Parliament to introduce the new offence of money laundering in the GCC by January 1993. The implementation of the law was to be funded by both the federal government and the states, but the amounts needed still had to be calculated. In particular, due to the introduction of new offences and of an enhanced international co-operation, public authorities were required to tighten monitoring measures and activities, the costs being covered by the states or by the federal state.[27] However, since public institutions were expected to profit from asset recovery measures, which were estimated to yield a yet to be quantified income, it was not expected of the public to bear this burden.[28]

Money laundering was defined in the draft law of the government that implements the Vienna Convention as the systematic concealing of objects through the financial system with the purpose of avoiding access by law enforcement in order to maintain its economic value (own translation).[29] The offence was included in the particular part of the German penal code, Chapter 21, dedicated to the assistance after the fact and handling stolen goods and was listed among the *Anschlussdelikte*, the derivative offences, namely the offences built on the commission of other offences, defined as the antecedent or predicate offences. The formulation introduced with the law OrgKG under Article 261 GCC reflected Article 3 b, c (I) of the Vienna Convention, which differentiated between the concealing-offence (*Verschleierungstatbestand*) according to Article 261(1) GCC and the acquisition, the possession and the use of the criminal property, (*Erwerbs-, Besitz- und Verwendungstatbestand*) regulated under Article 261(2) GCC. The first conduct, constituting of acts directed at ensuring the enjoyment of proceeds of crime without fearing law enforcement repression, was considered harmful for the administration of justice. The second one, instead, was directed at hampering the procurement, the use, and the keeping of contaminated objects also by third parties. By punishing any contact with the ill-gotten property, the legislator aimed at isolating perpetrators. The legislature aimed at isolating criminals by impeding them the access to the

(Footnote 26 continued)

(1) above committed abroad shall be equivalent to the objects indicated in subsections (1), (2) and (5) above if the offence is also punishable at the place of its commission. (9) Whosoever 1. voluntarily reports the offence to the competent public authority or voluntarily causes such a report to be made, unless the act had already been discovered in whole or in part at the time and the offender knew this or could reasonably have known and 2. in cases under subsections (1) or (2) above under the conditions named in No 1 above causes the object to which the offence relates to be officially secured shall not be liable under subsections (1)–(5) above. Whosoever is liable because of his participation in the antecedent act shall not be liable under subsections (1)–(5) above, either.

27 BT-Drucks 12/3533, p. 10.

28 BT-Drucks 12/3533, p. 11.

29 The original wording is the following: *systematische Tarnung von Vermögenswerten mit den Mitteln des Finanzmarktes, um sie dem Zugriff der Strafverfolgungsorgane zu entziehen und in ihrem wirtschaftlichen Wert zu erhalten.* BT-Drucks 12/3533, p. 12.

legitimate economy, and this was especially achieved by criminalising the providing, the storage, and the use also by third persons of the criminal property (Article 261(2) GCC). This function earned the second paragraph the name of 'isolation conduct'.[30]

The legislature used the term 'object' (*Gegenstand*), instead of property, because the latter was not legally defined and because it was meant to cover a broad range of items of economic value, regardless of the specific value. The expression *herrühren*, which means 'derived from an unlawful act', refers to the link between the antecedent illegal act and the subsequent acts. Both terms are subject of vivid controversies, as it will be shown in the third part.

Article 261(4) envisages an aggravating punishment, from 6 months to 10 years, for serious cases, namely, 'if the offender acts on a commercial basis or as a member of a gang whose purpose is the continued commission of money laundering'. With this provision, the legislature tried to include the link with organised crime and terrorism. This provision comes into play especially where the crime is committed by a gang member and where the offender of the antecedent crime acted in her or his interest or belongs to a mixed gang formed for the specific purpose of laundering the proceeds of crime. The legislature set a low burden of proof to facilitate the prosecution of organised criminal groups and terrorist organisations.[31]

Article 261(5) criminalises the reckless conduct. The decision to punish on the assumption of recklessness was debated at length in Parliament. The legislature declared that the introduction of the provision was necessary to avoid problems of evidence and thus allow a more effective fight against money laundering.[32] There were conflicting opinions about the degree of *mens rea* required with respect to the illegal provenance of the assets in order to punish the offender.[33] The SPD supported the criminalisation of the mere negligent behaviour so as not to undermine the seriousness of the offence of money laundering.[34] On the contrary, it was argued that this proposal would have been cumbersome for the economic cycle and for the free circulation of goods, to the point that anyone taking part in these activities could have been prosecuted for money laundering. The debate reflects the underlying question whether the norm should be make law enforcement more effective or to safeguard business operations (*Geschäftsverkehr*). The solution was found in the following compromise: only the reckless money laundering (*leichtfertige*), under paragraph 5 of Article 261 of the GCC (*leichtfertigen Begehung*), but not the mere negligent (*fahrlässig*), was criminalised. Recklessness is a heightened degree of negligence; its negative definition is that it constitutes negligent but not intentional

[30] According to some scholars, the provision criminalises three typologies of conduct: the concealing offence described in Article 261(1) of the GCC, the avoidance of prosecution and confiscation, according to Article 261(1) 1, 2 of the GCC, and the isolation conduct regulated in Article 261(2) of the GCC. *See* NK-Altenhain 2013, § 261, mn. 8, 9.

[31] *See* NK-Altenhain 2013, § 261, mn. 43.

[32] BT-Drucks 989, p. 27.

[33] BT-Drucks 12/2720, p. 43.

[34] BT-Drucks 12/731, p. 3.

behaviour. Yet, under German law, property crimes and derivative crimes are always committed intentionally and not negligently.

The commission of the predicate offence has to be demonstrated along general lines. Previous convictions for a predicate offence can be taken into account in deciding on the culpability of the predicate offence for money laundering.[35] However, the judge in the money-laundering case would have to determine the existence of the predicate offence.[36] The German provision included proceeds of other offences committed by a member of a criminal organisation (as defined by Article 129 of the GCC) and proceeds of any crime (Article 261(1) 1 and 3 of the GCC). Three categories of predicate offences were included, namely, serious crimes, offences in violation of the law on psychotropic substances, and offences committed by a member of a criminal organisation. The government expressively did not opt for the all-crimes approach in order not to extend the reach of the crime too widely.[37] However, according to other statements published by the Parliament, the legal provision ought to have blocked the entry of criminal money into the lawful economy. While this was the immediate aim, the indirect aim of the legislature was to avoid the distortion of the existing economic system.[38]

4.2 Following Significant Amendments to the Anti-Money Laundering Regime

Article 261 of the GCC has been amended very often, mostly to extend the list of predicate offences. The most recent amendment entered into force on the 26th November 2015. The *Gesetz zur Bekämpfung der Korruption* (Anti-corruption Act), in particular, introduced two new predicate offences contained in Article 299 of the GCC, namely, 'Taking and giving bribes in commercial practice', and in Article 355a of the GCC, which punishes the '[t]aking of bribes meant as an incentive to violating one's official duties' and the 'giving of bribes as an incentive to the recipient's violating his official duties' in relation to international civil servants. The most important and most discussed novelty introduced by the Anti-corruption Act is the elimination of the exemption from punishment.[39] The provision deletes the exclusion of criminal liability for those who participated in the predicate offences, and put in circulation the objects deriving from the crimes they commit to conceal the criminal origin (Article 261(9) 2 of the GCC). In Germany 'self-money laundering' had remained unpunished for long time, despite the fact that Germany had incurred an international obligation to criminalise it. The jurisprudence confirmed

[35] *See* NK-Altenhain 2013, § 261, mn. 49.

[36] *See* NK-Altenhain 2013, § 261, mn. 48.

[37] BT-Drucks 12/989, p. 27.

[38] BT-Drucks 12/989, p. 26; BR-Drucks 507/92. *See also* Müko-Neuheuser 2012, § 216, mn. 2, 3.

[39] Article 1, BGBI I S. 2025.

the decision of excluding personal criminal liability for someone who was already involved in the antecedent act, also if the act was committed abroad.[40] The Ministry of Justice and other actors took a strong position to protect the rule, yet Germany was bound both by the FATF Recommendations and by the EU to introduce a new criminal liability.[41] In June of the same year, the legislature introduced in the list of predicate offences the crime of terrorist financing, which is regulated by the new Article 89 c of the GCC.[42] In 2014, along with the introduction of a new provision that punished the bribing of members of Parliament under Article 108 e of the GC, which allowed Germany to finally ratify UNCAC,[43] the scope of Article 261 of the GCC was extended to include as an antecedent act the 'bribing of delegates'.[44] To improve the fight against money laundering and tax evasion, the German legislature enacted in 2011 the *Gesetz zur Verbesserung der Bekämpfung der Geldwäsche und Steuerhinterziehung*. This law included fiscal offences in the list of predicate crimes.[45] Other major enactments were introduced in 2008 to increase efforts to combat money laundering and the financing of terrorism were introduced with the *Gesetz zur Ergänzung der Bekämpfung der Geldwäsche und der Terrorismusfinanzierung, Geldwäschebekämpfungsergänzungsgesetz - GwBekErgG*,[46] which also implemented the Third EU Anti-Money Laundering Directive.[47]

From the start, it was clear that Article 261 of the GCC was closely linked to the regulations regarding the banking system. It had become obvious that money laundering could have be dealt with more effectively only if the banks collected information and reported suspicious transactions to law enforcement agencies.[48]

[40] BGH NStZ 1995, 500. *See also* Schmidt and Krause 2010, StGB-Fischer, § 261, mn. 50.

[41] *See*, in particular, Schröder 2013. The German federal bar association published an official opinion on the proposal of excluding the exemption of punishment pursuant to Article 261(9) 2 of the GCC, in which it expressed a strong scepticism. In particular, the bar association argues that the novelty would have been constitutional illegitimate because it would have infringed the principles of *ne bis in idem* and of legality. Bundesrechtsanwaltkammer 2015, p. 3.

[42] Article 1 of the GVVG-Änderungsgesetz (GVVG-ÄndG) of 12/06/15, BGBI I S. 926.

[43] BT-Drucks 449/14.

[44] Article 1 of the Achtundvierzigstes Strafrechtsänderungsgesetz-Erweiterung des Straftatbestandes der Abgeordnetenbestechung of 23/04/14, BGBl. I S. 410.

[45] BGBI I 676.

[46] BGBI I 37.

[47] Other amendments were introduced with the *Gesetz zur Verbesserung der Bekämpfung der Geldwäsche und der Bekämpfung der Finanzierung des Terrorismus, Geldwä schebekämpfungsgesetz*, BGBl I 02, 3105. Other major amendments to Article 261 were introduced by the *Steuerverkürzungsbekämpfungsgesetz* of 2002, the *Gesetz zur Neuregelung der Telekommunikationsüberwachung* of 2008, the *Gesetz zur Ergänzung der Bekämpfung der Geldwäsche und der Terrorismusfinanzierung* of 2008, which implemented the Directive 2005/60/EC, the *Geldwäschebekämpfungsergänzungsgesetz*, GwBekErgG of 2008, the *Gesetz zur Verfolgung der Vorbereitung von schweren staatsgefährdenden Gewalttaten* of 2009, which established the financing of terrorism as predicate offence for money laundering. BGBI I, 3922; BGBI I, 3198; BGBI I, 1690. *See* also amendments introduced with the *Gesetz zur Verbesserung der Bekämpfung der Organisierten Kriminalität*, BGBI I 845.

[48] Remmers 1998, p. 45.

In 1992, the Federal Government stated that an effective fight against money laundering was dependent on the ability of law enforcement agencies to obtain evidence of money-laundering transactions by gaining access to financial documents. To make this happen, the Money Laundering Act (*Geldwäschegesetz*, GwG) was enacted and it came into effect on 30 November 1993.[49] This law also implemented fully the EC Directive 91/308/EEC. The main provisions of the Money Laundering Act obligated credit and financial institutions to identify clients (Article 1(1) (2) of the Money Laundering Act) and beneficial owners (Articles 2, 6, 8 of the Money Laundering Act) in the public interest and for the benefit of law enforcement agencies.[50] The obligation to collect crucial information and to keep records on transactions with clients (Article 9 of the Money Laundering Act) was to facilitate the tracking of paper trails. The law required suspicious transactions to be reported to the designated authority that was empowered to authorise banks to interrupt suspicious transactions (Article 11 of the Money Laundering Act). Article 11 of the Act laid the ground for collaboration between the private sector and law enforcement agencies in the area of combating money laundering. In fact, financial investigations related to money laundering can be triggered by the collection of information in the context of another proceeding, which maybe related, for example, to the commission of a predicate offence, or a specific preliminary investigation based on a STR.

Among the most relevant amendments to Anti-money Laundering Act, in 2002 the Financial Intelligence Unit (FIU) was established in the *Bundeskriminalamt* BKA (Federal Crime Office), as an intermediary between law enforcement and obligated entities.[51] The FIU's is required to support the federal and state police forces in the prevention and prosecution of money laundering, and in particular, collecting and analysing suspicious transactions reports transmitted by obligated entities pursuant to Sections 11 and 14 of the Money Laundering Act.[52] The STRs are kept in a database and monitored to see whether there are grounds to justify an initial suspicion of money-laundering offence, or an underlying offence under Article 261 of the GCC, or any other criminal offence. The findings are summarised in a report, which is then passed on to the relevant specialised office or public prosecutor's office. Among the cases received by the FIU, some are classified as significant, based on indicators such as the number of the transactions reported, the persons involved, other significant case-specific features, or the high level of public

---

[49] BGBI 1993 I, p. 1770.

[50] For a critical view on the use of such information for fiscal purposes, *see* Dieter and Klos 1994, p. 135 ss.

[51] Recently, after the initiative taken by the Ministry of Finance to respond to the Panama Papers, the Federal Government has announced that the FIU shall be moved from the BKA to the customs, and should be supported with further personnel in order to improve its effectiveness. See Federal Government 2016.

[52] According to Articles 11(1) and 14(1) obliged entities shall report suspicious transactions both to the FIU and to the local police criminal office (*Landeskriminalamt*).

interest or media coverage.[53] In addition, the FIU maintains statistics on STRs received and analysed, follows up on the reported cases, the cases under investigation, number of prosecutions and convictions, property and assets frozen, seized or confiscated. All these findings are published in the annual report.

4.3 Considerations

The analysis of the national law-making process is important for depicting the divergent opinions and expectations relating to the criminalisation of money laundering. Whilst the manifested goal of the legislature for the introduction of the money-laundering offence was combating drug trafficking, external actors pushed the adoption of such law.[54] The vivid political debate shows that several issues cropped in the initial phase. Moreover, in line with the expansion of the international anti-money laundering legal regime, the scope of Article 261 of the GCC was extended to include new predicate offences. The ultimate impact of a law that generates such profound controversial issues will be discussed in the next part. The underlying hypothesis based on the reflections spelled out in the first chapter is that a provision that integrates with difficulty in a legal system may be doomed to be applied in a wrong way.

References

Aepfelbach R, Fülbier A (1994) Das Geldwäschegetz. Eine einführende Kommentierung. 2. Auflage. Verlag Kommunikationsforum GmbH, Cologne.

Altenhain K (2013) § 261 Geldwäsche; Verschleierung unrechtmäßig erlangter Vermögenswerte. In: Kindhäuser U et al. (eds.) Strafgesetzbuch. Nomos Kommentar (NK) 3 (4). Nomos, Baden-Baden, pp. 483–547.

Arzt G (1997) Das mißglückte Strafgesetz. Am Beispiel der Geldwäschegesetzgebung. In: Diedrichsen U, Dreier R (eds) Das missglückte Gesetz, 8. Symposium der Kommission "Die Funktion des Gesetzes in Geschichte und Gegenwart". Wandenhoeck & Ruprecht, Göttingen, pp. 17–38.

Bundesrat (1991) Plenarprotokoll 629. Sitzung 26/04/1991. http://www.bundesrat.de/SharedDocs/downloads/DE/plenarprotokolle/1991/Plenarprotokoll-629.pdf;jsessionid=66D04E3D152F3D9F8CD1AF3C44D78745.2_cid365?__blob=publicationFile&v=2. Last accessed on 16 September 2016.

Bundesrechtsanwaltkammer (2015) Stellungnahme Nr. 33/2015. http://www.brak.de/zur-rechtspolitik/stellungnahmen-pdf/stellungnahmen-deutschland/2015/september/stellungnahme-der-brak-2015-33.pdf. Last accessed on 16 September 2016.

Caesar P (1991) Das Gesetz gegen die Organisierte Kriminalität: Eine unendliche Geschichte? Zeitschrift für Rechtspolitik (ZRP): 241–244.

[53] FIU 2014, p. 27.

[54] Sotiriadis 2010, p. 174.

Dieter C, Klos J (1994) Das Bankgeheimnis. Steuerberater (StB): 135–143.

Federal Government (2016) Financial Intelligence Unit. Mit mehr Personal gegen Geldwäsche. https://www.bundesregierung.de/Content/DE/Artikel/2016/08/2016-08-09-spezialeinheit-geldwaesche.html. Last accessed on 17 August 2016.

FIU (2014) Financial Intelligence Unit (FIU) Germany - Annual Report 2013. https://www.bka.de/SharedDocs/Downloads/EN/Publications/AnnualReportsAndSituationAssessments/FIU/fiuJahresbericht2013Englisch.html?nn=39788. Last accessed on 16 September 2016.

Helmers G (2009) Zum Tatbestand der Geldwäsche (§ 261 StGB): Beispiel einer rechtsprinzipiell verfehlten Strafgesetzgebung. Zeitschrift für die gesamte Strafrechtswissenschaft 121 (3): 509–547.

Müko-Neuheuser S (2012) § 261 Geldwäsche; Verschleierung unrechtmäßig erlangter Vermögenswerte. In: Joecks W (ed.) Münchener Kommentar zum Strafgesetzbuch 4 2. Auflage. C H Beck, Munich.

Nestler C (2010) Geldwäsche; Verschleierung unrechtmäßig erlangter Vermögenswerte. In: Herzog F (ed.) Geldwäschegesetz (Gwg). 1. Auflage. C H Beck, Munich.

Nestler C (2014) Geldwäsche; Verschleierung unrechtmäßig erlangter Vermögenswerte. In: Herzog F (ed.) Geldwäschegesetz (Gwg). 2. Auflage. C H Beck, Munich.

Remmers B (1998) Die Entwicklung der Gesetzgebung zur Geldwäsche. Lang, Frankfurt am Main.

Schmidt W, Krause J (2010) § 261 Geldwäsche, Verschleierung unrechtmäßig erlangter Vermögenswerte. In: Laufhütte H W et al. (eds) Strafgesetzbuch. Leipziger Kommentar 8. 12. Auflage. De Gruyter, Berlin.

Schröder C (2013) Warum die Selbstgeldwäsche straffrei bleiben muss: Why self-money laundering must remain exempt from punishment. Berliner Wissenschafts-Verlag, Berlin.

Sotiriadis G (2010) Die Entwicklug der Gesetzgebung über Gewinnabschöpfung und Geldwäsche. Unter Berücksichtigung der jeweiligen kriminalpolitischen Tendenzen. Duncker & Humblot, Berlin.

Part III
The Integration of Article 261 in the German Criminal Code

Gegen Kriminalität, deren Bekämpfung sich nicht lohnt,
sind primär symbolische, wenig bis nichts kostende Massnahmen zu ergreifen.[1]

Arzt 2013, p. 1136

[1] Own translation: In order to combat criminality, which in itself is not worthwhile, one has to resort primarily to symbolic measures, which cost little to nothing.

Chapter 5
The Doctrinal Legal Debate on Article 261 of the German Criminal Code

Abstract This part looks at one of the determining factors for sociological research on the effectiveness of law mentioned in Part I, namely, how scholars, who are experts in the field, welcome a law. It questions whether the offence of money laundering is an adequate tool to combat money laundering from a theoretical perspective. In other words, does the legal provision on money laundering have the potential or not to achieve its goals. After having analysed the manifest and latent intentions of the legislature in making money laundering a crime, and having looked at the ultimate symbolic functions ascribed to the law, this study proceeds to examine how legal scholars have received the statutory provision that regulates the crime of money laundering. It deals with the following issues, in particular; the interests protected by Article 261 of the GCC; the wording of Article 261; the criminalisation of reckless conduct (*leichtfertige Geldwäsche*); and a summary of the critical opinions as to whether the provision regulating the crime of money laundering serves the purpose for which it was enacted or whether it has merely a symbolic function.

Keywords Article 261 of the German Criminal Code · Legally protected interests · Predicate offences for money laundering · Defence attorneys and money laundering

Contents

V. Zoppei, *Anti-Money Laundering Law: Socio-Legal Perspectives on the Effectiveness of German Practices*, International Criminal Justice Series 12,
DOI 10.1007/978-94-6265-180-7_5

The opinions expressed in the legal literature reflect what *Friedman* refers to as the internal legal culture.[1] This part looks at the perception of legal scholars, while Part V deals with how legal practitioners receive a law. Given existence of the huge body of literature on the topic at hand, it would have been superfluous to conduct interviews with legal scholars.[2] The paragraphs below draw attention to the specific controversial challenges that arise because of the wider formulation of the money-laundering offence and how this hinders the effective application and enforcement of the law. The underlying assumption is that the degrees to which legal scholars express how they accept a law mirrors the degree to which the law integrates itself into the legal system. In turn, the degree to which the law is perceived to be legitimate is a factor that determines how effective the law will be. Given that the national law-making process has been largely influenced by international efforts to combat money laundering, controversy is bound to arise when international norms are transplanted into the national legal system. The fact of the matter is that states are still reluctant to relinquish their sovereignty, particularly about criminal law. It is, therefore, crucial to determine whether overarching international anti-money laundering policies lend themselves to be accommodated in national legal cultures.

5.1 The Interests Protected by the Law: All Interests or no Interest?

Before looking at the controversial debate about the interests protected by Article 261 of the GCC, it is useful to contextualise the issue in the general discussion on the limits and the functions of criminal law, particularly in regard to the legal interests that criminal law protects. As pointed out in Part I, research on the effectiveness of criminal law must take into account the peculiarities of criminal law, one of them being that, by definition, criminal law is a harmful tool, which harms offenders in order to protect some interests. Given that the criminalisation of conduct is a question of labelling some behaviour as deviant as opposed to being compliant, it is essential that such respects the reasonable constraints of repression. Specifically,

---

[1] Friedman 1975, p. 135.

[2] When contacted for an interview, one of the scholars suggested that the author reads his numerous publications on the topic. This led the author to decide to peruse the legal literature rather than to interview legal scholars face to face.

criminal law should be used sparingly if it wants to achieve certain goals.[3] A useful tool to limit the boundaries of criminal law in civil law systems is the concept of legally protected interests (*Rechtsgut*).[4] The so-called '*Rechtsguts*-theory'[5] was based on the presumption of the existence of some particularly relevant goods, the protection of which legitimises the use of the repressive public power. The resort to criminal law ought to be limited to protect those goods. The doctrinal debate is particularly lively among Germans legal scholars,[6] who have occupied themselves especially in attempts to define the concept of a *Rechtsgut* (legal interest). A modern definition refers to 'the conditions and the aims needed for free development of the individual, for realisation of his fundamental rights, and for the proper functioning of state institutions that are needed for these purposes'.[7] Recent discussions focus on the question whether the legally protected interest represents a 'critical, liberal' boundary for a criminal policy that limits state intervention to the protection of only certain qualified interests, or whether it is a discretional tool that perpetuates class inequalities through selective penal sanctions.[8] Given the uncertainty surrounding the concept, the German Federal Constitutional Court has thus far preferred to apply the well-established principle of proportionality when weighing the legitimacy of criminal law provisions.[9] But the debate is still open for the reason that to some scholars, even the principle of proportionality does not have a predictable consequence.[10] 'In fact, it is fair to say that the constitutional processes and value judgments have proven to be open enough to justify almost any outcome [...]. This, in turn, shows that the *Rechtsgut*-concept is, at least when compared to any constitutional standard, not as empty and vague as some have criticised it to be.'[11]

---

[3] Von Liszt 1882.

[4] Binding 1872; and Birnbaum 1834. Common law applies instead the harm principle.

[5] The term '*Rechtsguts*-theory' is used by Ambos 2015, pp. 305 ss.

[6] *See* among others, Amelung 1972, pp. 302 ss; Appel 1998, pp. 344, + 381 ss; NK-Hassemer 2010, § 1 mn. 108 ss, 146 ss; and Roxin 2006, § 2, mn. 1 ss.

[7] Definition provided by Roxin 2010, § 2 mn. 7–9.

[8] According to the first approach, the state is allowed to punish only conduct that harms or, at least, endangers legally protected interests. In other words, this means that there is no offence which does not harm a legally protected interest and that the harm to a legally protected interest is a conditio sine qua non for criminalisation. *See* Marinucci and Dolcini 2006, p. 6; and Paliero 1992, p. 449. The second viewpoint has criticised the *Rechtsguts*-theory for being imprecise, arbitrary and inconsistent, because the concept of *Rechtsgut* is still controversial, and thus the theory does not rely on pre-existing goods, nor does it provide criteria for determining those goods. *See* Amelung 1972, pp. 261–272; Frisch 2003, pp. 216–218; Helmers 2009, pp. 514–515; Hörnle 2005, pp. 11 ss; Stratenwerth 1998, pp. 378–381; Wohlers 2000, pp. 213 ss.; and Von Hirsch 2003.

[9] *See*, for example, BVerfG Decision 2 BvR 392/07 of 26 February 2008, para. 39; BVerfGE 120, 224–273. About this case, *see also* Ambos 2015, p. 307; Roxin 2010, pp. 580–582; 2006, § 2 mn. 86–87, 89; and Schünemann 2003, pp. 142–149.

[10] For example, Roxin argued that the proportionality test gives too much discretion to the legislator. *See* Roxin 2010, pp. 584–585; 2006, § 2, mn. 93.

[11] Ambos 2015, pp. 308–309.

Far from being a philosophical question, this limitation affects the manifestation of state power in a very concrete way, as it restricts public action at both the law-making and implementation level. Among European countries, for example, there is yet no consensus on the interests protected by the offence of money laundering.[12] These differences show that states have varying perceptions of the purposes of anti-money laundering law, to the point that some perceive it as an anti-drug policy, some as a measure against tax evasion, and some as a tool to curb corruption. The European Directives have justified the criminalisation of money laundering mainly on the ground that it is necessary for maintaining public confidence in the soundness of the financial system, and secondarily because there is a need to co-operate transnationally in fighting organised crime.[13] The offence protects various interests, 'ranging from individual ones, such as property, to collective ones such as state security'.[14] Given the different manifest and latent functions attributed to the offence of money laundering during the law-making process and in the widening of the ambit of the crime, which was discussed in the previous Part, it is unsurprising that there is no unanimity on the legally protected interests.

Furthermore, the tendency of criminal policy to endorse universal legal interests, *Universalrechtsgüter*, such as the administration of justice, or the economic order, has widened the realm for the legislature to enact criminal law, to the extent that criminal law could be used to minimise insecurity and to regulate global complex issues. This results in sanctioning behaviour which is already regulated in the field of private law. While this phenomenon can partly be explained by the fact that there is a general tendency in Europe to regulate the private sector, too, through criminal law, it bears testimony to a regression towards an authoritarian state that abuses its monopoly of violence.

In Germany, the controversy surrounding the demarcation of the interests protected by the offence of money laundering is particularly vibrant. According to *Helmers*, the debate is even overwrought in the attempt to arrive at a decision on what legitimizes the offence, and at the same time function as yardstick to restrict its scope.[15] In other words, the scholar considers the doctrinal debate biased, because it aims to legitimize the provision *ex-post facto* by ascribing to the offence the function of protecting an interest. This is particularly dangerous, as it tends to justify any

[12] *See* Unger et al. 2014, p. 237. For instance, in England the offence has been classified as a drug-related offence (Sections 49–52 of the English Drug Trafficking Act of 1994). Articles 305 *bis* and 305 *ter* of the Swiss Criminal Code are classified as offences against the administration of justice. Article 301 of the Spanish Penal Code is classified as an offence against the patrimony and against the socio-economic order. The Italian money laundering offence, regulated by Article 648 *bis* of the Italian Criminal Code is included among the offences against property; Article 324(1) of the French Criminal Code belongs to the third book of the code that regulates the offences against property, too.

[13] Vogel, ZStW 109, 1997, p. 351.

[14] Mitsilegas 2003, p. 105.

[15] Mitsilegas 2003, p. 105.

means to have a general protective function.[16] More critical is *Helmers*, who contends that the legitimacy of a criminal norm should be grounded in a different way than ascribing to it any kind of function for the achievement of any type of purpose.[17] Even the German Federal Constitutional Court has declared that the determination of the legal interest (*Rechtsgutsbestimmung*) protected by Article 261 is vague, and has recognised how complex it is to assign a certain interest to the offence. Unfortunately, the Court has not taken the opportunity of clarifying the legal interest protected.

The doctrinal dispute reflects the various intentions underlying the anti-money laundering that have been expressed in the different types of conduct criminalised under the common umbrella of Article 261 of the GCC. The legislature did, in fact, indeed, categorise the different interests protected by the punishment carried paras 1 and 2 of Article 261 of the GCC. According to the statements issued by the legislature, the legal interests protected by Article 261(1) of the GCC should be the task of Germany's administration of justice to eradicate the impact of crime,[18] while Article 261(2) of the GCC should protect not only the administration of justice but also any interest endangered by the predicate offences.[19] The German Parliament specified furthermore that the money-laundering offence protect the rule of law by decreasing the perpetration of more crimes.[20] However, legal scholars were not placated by the explanations emanating from Parliament, because of the continuous expansion of the scope of the offence. Despite the legal uncertainty, the judiciary has not done anything to narrow down the question.[21]

5.1.1 The Interests Protected by Predicate Offences

There are four main recognisable interests protected by Article 261,[22] but all of them have been criticised and scholars disagree on this subject. Given its nature as a derivative offence, the offence of money laundering is said to protect interests protected by predicate offences, which range from human life, property, the social fabric and public order.[23] This is acknowledged with particular reference to the isolation clause contained in the second paragraph, which is directed at preventing

---

[16] Ibid.

[17] Helmers 2009, p. 518.

[18] BT-Drucks 12/3533, p. 11.

[19] BT-Drucks 12/3533, p.13.

[20] BT-Drucks 12/989, p. 27.

[21] GwG-Herzog 2014, § 261, mn. 28; and BGH, NJW 1997, 3323, 3325.

[22] GwG-Herzog 2014, § 261, mn. 22 ss.

[23] BGHSt 55, 36(49); Eisele, 2015, § 49, mn. 1172; StGB-Fischer, § 261, mn. 2, 3; MüKo-Neuheuser 2012, § 261, mn. 12; Rengier 2015, § 23, mn. 4; SK-Hoyer, § 261, mn. 1; Wessels and Hillenkamp 2015, § 261, mn. 891. *See also* Althenhain 2002, p. 402; GwG-Herzog 2014, § 261, mn. 24; and Oswald 1997, p. 63. Article 261(2) is said to intensify the protection of the predicate offences' interests, *see* Arzt, ZStW 111, 1999a, b, p. 758.

the commission of the predicate offences by making them less attractive, and by depriving criminals of their financial means.[24] In view of the fact that the law functions to discouraging the commission of any offence by blocking the criminal from enjoying the proceeds of the crime committed, Article 261(2) of the GCC would protect all interests of the criminalised predicate offences.[25] This potentially expands the *Rechtsgut* protected by the money-laundering offence, consequently adding to the growing catalogue of predicate offences. As a result, the provision becomes a multifaceted offence that serves to combat a broad range of practices, thus attributing to it the function of serving to protect a global legal interest (*Globalrechtsgut*) or a universal legal interest (*Universalrechtsgut*).[26] Such a boundless offence is considered dangerous, as it extends the boundaries for the application of criminal law, which imparts a banality to the legal interest protected.[27] This consequence, combined with the vague definition of the *actus reus,* may lead to 'an unlimited power to prosecute and to punish'.[28] In addition, given the intimate connection between the criminal law provision and the preventive regulations, the broadening of the scope of the offence devolves continually increasing policing powers to designated professions by imposing on them the duty to report suspicious transactions.[29] Furthermore, seen from a substantive point of view, 'the threat of money laundering to the interests protected by the predicate offences […] appears only indirect, if not tenuous'.[30] General comments have been made regarding the question of criminal law policy to the effect that, if the aim of the law is to reduce the rate at which antecedent crimes are committed predicate offences should have not been ignored. Taking drug trafficking as an example, the money-laundering discourse does not include a discussion on the appropriateness of legalising certain types of narcotics in order to diminish criminal activities linked to them.[31] The broadening of the catalogue of designated offences, directed at increasing the effectiveness of general deterrence, should not suppress local debates on the (de)criminalisation of those offences.[32] Finally, the protection of the interests envisaged by the predicate offences does not exhaust the interests protected by the legal provision. While this might be appropriate for the conduct described in para 2 of Article 261 of the GCC, it does not seem to be suitable for the offence of concealing listed in para 1.

---

[24] *See* Burr 1995, p. 25; Müko-Neuheuser 2012, § 261, mn. 13; Salditt, StraFo, 1992, pp. 121–122.

[25] *See* Leip 1999, p. 54; Dionyssopoulou 1999, p. 78; and Hefendehl 2001, p. 145.

[26] *See* NK-Altenhain 2013, § 261, mn. 11; Arzt et al. 2015, § 29, mn. 7; and Sotiriadis 2010, p. 209.

[27] Arzt 1997, p. 34.

[28] Mitsilegas 2003, p. 12.

[29] Arzt et al. 2015, § 29, mn. 8.

[30] Mitsilegas 2003, pp. 105–106.

[31] A discussion about the necessity of changing the current drug policy is taking place in some countries and within the UN. *See also* Garzòn Vergara 2014, p. 2 ss.

[32] Alldridge 2008, p. 458.

5.1.2 The Administration of Justice

Due to its proximity to Article 257 of the GCC, which criminalises aiding and abetting (*Begünstigung*), the offence of money laundering is regarded as protecting the administration of justice (*Rechtspflege)* as well.[33] Parliament expressed this opinion already during the law-making process,[34] with particular regard to what legal scholars have called the 'real money-laundering offence', which criminalises the integration of illegal proceeds into the legitimate economy pursuant to Article 261(1) of the GCC. In particular, by interpreting Article 261(1) as a tool used to avoid investigations, prosecutions and forfeiture, it has been said that it serves the purposes of defending the public interest in investigating, prosecuting and freezing and confiscating criminal assets.[35] Yet, the legislature initially introduced the offence of money laundering in the context of the fight against organised crime, especially drug trafficking. The purpose was, therefore not to protect the whole criminal justice system from criminal conduct, but rather to protect those interests connected to those specific predicate offences.[36] Given the massive expansion of the catalogue, however, one could argue that the legislature, in fact, attributed to the money-laundering offence the function of protecting the whole criminal justice system. *Dionyssopoulou* maintains that it is necessary to restrict the notion of *Rechtspflege* (the administration of justice), in order to curb the scope of the offence as well, otherwise it would be too broad.[37] He specifies that the interest of the administration of justice should be understood as general deterrence, in line with the legislature's intention to eliminate the incentives for the commission of crimes through the threat of punishment, specifically through the risk of investigation and confiscation of the ill-gotten assets. This should remain the foremost, while the specific interests protected by the different predicate offences should remain subsidiary. Since all offences contained in Chapter 21 of the GCC derive from Article 258 of the GCC, the crime of assisting someone to avoid prosecution or punishment, which was introduced with the goal of strengthening general deterrence, the other new offences should be interpreted as also serving the same function. In this manner, the exegesis approach can be used to limit the scope of the money-laundering offence.[38] *Dionyssopoulou* argues, particular, that the historical and taxonomic standpoint excludes the punishment of common social practices and

---

[33] Among others, *see* Otto, Jura 1993, p. 331; Vogel, ZStW 109, 1997, pp. 349 ss. Other scholars consider this function as rather minimal; *see* Barton, StV, 1993, p. 156 or critically Hefendehl 2001.

[34] BT-Drucks 12/989, p. 27.

[35] According to some scholars, the offence of money laundering should have facilitated seizure and confiscation. *See* Arzt, JZ 1993, pp. 913–917; Gwg-Herzog 2014, § 261, mn. 23; *see also* Arzt et al. 2015, mn. 8. Critical about this approach: Müko-Neuheuser 2012, § 261, mn. 10.

[36] Burr 1995, p. 25.

[37] Dionyssopoulou 1999, p. 170.

[38] Dionyssopoulou 1999, p. 130.

actions aimed at procuring necessities, because to punish them would not lead to general deterrence, but would, instead, constitute a strong interference with the rights of the individuals.[39] Of a completely different opinion is another scholar, *Bottke*, who argues that an effective money-laundering offence should punish every negligent conduct, which should extend to the gate-keepers of the law, for they are entrusted with the duty to monitor suspicious transactions and operational risks, and they should have the responsibility of monitoring transactions and operations at risk and should therefore be held liable even for a negligent conduct.[40]

5.1.3 The Economic Interest

Article 261 of the GCC is said to protect the state's interest in the surveillance of financial transactions much as the anti-money laundering preventive regulation does.[41] According to this line of reasoning, the provision should protect the lawful economy from being infiltrated by criminal money.[42] Consequently, the law defends public confidence in the soundness of the financial system. The protection of economic interests brings to the fore the European Directive's considerations on the need to defend the soundness of the Single Market.[43] This philosophy embraces the prudential strategy at the basis of the anti-money laundering act. However, this being the domain of criminal law, criticisms are raised with regard to the need to limit the ambit of criminal law.[44] Critical scholars contend that this interest is somewhat nebulous, '*wolkig*' or '*luftig*',[45] because of the unexplained connection between the use of illegal property within the lawful economy and the harm to public confidence.[46] *Vogel* has further made the point that, from a legal point of view, public confidence in the financial system is no longer affected once the property deriving from a crime is not contaminated anymore due to an in-between transaction with a third person in good faith.[47] Another argument that has been raised against those who maintain that the 'economic order' is an interest protected

[39] Dionyssopoulou 1999, p. 131.

[40] Bottke, wistra, 1995, p. 89. The scholar's thoughts on this topic will be further explained in the following paragraphs.

[41] Among others Burr 1995, p. 26; Findeisen, wistra 1997, pp. 121 ss. (the legal economy); Lampe, JZ, 1994, p. 123; and Vogel, ZStW 109, 1997, pp. 351–356.

[42] Some scholars suggest that the protection of the economic order goes hand in hand with the protection of other interests for example, with the protection of the administration of justice. *See* Hassemer, WM 1995, p. 14 (national economy). Critical about Lampe's statement Müko-Neuheuser 2012, § 216, mn. 9.

[43] Lampe, JZ, 1994, p. 125; and Mitsilegas, 2003, p. 106.

[44] *See* among others Arzt 1997, p. 34.

[45] Vogel, ZstW 109, 1997, p. 351.

[46] Ibid.

[47] Vogel, ZstW 109, 1997, p. 355.

by the law is the following: The economic order may coincide with the purpose of the policy rather than with the legally protected interest, and therefore this does not justify resorting to a repressive intervention. According to *Hassemer* and *Baratta*, the difference between the rationale of a law and the interests it protects is fundamental; whereas the former coincides with the overall goal of the policy maker, the latter should limit such policy.[48] The protection of the financial interest may be supported by interpreting the notion of an economic order in a way that entails personal rights. In particular, this argument can be supported by interpreting property as a modern, dynamic concept that entails material and immaterial goods and economic relations aimed at human development. When the offence of money laundering is considered to harm property, it can be said that acts of money laundering, by distorting economic relations, undermine the individual's capacity to develop economically.[49] This notion of property would, thus, include the economic potential of the individual to act in a context in which certain rules are respected. According to this approach, a criminal offence against the protected economic asset would consist of any act *contra ius* that would limit the economic potential of the individual, and thus acts of money laundering. According to this reasoning, the gravity of the harm caused by money laundering should justify resorting to criminal law to protect law-abiding individuals disadvantaged by the unlawful economic competition acted out also through the laundering of illegal capital, by anchoring the offence of money laundering to the protection of the individual's rights.[50] For instance, scholars have suggested that the offence of money laundering protects fair competition.[51] This approach regards *Hassemer's* and *Baratta's* notion of a 'minimum criminal law'[52] as antiquated and dangerous because it results in the use of a selective repressive tool that supports a class system, by reducing the scope of criminal law in the field of white-collar crimes.[53] By referring to the category of white-collar criminality, *Dionyssopoulou* argues that the economic interest protected by these offences is twofold: On the one hand the fair competition, on the other hand economic institutions.[54]

Fair competition is understood to mean that everyone who participates in the economy actor in the economy expects to operate in an environment of fair competition in which money launderers should not be advantaged by the fact that they can profit from crime. The protection of economic institutions can be interpreted through the so-called game theory, namely, as the protection of the rules of the

[48] Moccia 1995, p. 739; and Hassemer 1989, p. 557.

[49] Moccia 1995, p. 740.

[50] Bottke instead contests the categorisation of the money laundering offence as a property crime, and justifies the offence as one that protects the global financial economic system and not someone's property. Bottke, wistra 1995, p. 89.

[51] Bottke, wistra 1995, p. 121–124; Fiandaca and Musco 1992, p. 379; and Diéz Ripollés 1994, pp. 591, 595 ss.

[52] Baratta 1985; and Hassemer 1992, p. 378.

[53] *See* among others Flick 2005, p. 1303; and Silva Sánchez 2004, p. X.

[54] Dionyssopoulou 1999, p. 16.

economic system.[55] The protection of the rules of the game could be seen as a legal interest. But what still needs to be clarified is which rules need such enhanced safeguarding; whether it is those that regulate access or those that regulate actions. One option would be to limit the scope to those rules that aim to maintain the trust of money savers. However, once again, the protection of the confidence in the economic system does not improve personal situations. Moreover, this approach has also been contested, because the concept of economy is a versatile concept that encompasses different philosophical perspectives, which raises the following question; if the money-laundering offence is said to protect the economic system, which system are we talking about? Arguing from a pro-state interventionist perspective, but with a still critical approach towards the protection of economic interests through criminal law, one can say that 'simultaneously with the request for "less state" in the economic and social ordinance, "more state" is required to conceal and contain the destructive social consequences where the deterioration of social protection is also evident'.[56] There is indeed a link between a lower degree of state intervention in the social sector and the use of the repressive arm. In other words, advocating for a reduction of the use of criminal law to punish misconduct does not mean preventing state intervention in the economy. On the contrary, it means requiring that public action be directed at social policies rather than at repressive ones. Even if one considers criminal law a necessary and legitimate tool, it should aim to protect the individual or collective positions within the financial system, rather than aim at protecting the financial system's reputation. The goal should be the concrete protection of potential victims' rights and not their intangible confidence in the sector.

To protect client confidence in the financial system is a typical interest of the banking sector, as was shown, too, in Part II. Financial institutions are concerned about their reputation, without necessarily showing themselves willing to impede the influx of illegal money, while weaker actors are interested in a more concrete safeguarding of their economic potential from unfair competition. A money-laundering offence that aims at regulating the already deregulated economic sector cannot operate within the frame of the actual system. Otherwise, as underlined by *Burr*, the law would protect those actors who are corrupted through illegal capital and who are, therefore, the offenders and not the victims.[57] This diatribe, which reflects a more general question about the use of criminal law to sanction economic misbehaviour and to protect financial interests, mirroring the even more general tension between a liberal-civil libertarian and a socialist approach to the role of the state in the economy, will be looked at again later in the last chapter through the lenses of the interviewees.

[55] Severino 2014, p. 676.

[56] Miranda Rodriguez 2003, p. 191.

[57] Burr 1995, p. 27.

5.1.4 Internal Security

The last interest taken into account by only a few legal scholars, and also probably the most contested one, is the one of internal security. Article 261 of the GCC is said to protect especially the security of citizenry by prohibiting the entrance of organised crime into the society and the consequent undermining of social structures.[58] The indefiniteness of the concept of internal security, which by itself constitutes a ground for its denial, might be restricted to the concept of internal security protected by any criminal law enacted against organised crime. But this attribution does not justify the designation 'national security' as an interest protected by Article 261, for the scope of the provision is not limited to organised crime-related offences.[59] The German doctrinal discussion on the topic of security as a constitutional principle and a legally protected interest is very extensive. Some scholars recognise the subjective feature of security, and thus the risk of its vulnerability to manipulation.[60] Others elevate the feeling of insecurity as a factor justifying legal intervention.[61] Both approaches do not specify the specific threats; instead, they infer that security is a matter of perception and not an objectively quantifiable value. These viewpoints transform the protection of fundamental rights to a dangerously arbitrary question of interpretation.[62] Other critics have referred to the use of this broad and undefined concept of security as justifying the adoption of laws that would otherwise not be accepted because of their high social costs and to their sheer inefficacy. Governments have, in fact, been accused of jumping on the horse of internal security when expanding the scope of the money-laundering offence beyond the limits of the principle underpinning criminal law. They have been criticised for imposing legally protected interests from 'above'. Against the background of the securitisation rhetoric, scholars have also observed that types of conduct constituting money laundering consist of quite common daily actions, so much so that the offence has been defined as 'everyone's misdemeanour' (*Jedermannsdelikt*).[63] Consequently, the harm caused by these types of conduct is not a direct harm to security, and therefore it should not legitimatise the recourse to criminal law. On the contrary, some argue, certain interests are socially so important that they require an anticipated safeguarding and that criminal law should punish acts that endanger those interests, although the interests have not yet been harmed.

---

[58] Barton, StV 1993, p. 160. Critical against Barton's approach is Müko-Neuheuser 2012, § 261, mn. 11.

[59] GwG-Herzog 2014, § 261, mn. 26.

[60] According to Pitschas, security coincides with internal peace and is, thus, conceived as a constitutional inalienable principle, which entails both the subjective and the state dimensions. *See* Pitschas 1993, pp. 857 ss.

[61] Isensee claims that security is a fundamental right, which refers to the rule of law and public security. *See* Isensee 1983 pp. 22–23.

[62] Lisken 1994, p. 50.

[63] Bottke 1995, p. 89; Vogel, ZStW 109, 1997, p. 351.

This kind of thinking, known as the 'remote harm theory', would allow states to sanction conduct that represents a threat to specific interests but does not harm any of them directly.[64] However, this would allow criminal law to be a mere tool for sanctioning socially dysfunctional conduct, without necessarily protecting the individual from materially damaging acts.[65] Also, by criminalising conduct that do not cause direct harm to legally protected interests, the latter would no longer serve to limit criminal policy.[66]

In conjunction with this debate, scholars have also stressed the role of the securitisation rhetoric shaping public perception of crime, with result political intervention is legitimised. For instance, as regards terrorism there has been a proliferation of policies directed at eliminating or controlling the risks posed by terrorism. The social perception of risk can be influenced in order to create a fertile environment for the adoption of particular legislation that would otherwise not be readily accepted, for example, regulations limiting personal liberties or invading the individual's privacy. Through this rhetoric, policy-makers have anticipated their intervention for purposes of neutralising potential risks, thus missing the link between criminal law and the existence of concrete dangers to legal interests. This phenomenon has been animated by what *Baratta* calls a 'renouncement of the subsidiarity principle of criminal law', which takes criminal law from being an instrument to protect society to being an instrument that controls society. *Baratta* connects this switch to the failure of the criminal law's aim of re-socialisation, hence a general loss of legitimation, which has been substituted with the function of general prevention.[67] Yet, because criminal law is anchored to the principle of ultima ratio, the legislature is supposed to balance the interests and protect only those that prevail to the detriment of others.

Due to the uncertainty surrounding the issue of the interests protected by Article 261, German scholars still define the offence of money laundering as a crime '*ohne Herz und Hirn*' (without heart and brain), a pointless offence, whose legally protected interest has been trivialised.[68] Particularly critical about this issue is *Arzt*, who already in 1997 drew attention to the offence of money laundering as an example of a deficient criminal law in the book, *Das missglückte Gesetz* (The failed law),[69] basing his criticism mostly on the trivialisation of the legally protected interests. In his opinion, the more the offence is enforced, the clearer it becomes that the provision aims at monitoring financial transactions. This means that the criminalisation of money laundering protects the same public interest in controlling the

---

[64] For a complete discussion on the remote harm theory, *see* Ashworth 1999; Von Hirsch 1996; and Wallerstein 2007.

[65] Patalano 1991, p. 634.

[66] Fiandaca 1982, p. 72; and Volk 1985, p. 871.

[67] Baratta 1982 and 1985.

[68] Althenhain 2002, p. 402; Arzt 1997, p. 34; and Arzt et al. 2015, § 29, mn. 7.

[69] Diederichsen and Dreier 1997.

economy as the preventive regulatory body does.[70] Consequently, the legally protected interest has lost its fundamental function of limiting criminal law. *Arzt's* reflections also shed light on the legislative intents since they show that the ultimate function of the offence criminalising money laundering is to control the financial system. As the scholar highlights, the real goal is not eliminating money laundering but rather classifying all money-laundering acts as infringements.[71] What remains to limit the action of the legislature is the general limit for the enlargement of the offence of money laundering, which narrows the preventive purpose of the offence of money laundering that should instead be pursued by other means.[72]

5.2 Too Broad or Too Narrow?

Interestingly, criticisms of ineffectiveness are levelled against the money-laundering offence because the provision is considered both too narrow and too broad.[73] One of the main controversies is whether Article 261 of the GCC envisages punishing also conventional social conduct. On the one hand, the legislature aimed at punishing any act linked to the illicitly gained property in order not to miss the link with the predicate offence due to laundering schemes; on the other hand, it tried to limit the potential criminalisation of widespread economic activities to avoid encumbering the economy too heavily. The Federal High Court held that Article 261 of the GCC should also have been applied to actions undertaken to cover life needs. The offence indeed tends to target unobtrusive actions, such as the exchange of cash money in a bank. In practice, the purchase of food or clothes is not seen as a potential act of money laundering. However, the elimination of some trivial acts from the scope of the money-laundering offence would allow money launderers to exploit those activities.

Given the boundless formulation of the offence and the various and vague functions assigned to the law, the conclusion is justified that Article 261 aims at penalising as many types of conduct as possible.[74] This clashes with the neutral character of money, expressed in the well-known sentence 'pecunia non olet', since it would make every transactions suspicious. According to *Barton* and *Bottke*, different theories have been proposed on how to limit the scope of application of the

[70] This violates the criminal law principle of *ultima ratio* since it shows that the repressive tool is not the only mechanism to pursue such goal.

[71] Arzt 1997, p. 34.

[72] GwG-Herzog 2014, § 261, mn. 19, 20.

[73] Bottke describes the wording of Article 261 as partly too broad, partly too narrow. *See* Bottke 1995, Wistra, p. 89.

[74] Dionyssopoulou 1999, p. 118.

money-laundering offence, with reference to the concept of social adequacy '*Sozialadäquanz*' of *Welzel*,[75] or through the use of the *Rechtsgut* as a limiting factor.[76] *Barton* claims that the function of isolating criminals should limit the liability under Article 261 by eliminating the criminalisation of actions directed at the procurement of necessities. These, indeed, do not endanger national security. Once again, national security is considered a too vague concept to limit the applicability of the money-laundering offence.[77] *Bottke*, instead, argues that if one accepts the financial market as the legally protected interest, trivial misbehaviour (*Bagatellen*) should not be included because it poses no danger.[78] According to the scholar, the scope of the offence should include all individuals and actions that are related to economic transactions and can be thus potentially abused by money launderers.

5.2.1 The Catalogue of the Predicate Offences: A Wide Scope for a Limited Application

On the one hand, the decision of the legislature to avoid the all crimes approach is perceived as complicating law enforcement activity, due to the added level of evidence required. Narrowing the scope of the offence by listing only certain predicate offences for Article 261 of the GCC is considered cumbersome. On the other hand, the money-laundering offence is viewed as too broad, not only because of the continual expansion of the catalogue of predicate offences, but also because the wording of the provision and the decision to criminalise reckless conduct, may lead to legal uncertainty, which can result in the law losing its legitimacy and being applied wrongly.[79]

The catalogue of the predicate offences has been expanded on the assumption that the polluting capacity of money laundering derives not only from the proceeds of drug trafficking, but also from other crimes. In addition, the expansion of the catalogue of predicate crimes ought to have increased the effectiveness of the law, by way of facilitating the work of prosecutors and obligated entities. Moreover, the FATF and other international organisations took advantage of the legal framework set out to prevent money laundering and decided to use it to tackle other "similar" phenomena, such as terrorism. The flexible wording of the money-laundering offence also facilitates the harmonisation of national laws. The financial system evolves very quickly. Thanks to technological innovations, such as the cyber economy, the expansion of the catalogue of predicate offences can allow

[75] Welzel, ZStW 58, 1939, p. 517.

[76] Barton, StV, 1993, p. 156; and Bottke, wistra 1995, p. 124.

[77] Dionyssopoulou 1999, p. 125.

[78] Bottke, wistra 1995, p. 124.

[79] For a complete overview on the different opinions, *see* Dionyssopoulou 1999, pp. 119 ss.

legislatures to contemplate continually emerging vehicles and subterfuges to transfer criminal money, thus enabling e novel ways of combating laundering money. The broad catalogue of predicate offences also facilitates, at a domestic level, the gathering of information by public prosecutors. Despite the declared goal of the 1992 legislature of fighting organised crime, the catalogue of the predicate offences does not comprehend only offences linked to organised crime activities. For example, from the outset it included the cultivation and the production of psychotropic substances for personal use.[80] As already pointed out in Part II, when looking at the wording of the offence, the provision does not refer only to those typical types of conduct that are commonly understood as money laundering, but also to any act that is connected with the incriminated object.[81] *Arzt* describes the expansion of the scope of the money laundering as a fruitless attempt of the legislature to improve the effectiveness of the money-laundering offence.[82] The scholar speaks of a legislature's '*Flucht nach vorne*' (taking the bull by its horns)[83] and cautions against the introduction in the catalogue of dubious offences.[84] Especially in countries with strongly embedded criminal law principles, the versatile use of the offence of money laundering to tackle emergencies that crop up has elevated the legal challenges that, far from being purely dogmatic, may hinder the effective implementation of such measures, because they undermine the acceptance of that law.

5.2.2 The mens rea *Element: Punishing Reckless Bakers Instead of Mafia Bosses*

The controversial parliamentary debate that preceded the decision to criminalise reckless money laundering in Article 261(5) of the GCC, which was analysed in the previous chapters, revealed that the different parties agreed on including reckless conduct in order to lessen the difficulties in adducing evidence of the knowledge of the criminal provenience of the proceeds.[85] This doctrine has provoked severe criticism that is grounded in the fact that it is not the function of substantive criminal to facilitate the way procedural law is implemented.[86] Moreover, it was the first time that the recklessness with regard to property was made punishable, and this happened without the matter being subjected first to rigorous legal debate.

---

[80] Burr, 1995 p. 30.

[81] Burr, 1995 p. 32; and StGB-Fischer, § 261, mn. 4c.

[82] Arzt et al. 2015, § 29, mn. 8.

[83] The sentence can be translated with the saying: 'The best defence is offence'.

[84] Arzt et al. 2015, § 29, mn. 8.

[85] BT-Drucks 12/989, p. 27.

[86] Lampe, JZ 1994, p. 129; and Vogel, ZStW 109, 1997, p. 347.

According to one scholar, *Vogel*,[87] this decision was taken notwithstanding the fact that Germany was under no international obligation to criminalise reckless behaviour. The Federal High Court, however, was of different view.[88] The European Directives require intention and knowledge about the illicit origin of the property; on the contrary, the Warsaw Convention of 2005 offered member states the opportunity to extend the *mens rea* element to encompass negligent behaviour by widening the criminalisation to include situations where the offender 'ought to have assumed the criminal provenience of the property'.[89] The punishment of reckless money laundering conduct may potentially infringe the criminal law principles of culpability (*nullum crimen sine culpa*) and certainty (*nullum crimen sine lege*).[90] Nevertheless, the Supreme Court denied the possible violation of these principles, and held that the law was in line with the Constitution.[91] Many scholars are agreed that, by punishing reckless economic conduct, the provision breaches the interests of a free market system.[92] To require that every single person should act with diligence effecting a financial transaction is viewed as having the effect of burdening the market by holding up transactions. In addition, obligating every participant in the market to avoid recklessly money laundering might affect the free movement of goods negatively. In fact, the criminalisation of recklessness brings with it the danger that everyday professional conduct which is unconnected to money laundering, could be punishable.[93] Ordinary citizens cannot be expected to monitor transactions for their legitimacy, as this would constitute too high a burden on the financial sector. In fact, even the preventive regulations are not a guarantee of complete control, since bank employees cannot be expected to identify all money laundering transactions correctly.[94] Moreover, while reckless conduct can constitute a money-laundering offence, recklessness in respect of some of the predicate offences is not punishable. This results in the anti-money laundering being glaringly incoherent.

Given this state of affairs, one scholar has concluded that Article 261(5) of the GCC should be repealed.[95] This incoherence became manifest when offences against the tax laws were included in the catalogue of predicate offences: even if the legislature considered this extension as to be indispensable, the inclusion of fiscal crimes under the umbrella of the money-laundering offence has exacerbated the

---

[87] Vogel, ZStW 109, 1997, pp. 335–337.

[88] BGHSt 50, 347, 354 ss.

[89] Article 6(3) a of the Strasbourg Convention of 2005. Interpretation challenges have raised also in other jurisdictions that adopted the restrictive approach, such as Italy, England and Wales. *See* Mitsilegas 2003, pp. 112 ss.

[90] *See* among others: Hassemer 1995, p. 14; Leip 1999, p. 146 ss; and StGB-Fischer, § 261, mn. 42 a.

[91] BGHSt 43, 158, 166 ss; and Arzt, JR 1999a, b, p. 79.

[92] GwG-Herzog, § 261, mn. 120; StGB-Fischer, § 261, mn. 42 a; and Hetzer, NJW, 1993, p. 3299.

[93] GwG-Herzog, § 261 mn. 120.

[94] Dionyssopoulou 1999, p. 156.

[95] Dionyssopoulou 1999, p. 157.

highlighted problems. Indeed, because tax evasion does not result in a profit but rather a saving, the assets in possession of a tax evader might have a legal provenience. Therefore, punishing reckless failure to acknowledge the criminal origin of property deriving from tax evasion, which might be used in daily transactions, seems to go beyond what the legislature intended.[96] Yet, according to the provocative article of *Bottke* published in 1995, the impunity of property crimes for negligent behaviour was not sacrosanct.[97] The scholar contends that only by incriminating all transactions that integrate ill-gotten gains into the legal economy and committed both intentionally or negligently, would the law would fulfil its function adequately. In fact, *Bottke* acknowledges that this hypothesis would be cumbersome for the whole economic system. He acknowledges the excessive broad scope of the money-laundering offence and specifically criticises the fact that the formulation of the offence results in it being a '*Jedermannsdelikt*'. The provision should instead punish only the so-called 'gatekeepers', namely, individuals who in the exercise of their professional or economic duties may permit the infiltration of illegal money into the legitimate economy.[98] This line of reasoning is similar to that of *Moccia*, who prefers to define the offence of money laundering as a '*reato d'obbligo*' (a compulsory offence meant for individuals who have the function of guarantor).[99] In the specific case of money laundering, for instance, financial services providers should have a 'security function' and therefore a specific criminal liability.[100] However, certain professionals would experience a conflict of interests between the interest to practise their profession properly and the public interest in having crimes prosecuted.[101] In recalling the parliamentary debate, we should not overlook that one of the functions assigned to the money-laundering offence was the isolation of criminals through the criminalisation of any actions of third parties dealing with the incriminated object, pursuant to Article 261(2) of the GCC. In other words, the legislature aimed at hitting the gatekeepers, although this was not stated expressly.

In order to stop the drifting of such an offence, the courts have intervened and determined the limits within which recklessness can attract a charge of money laundering. The jurisprudence has fastened recklessness in this context to the civil law notion of culpable negligence.[102] The courts have interpreted recklessness

[96] The typical example used to clarify this absurdity is that baker who sells bread to a notorious tax evader, can be held liable for money laundering only because he or she has accepted money that could derive from tax evasion. As a consequence, someone charged with tax evasion would not be able to purchase commodities.

[97] Bottke, wistra 1995, p. 89.

[98] Ibid.

[99] Actually, money laundering can be committed also through omission. The guarantor position is set for competent authorities (e.g. law enforcement and customs) and witnesses. *See* NK-Altenhain 2013, § 261, mn. 93; Leip 1999, p. 138; and Müko-Neuheuser 2012, § 261, mn. 92.

[100] Moccia 1995, p. 747.

[101] Müko-Neuheuser 2012, § 261, mn. 77.

[102] BGHSt 43, 158, 168; and BGH NJW 2008, 2516, 2517.

closer to intention, so that it coincides with particular degree of negligence or gross carelessness. The *mens rea* required is a particular degree of negligence or gross recklessness.[103] The latter premise applies, too, where the accused is unable to know about the provenance of the property.[104] The inclusion of the recklessness and the extension of the scope of the offence to commercial and organised tax evasion have an impact mostly on categories of designated businesses and professions which are required to take particular care when receiving fees from clients, such as defence attorneys. In order to prevent some obligated categories of businesses and professions from being abused for the purposes of laundering the proceeds of crime, specific duties have been imposed on them to detect suspicious transactions.[105]

5.2.3 *Defence Attorneys Under Threat*

Within this scenario, the situation of defence attorneys is particularly precarious because of attorney-client privilege, which places a high premium on the confidentiality in the relationship on the one hand, and the public interest in the prosecution of crimes on the other hand. The matter can be summarised as follows. When a client is suspected to have committed one of the predicate offences for money laundering and to have gained some profit out of it, the defence attorney must ask her or himself whether the fee that she or he receives from the client is derived from that offence. In the case of receiving stolen goods, the question can be answered by looking at whether the attorney knew at the moment of receiving the fee that it had a criminal provenance. With respect to the lawyer-client relationship, issues linked to the peculiarity of the relationship are crucial. On the one hand, lawyers might be held liable, as many other professions, for receiving fees derived from the commission of predicate offences, and on the other hand, everyone has a right to legal representation, including money launderers. In Germany, there is abundant jurisprudence on this topic. Legal scholars, too, have been actively engaged in the discussion. One of the groundbreaking cases dealt with a defence attorney who allegedly received drug money from a gangster, and who could have suspected the illegal provenance of the money, as he had previously defended gangsters belonging to the same gang.[106] The Provincial High Court of Hamburg ruled on the matter by interpreting the provision according to the Constitution, and held that defence attorneys may not be held liable for receiving fees, except in particular cases. The three exceptions are firstly, if the lawyer's actions frustrate the enforcement of the law; second, if the attorney receives money that should have

[103] GwG-Herzog, § 261, mn. 122.

[104] BGHSt 43, 158, 169; and BGH NJW 2008, 2516, 2517.

[105] StGB-Fischer, § 261, mn. 44.

[106] OLG Hamburg, Decision of 6 January 2000-2Ws185/99, NJW 2000. 673 = StV 2000, 140.

been given back to victims; and third, if the attorney and the client struck a 'kick-back' deal, according to which the offender would receive the money back.[107] The Federal Constitutional Court was called upon to express its opinion on this topic in a matter that came before it from the Federal High Court, which convicted an attorney for money laundering for having received a fee of 200,000 DM (Deutsche Mark, the former German currency) in cash from a client suspected of fraud committed on a commercial and organised basis.[108] The Supreme Court inferred the liability of the attorney from the unusual high fee, from the fact that the fee was paid in cash carried in suitcases, from the circumstance that there were no written documents regulating the transaction, and from the fact that the alleged offence was a predicate offence for money laundering. The court motivated the decision by proclaiming that attorneys, in particular, should not have been exempted by the money laundering provision, since the legislature did not provide for exceptions under Article 261(2), the aim of which is to isolate offenders. The Federal Constitutional Court overruled the Federal High Court by holding that as regards case at hand; the *mens rea* required a certain degree of certainty as to the illegal origin of the asset. The Court, accordingly, established an exception for defence attorneys, who cannot be held liable for gross negligence. Instead, it is required evidence of knowledge (*dolus eventualis*).[109]

This decision caused a spirited doctrinal debate. Some scholars supported the privilege afforded defence attorneys, while others severely contested it vigorously. Arguments brought up in support of the privilege are the following: The suspect has the right to be represented by counsel of his choice; the confidentiality between defence attorney and client should be maintained; the defence attorney has an exclusive interest in the client; the client suffers harm where the defence attorney resigns from the case of refuses the brief; suspects of serious crimes should not be discriminated against by denying them legal representation; the principle of presumption of innocence is fundamental; attorneys have a right to the free exercise of their profession; the accused should not be denied the right to a fair trial; there is a need to protect professional secrecy; and defence attorneys should not be manipulated by public prosecutors.[110] The last argument refers to the criminal law policy goals of the money-laundering offence. Scholars argue that the law was enacted especially to fight organised crime, whereas the receiving of a fee by a defence attorney does not represent a typical conduct related to organised crime activities. Through the payment of a fee, indeed, money launderers are not able to integrate ill-gotten gains into the legal economy; in fact, they do not get back anything from the lawyer. Moreover, hindering the payment of attorneys' fees does not make the commission of predicate offences less attractive. Offenders do not engage in crime

[107] Fernandez and Heinrich, ZStW 126, 2014, p. 417.

[108] BGH, Decision of 4 July 2001-2 StR 513/00, BGHSt 47, 68 = NJW 2001, 2891 = JR 2002, 27 = JZ 2002, 102.

[109] Fernandez and Heinrich, ZStW 126, 2014, p. 419.

[110] Fernandez and Heinrich, ZStW 126, 2014, pp. 421–436.

to pay a more qualified defence lawyer; and if they do not commit a predicate offence, they would not need any defence attorney.[111] However, criminal organisations might be interested in obtaining a very qualified lawyer in order to be represented when charged with other serious crimes. They would commit predicate offences in order to accumulate the money to pay a qualified defence counsel. In addition, even though the payment of an attorney's fee does not represent a typical organised crime activity, nor is it a way to integrate illicit funds in the legitimate economy, it does represent an action that, if it is impeded, would isolate offenders and thus demotivate them from the commission of crimes, in accordance with the legislative intentions s related to Article 261(2) of the GCC. The opinion against the attorney-client privilege is sustained with the following arguments: The law should apply equally to all attorneys; attorneys are organs of the administration of justice, and it would be consequently inappropriate for them receive unlawful money consciously; suspects who commit predicate offences and who are able to afford highly qualified expert defence counsel would be placed in an advantageous position; and a defence attorney can apply to the court to have him appointed as a legal aid counsel.[112]

For the purposes of this study, this discussion is relevant to the extent that shows the controversial matters arising from the criminalisation of money laundering. It is striking that there is still strong resistance to this '*Fremdkörper*' (alien element)[113] within the criminal legal system, because blatant inconsistencies between the offence and the principles, some of which are of a constitutional nature, embedded in the national legal culture. Another relevant question connected to this discussion concerns the functions assigned to the offence. If on the one had the function of isolating the criminal is said to serve the purpose of fighting organised crime and that it therefore trumps confidentiality principle, on the other hand, the client-attorney privilege is perceived as deserving of more protection than public's interest in prosecuting crimes. The defence attorney doctrinal debate is important in relation to the issue effectiveness because it is a discussion triggered by the implementation of the law. Therefore, it shows that the law creates challenges not only 'in the books' but also in practice.

5.2.4 Definitions of '*Gegenstand*' and of '*herrührt*'

Given that the offence of money laundering was created to close the loopholes left by the other derivative offences that required a close link between the commission of the predicate offence and the main conduct, the legislature adopted the term '*herrühren*' (deriving) in order to attenuate that link. Moreover, given that the

[111] Fernandez and Heinrich, ZStW 126, 2014, p. 436.

[112] Fernandez and Heinrich, ZStW 126, 2014, pp. 436–441.

[113] Vogel, ZStW 109, 1997, p. 346.

offence of handling of stolen goods (Article 259 of the GCC) refers only to goods, leaving money out of the scope, the legislature chose to use the undefined term '*Gegenstand*' (object) in order to encompass any type of object with an economic value. Thanks to the broad interpretation of these terms, conduct in respect of the original criminal asset that changed its nature but maintained its economic value is considered to incur liability. The aim was to have access to those surrogate assets that are not connected with the commission of the antecedent act.

Parliament specified that the object in possession of the offender or of third parties is supposed to derive from a predicate offence.[114] However, this causal link was criticised by legal scholars because it could have been extended to any act of contamination with the illegal property.[115] The legislature conceived the concept of *herrühren* but did not clarify what it means, with the only guideline as to its meaning being the wide criminalisation.[116] In addition, the declared legislative intentions do not place limitations on the applicability of the term since, according to the follow the money strategy, any action linked to the paper trail is relevant. The legislature opted for such a broad criminalisation in order not to sever the link with the illegitimate conduct due to laundering process.[117] The legislature recognised the risk of too wide a criminalisation and placed a restriction, which should have not transformed the legitimate economy in a place full of somehow incriminated assets.[118] Yet, this restriction does not reply to the question as to how to define the provenance of property from a predicate crime. Scholars have also tried to tie the provenance of the object to the rules governing forfeiture. But those rules apply only to assets of the offenders, while the money-laundering offence relates only to predicate offences committed by third parties.[119] *Dionyssopoulou* considers the term *herrühren* as an important element to determine the scope of the money-laundering offence because it constitutes the link between the predicate offences and the object[120]; one could even see it as the link between the antecedent act and the main act. Yet, the vague definition of the interests protected by the law does not serve the purposes of limiting the scope of the offence and thus does not help to narrow the meaning of the term *herrühren*.[121] As concerns the burden of proof, the state is required not only to prove that the object stems from any of the offences of the catalogue, or that the object does not have a legitimate origin; instead, it has to adduce evidence of the concrete situation of the antecedent act.

---

[114] BT-Drucks 12/3533, p. 12.

[115] NK-Altenhain 2013, § 261, mn. 52; GwG-Herzog, § 261 mn. 50; Leip 1999, p. 71; and StGB-Schönke, § 261, mn. 8.

[116] On this topic *see*, among others, Wohlers, StV 2001, p. 425; Hefendehl, FS Roxin 2001, pp. 145, 163; and GwG-Herzog, § 261, mn. 48.

[117] BT-Drucks 12/989, p. 27.

[118] Ibid. *See also* NK-Altenhain 2013, § 261, mn. 55.

[119] GwG-Herzog, § 261, mn. 52; Arzt, JZ 1993, p. 914; NK-Altenhain, § 261, mn. 58; Vest, FS-Schmid 2001, p. 417; Leip 1999 p. 76; and Voß M 1989, p. 40.

[120] Dionyssopoulou 1999, p. 171.

[121] GwG-Herzog, § 261, mn. 49.

This higher burden of proof is required in order not to violate the principles of *in dubio pro reo* and of culpability, and the rights of the accused.[122]

Section 261 of the GCC does not refer to the term property; it refers instead to the term object (*Gegenstand*), which is not defined under German law. The legislature chose the term precisely because it was not legally defined, with the goal of including the whole chain of uses and substitutions of the original property.[123] Indeed, the term was meant to cover a broad range of things and even surrogates of the original asset with some kind of economic value, including, for instance, movable and immovable property, money, securities and accounts receivables.[124] A classification has been proposed, which refers to the economic nature of the money-laundering offence and considers only those objects that economically substitute the laundered value. Yet, in the literature, there is, at the time of writing, no consensus on the definition of the term. The decision to adopt a broad concept may be related to the approach taken in the European Directives, which also adopted the broadest definition possible of proceeds of crime: 'Assets of every kind whether corporal or incorporeal, movable or immovable, tangible or intangible, and legal documents or instruments evidencing title or interests in such assets'.[125]

5.3 Doctrinal Opinions on the (Symbolic) Effectiveness of the Money-Laundering Offence

After 1 year of its entry into force, the law criminalising money laundering was the focus of a speech about symbolic legislation in the field of organised crime held by *Pieth* at the German Conference of Criminal Defence Lawyers in Münster.[126] *Pieth* dealt with the new anti-money laundering regime in the context of the then current fight against drug criminality and criticised fundamentally the fact that the anti-drug policy, as a prohibition tool, notoriously, has the opposite effect of increasing criminal proceeds derived from the illegal drug market. At the same time, the money-laundering offence, which is part of the drug policy, aims at confiscating the proceeds of drug-related crimes. On the one hand, the state provokes the accumulation of illegal assets, and on the other hand, it confiscates them, so that it seems that 'the left hand does not know what the right hand does'. He also deliberated on

[122] At the moment the German Parliament is debating draft legislation to reform criminal law on asset forfeiture (BT-Drucks. 18/9525), which will allow, in the context of organised crime investigations, the confiscation of assets that cannot be proved to have been lawfully obtained, based on substantiated suspicion of their illicit origin.

[123] BT-Drucks 12/989, p. 27; BT-Drucks. 12/3533, p. 12.

[124] Leip 1999, p. 116; Altenhain 2002, p. 419.

[125] Article 1(8) Directive 2005/60/EC.

[126] Pieth 1993, p. 101.

the complicity theory.[127] The symbolic dimension of the money-laundering offence has been the subject of legal scholarship. Based on reflections about the legislature's intent of using the offence to overcome investigative challenges and on the better suitability of other measures to tackle organised crime rather than the criminalisation of money laundering, *Kilchling* defines the law as 'symbolic policy'.[128] *Dionyssopoulou* as well draws attention to the latent functions of the money-laundering offence. He writes that the underlying motive for the introduction of the crime suggests that it was intended to overcome the difficulties of proving the crime of laundering in a criminal trial.[129] Yet, according to the *Dionyssopoulou,* the use of criminal law for procedural purposes violates the principles of culpability and of presumption of innocence and therefore the offence should be repealed. *Bottke*, in his article published in 1995, expresses a quite provocative opinion by stating that the money-laundering offence, as it is formulated, consists of symbolic paper, excitement and lip service.[130] In his opinion, a money-laundering offence that would slow down the flow of money across the globe would effectively hinders the infiltration of illegal money into the legitimate economy, despite being a heavy burden for the private sector. Such an offence would require that not only citizens, desk personnel, and subordinates but also managers would not be able to discharge their preventive duties.[131] Such an offence, concludes the scholar, would be harmful to the whole society.

Dionyssopoulou interestingly recognises a symbolic dimension of the norm, in relation to the function of tackling organised crime.[132] The author contextualises his reflections in the framework of the law against organised crime (OrgKG) and infers the symbolic effectiveness of the money-laundering offence from its proven ineffectiveness in practice. The scholar believes that the OrgKG had a symbolic function.[133] However, the non-application of the law frustrates even the symbolic function because the addressees would not be deterred by the threat of prosecution and could count on impunity. Therefore, the scant effectiveness of the criminalisation of money laundering can be related on the one hand to the fact that this measure can tackle only subsidiary issues, and on the other hand to the symbolic effectiveness attributed to the crime within the context of the fight against organised crime. By assuming that organised crime does not pose a threat to Germany, the scholar suggests that the money-laundering offence be regarded as a new form of handling stolen goods, so that it can really overcome legal loopholes and thus have instrumental efficacy.[134]

---

[127] Pieth 1993, p. 105.

[128] Kilchling, wistra 2000, pp. 243–244.

[129] Dionyssopoulou 1999, p. 157.

[130] Bottke, wistra 1995, p. 89.

[131] Ibid.

[132] Dionyssopoulou 1999, p. 174.

[133] Ibid. p. 169.

[134] Ibid. p. 168.

Quite a vast body of literature has been criticising the law for not being suitable to achieve the declared goals. Adopting a very critical approach towards the basis of criminal law policy behind the criminalisation of money laundering, namely the fight against organised crime, *Arzt* has levelled very strong criticism in 1997 when he said that the offence of money laundering was a conceptual failure, because criminal control is not a conflict that the state can win, therefore it should not aim at winning, but rather at finding a bearable balance.[135] In other words, a society without crime is not realistic, and thus a society without organised crime, therefore the goal of the criminal justice system should not be the 'fight against organised crime', but rather to diminish the crime rates. The same scholar adds that the system has so far managed to create only a form of new professionalism.[136] Other scholars, too, have voiced their criticism stringent approach to organised crime. *Hassemer*, for example, theorised that social fear of organised crime was exploited to introduce new repressive measures.[137] Along with this critical approach, other scholars have emphasised the exploitation of the threat of organised crime to expand criminal law by adopting the securitisation rhetoric of the enemy. This philosophy, which negates the idea of using criminal law against the enemy (*Feindstrafrecht*), regards the threat of organised crime as an excuse to introduce preventive regulations.[138] Concerns that are more specific were raised with regard to the money-laundering offence's suitability to tackle organised crime. Since the risk posed by organised crime was not unanimously recognised,[139] the introduction of the offence of money laundering for the purposes of dealing with it was not considered necessary. Some scholars, in fact, believed that the commission of crimes in an organised and collective way was normal and that therefore organised crime was not posing a particular threat. In addition, Article 261 was not considered suitable for combating gangster criminality.[140]

Another critical issue that has been raised is the incapacity of the money-laundering offence to tackle the grey area, namely, the fine line between legality and illegality. This is because of the proximity of money laundering types of conduct and legitimate financial transactions. Already in 1999, in his Ph.D. thesis, *Dionyssopoulou* underlined that it is quite impossible to find out about the origin of sums of money used for financial transactions without disturbing the

---

[135] The scholar quotes the 'Gesetzgebungslehre' by Noll, where the author states that criminal law has never developed an idea of a society free from crime or the purpose of a total elimination of criminality. *See* Noll 1973, p. 85; and Arzt 1997, p. 28.

[136] Arzt 2013, p. 1130.

[137] Hassemer and Starzacher 1993, pp. 16 ss.

[138] Dionyssopoulou 1999, p. 28.

[139] Rebscher and Vahlenkamp have stated that criminality in Germany at that time was organised but was not often violent. Weschke found that there was an existing network of gangs but that they did not have a hierarchical system; *see* Rebscher and Vahlenkamp 1988, pp. 181 ss; and Weschke, Kriminalistik 1986, p. 298.

[140] Dionyssopoulou 1999, p. 27.

market.[141] Investigations of customers, of legal entities, or of businesses are cumbersome for the functioning of a free economy. Given the neutral nature of money as a universal payment method and the ability of criminals of exploiting all legal loopholes, the scholar is very sceptical about the efficacy of the anti-money laundering regulations. In addition, he highlights that some countries, without naming which ones, profit from financial flows and are thus not interested in restricting liberties of this lucrative business through public control.[142] In other words, he reveals a fundamental truth about the anti-money laundering regime which is still very real, namely, the fact that the regulation of the financial sector through public interference to monitor transactions is not regarded favourably by those who profit from the '*laissez faire*' philosophy.

Along the same lines, *Pieth* underlines that the financial system often profits from the flow of dirty money deriving from fiscal crimes, or violations of currency export laws.[143] He distinguishes between proceeds of organised crime and capital flight. While the first is perceived as being more serious because of the human rights violations allegedly implicated, the second type of illegal money appears less harmful. The distinction between the two is what especially interests those countries that profit from financial flows. Switzerland, for instance, was, according to *Pieth*, very much concerned about its reputation as banking centre. Therefore, the country would not want to be known for being an offshore centre where criminals launder their profits, but without renouncing its practice of conducting financial business behind the veil of bank secrecy.[144]

5.4 Considerations

This chapter has shown that the wording of Article 261 of the GCC has the potential of frustrating some of the intentions expressed by the legislature in enacting the provision. For instance, while the vague wording of the money-laundering offence was thought to tackle permanently surfacing emergencies and has been justified by legislatures as necessary to ensure a more effective fight against money laundering, it has also raised issues that, far from being purely dogmatic, have undermined the acceptance of such a law. In addition, criminalising reckless conduct without envisaging a specific criminal liability for those charged with the task guaranteeing security, has widened the scope of the offence to the point that the law has missed its function of isolating criminals by criminalising gate-keepers' activities. The analysis has also revealed underlying controversies, for example the interests protected by Article 261 of the GCC, which may, if not solved, affect its

[141] Ibid. pp. 168 ss.

[142] Ibid. p. 168.

[143] Pieth 1993, p. 105.

[144] Ibid.

implementation. For instance, if on the one hand state intervention is considered necessary to contain the impact of economic misbehaviour to protect the public, on the other hand it is important to limit the resort to criminal law only for the sake of safeguarding individual or collective situations and not for defending an existing economic structure. In fact, the economic system may not be considered as a collective interest that needs protection. Also, safeguards provided by criminal law need to be substantial and not symbolic, because they change a given situation of inequality, where criminals can profit from illegal practices while legitimate economic actors undergo unfair competition. The fact that the criminalisation of money laundering causes so much uncertainty at a domestic level should be taken into account when evaluating how it is enforced; therefore, instead of perpetuating the process of expanding the reach of anti-money laundering law, legislatures should clarify the goals of such a cumbersome policy.[145]

Against the background of the analysis conducted in this chapter, it can be said that the hypothesised symbolic nature of Article 261 of the GCC is generally supported by legal scholars, who have revealed the technical hindrances that undermine the legitimacy of the provision legitimacy and thus hamper a positive integration of the law in the criminal justice system. In addition, given that most controversial issues are caused by the wording of the offence, the chapter upholds the idea of an intentional potential decriminalisation of money launderers.

References

Alldridge P (2008) Money Laundering and Globalization. Journal of Law and Society 35 (4): 437–463.

Altenhain K (2002) Das Anschlussdelikt. Grund, Grenzen und Schutz des staatlichen Strafanspruchs und Verfallsrechts nach einer individualistischen Strafrechtsauffassung. Mohr Siebeck, Tübingen.

Altenhain K (2013) § 261 Geldwäsche; Verschleierung unrechtmäßig erlangter Vermögenswerte. In: Kindhäuser U et al. (eds) Strafgesetzbuch. Nomos Kommentar (NK) 3 (4). Nomos, Baden-Baden, pp. 483–547.

Ambos K (2015) The Overall Function of International Criminal Law: Striking the Right Balance Between the Rechtsgut and the Harm Principles. A Second Contribution Towards a Consistent Theory of ICL. Criminal Law and Philosophy 9: 301–329.

Amelung K (1972) Rechtsgüterschutz und Schutz der Gesellschaft: Untersuchungen zum Inhalt und zum Anwendungs- Bereich eines Strafrechtsprinzips auf dogmengeschichtlicher Grundlage. Athenäum-Verlag, Frankfurt am Main.

Appel I (1998) Verfassung und Strafe. Zu den verfassungsrechtlichen Grenzen staatlichen Strafen. Duncker & Humblot, Berlin.

Arzt G (1993) Geldwäsche und rechtsstaatlicher Verfall. JuristenZeitung (JZ): 913–917.

Arzt G (1997) Das mißglückte Strafgesetz. Am Beispiel der Geldwäschegesetzgebung. In: Diedrichsen U, Dreier R (eds) Das missglückte Gesetz, 8. Symposium der Kommission "Die Funktion des Gesetzes in Geschichte und Gegenwart". Wandenhoeck & Ruprecht, Göttingen, pp. 17–38.

[145] Zoppei 2015, pp. 130, 144.

Arzt G (1999a) Wissenschaftsbedarf nach dem 6. StrRG. Zeitschrift für die gesamte Strafrechtswissenschaft (ZStW) 111 (4): 757–784.

Arzt G (1999b) Anm. zu BGHSt 43, 149, 1 StR 208/97 v. 17. 7. 97, betr. Geldwäsche, Fall EKC-Callmaster; BGHSt 43, 158, 1 StR 791/96 v. 17. 7. 97, betr. Geldwäsche durch Kuriere, Rückfluss an Drogengroßhändler. Juristische Rundschau (JR) 53: 75–81.

Arzt G (2013) Milliardenschwere Geldwäscherei im Untergrund Schweizer Banken - Eine Märchenhafte Rechtsgeschichte. In: Kuhn A et al. (eds) Kriminologie, Kriminalpolitik und Strafrecht aus Internationaler Perspektive. Festschrift für Martin Killias zum 65. Geburtstag. Stämpfli Verlag, Bern, pp. 1127–1139.

Arzt G et al. (eds) (2015) Strafrecht Besonderer Teil 3. Gieseking Verlag, Bielefeld.

Ashworth A (1999) Principles of Criminal law. Oxford University Press, Oxford.

Baratta A (1982) Criminologia critica e critica del diritto penale. Il Mulino, Bologna.

Baratta A (1985) Principi del diritto penale minimo. Per una teoria dei diritti umani come oggetti e limiti della legge penale. In: Baratta A (ed.) Il diritto penale minimo. La questione criminale tra riduzionismo e abolizionismo. Edizioni Scientifiche Italiane, Naples, pp. 443–473.

Barton S (1993) Sozial übliche Geschäftstätigkeit und Geldwäsche (§ 261). Strafverteidiger (StV): 156–163.

Binding K (1872) Die Normen und ihre Übertretung: Eine Untersuchung über die rechtmäßige Handlung und die Arten des Delikts. Engelmann, Leipzig.

Birnbaum J M F (1834) Über das Erfordernis einer Rechtsverletzung zum Begriff des Verbrechens mit besonderer Rücksicht auf den Begriff der Ehrenkränkung. Archiv des Criminalrechts 15: 149–194.

Bottke W (1995) Teleologie und Effektivität der Normen gegen Geldwäsche. Zeitschrift für Wirtschaft, Steuer und Strafrecht (wistra): 87–91; 121–130.

Burr C (1995) Geldwäsche: eine Untersuchung zu § 261 StGB. Respublica-Verlag, Siegburg.

Diederichsen U, Dreier R (1997) Das missglückte Gesetz. Wandenhoeck & Ruprecht, Göttingen.

Diéz Ripollés (1994) El blanqueo de capitales procedentes del tráfico de drogas. Actualida Penal 32: 583–613.

Dionyssopoulou A (1999) Der Tatbestand der Geldwäsche: eine Analyse der dogmatischen Grundlagen des § 261 StGB. Frankfurter kriminalwissenschaftliche Studien 66. Lang, Frankfurt am Main.

Eisele J (2015) Strafrecht Besonderer Teil 2. 3. Auflage. Verlag Kohlhammer, Stuttgart.

Fernandez L, Heinrich B (2014) Die Strafbarkeit des Strafverteidigers wegen Geldwäsche durch Annahme des Honorars nach Südafrikanischem und deutschem Recht. Zeitschrift für die gesamte Strafrechtswissenschaft (ZStW) 126 (2): 382–445.

Fiandaca G (1982) Il bene giuridico come problema teorico e come criterio di politica criminale. Rivista italiana di diritto e procedura penale: 42–81.

Fiandaca G and Musco E (1992) Diritto penale. Parte speciale. Zanichelli, Bologna.

Findeisen M (1997) Der Prävention im Geldwäschegesetz. Anforderungen der Bankenaufsicht an die internen Sicherungsmaßnahmen der Kreditinstitute gem. § 14 Abs. 2 GwG zur Bekämpfung der Geldwäsche. Zeitschrift für Wirtschaft, Steuer und Strafrecht (wistra) 16 (4): 123–128.

Fischer T (2014) Strafgesetzbuch: StGB. 61. Auflage. C H Beck, Munich.

Flick (2005) Problemi e prospettive del diritto penale dell'impresa all'alba del nuovo secolo: Il nodo dei beni protetti. In: Vv. AA. (ed.) Governo dell'impresa e mercato delle regole. Giuffré, Milan.

Friedman L M (1975) The Legal System: A Social Science Perspective. Russell Sage Foundation, New York.

Frisch W (2003) Rechtsgut, Recht, Deliktsstruktur und Zurechnung im Rahmen der Legitimation staatlichen Strafens. In: Hefendehl R et al. (eds) Die Rechtsgutstheorie. Nomos, Baden-Baden, pp. 215–238.

Garzón Vergara J C (2014) Fixing a broken system: modernizing drug law enforcement in Latin America. Series on legislative reform of drug policies 29: 1–11.

Hassemer W (1989) Symbolisches Strafrecht und Rechtsgüterschtutz. Neue Zeitschrift für Strafrecht 9: 553–559.
Hassemer W (1992) Kennzeichen und Krisen des modernen Strafrechts. Zeitschrift für Rechtspolitik (ZRP): 378–383.
Hassemer W (1995) Vermögen im Strafrecht. Zu neuen Tendenzen der Kriminalpolitik. Zeitschrift für Wirtschafts- und Bankrecht. Wertpapier Mitteilungen (WM) Sonderbeilage 3: 3–31.
Hassemer W (2010) Preliminary remark to § 1. In: Kindhäuser U et al. (eds) Strafgesetzbuch 1 (3) Nomos Kommentar. Nomos, Baden-Baden.
Hassemer W and Starzacher K (1993) Organisierte Kriminalität - geschützt vom Datenschutz? Nomos Verlag, Baden-Baden.
Hefendehl R (2001) Kann und soll der Allgemeine Teil bzw. das Verfassungsrecht miß-glückte Regelungen des Besonderen Teils retten? Die „Geldwäsche" durch den Strafverteidiger. In: Schünemann B et al. (eds) Festschrift für Claus Roxin zum 70. Geburtstag. De Gruyter, Berlin/New York, pp. 145–172.
Helmers G (2009) Zum Tatbestand der Geldwäsche (§ 261 StGB): Beispiel einer rechtsprinzipiell verfehlten Strafgesetzgebung. Zeitschrift für die gesamte Strafrechtswissenschaft 121 (3): 509–547.
Hetzer W (1993) Der Geruch des Geldes: Ziel, Inhalt und Wirkung der Gesetze gegen Geldwäsche. Neue Juristische Wochenschrift (NJW): 3298–3301.
Hoyer A (2012) In Wolter J (ed.) Systematischer Kommentar zum Strafgesetzbuch (SK) Wolters Kluwer, Cologne.
Hörnle T (2005). Grob anstössiges Verhalten: Strafrechtlicher Schutz von Moral, Gefühlen und Tabus. Vittorio Klostermann, Frankfurt am Main.
Isensee J (1983) Das Grundrecht auf Sicherheit. Zu den Schutzpflichten des freiheitlichen Verfassungsstaates. Walter de Gruyter, Berlin/New York.
Kilchling M (2000) Die vermögensbezogene Bekämpfung der Organisierten Kriminalität - Recht und Praxis der Geldwäschebekämpfung und Gewinnabschöpfung zwischen Anspruch und Wirklichkeit. Zeitschrift für Wirtschaft, Steuer und Strafrecht 9 (wistra): 241–249.
Leip C (1999) Der Straftatbestand der Geldwäsche: zur Auslegung des § 261 StGB. Berlin Verlag Spitz, Berlin.
Lisken (1994) 'Sicherheit' durch 'Kriminalitätsbekämpfung'. Zeitschrift für Rechtspolitik: 49–51.
Marinucci G, Dolcini E (2006) Manuale di diritto penale. Parte generale. Giuffrè Editore, Milan.
Miranda Rodriguez A (2003) Criminal Policy: New Challenges, Old Ways. Cahiers de defense sociale: 182–212.
Mitsilegas V (2003) Money Laundering Counter-measures in the European Union: A new paradigm of security governance versus fundamental legal principles. Kluwer Law International, The Hague.
Moccia S (1995) Impiego di Capitali illeciti e riciclaggio: la risposta del sistema penale italiano. Rivista italiana di diritto e procedura penale: 728–739.
Nestler C (2014) Geldwäsche; Verschleierung unrechtmäßig erlangter Vermögenswerte. In: Herzog F (ed.) Geldwäschegesetz (Gwg). 2. Auflage. C H Beck, Munich.
Neuheuser S (2012) § 261 Geldwäsche; Verschleierung unrechtmäßig erlangter Vermögenswerte. In: Joecks W (ed.) Münchener Kommentar zum Strafgesetzbuch 4 2. Auflage (MüKo). C H Beck, Munich.
Noll P (1973) Gesetzgebungslehre. Rowohlt, Reinbek.
Oswald K (1997) Die Implementation gesetzlicher Massnahmen zur Bekämpfung der Geldwäsche in der Bundesrepublik Deutschland: Eine empirische Untersuchung des § 261 StGB i.V.m. dem Geldwäsche. Max-Planck-Institut für ausländisches und internationales Strafrecht, Freiburg.
Otto H (1993) Geldwäsche § 261 StGB. Jura: 329–332.
Paliero C E (1992) Il principio di effettività del diritto penale. Rivista italiana di diritto e procedura penale: 430–478.

Patalano V (1991) Beni costituzionali e tutela penale degli interessi economici. In: Bassiouni M C et al. (eds) Evoluzione e riforma del diritto e della procedura penale: Studi in onore di Giuliano Vassalli. Giuffrè, Milan, pp. 629–648.
Pieth M (1993) "Symbolische Gesetzgebung" gegen Geldwäscherei und organisiertes Verbrechen? Vortrag am 17. Deutschen Strafverteidigertag, Münster, 7. - 9.5.1993. In: Strafverteidiger-vereinigungen, Organisationsbüro der Strafverteidigervereinigungen (ed.) Rechtsstaatliche Antworten auf neue Kriminalitätsformen. Der Andere Buchladen, Cologne, pp. 99–106.
Pitschas R (1993) Innere Sicherheit und international Verbrechensbekämpfung als Verantwortung des demokratischen Verfassungsstaates. JuristenZeitung (JZ) 19: 857–866.
Rebscher E, Vahlenkamp W (1988) Organisierte Kriminalität in der Bundesrepublik Deutschland. Bestandsaufnahme, Entwicklungstendenzen und Bekämpfung aus Sicht der Polizeipraxis. BKA-Forschungsreihe, Wiesbaden.
Rengier R (2015) Strafrecht Besonderer Teil II. Delikte gegen die Person und die Allgemeinheit. C H Beck, Munich.
Roxin C (2006) Strafrecht Allgemeiner Teil Band I: Grundlagen. Der Aufbau der Verbrechenslehre. C H Beck, Munich.
Roxin C (2010) Zur neueren Entwicklung der Rechtgutsdebatte. In: Herzog F et al. (eds) Festschrift für Winfried Hassemer. C F Müller, Heidelberg, pp. 573–597.
Salditt F (1992) Der Tatbestand der Geldwäsche. Strafverteidiger Forum (StraFo): 121–136.
Schönke A (2010) Strafgesetzbuch: StGB. 28. Auflage. C H Beck, Munich.
Schünemann B (2003) Das Rechtsgüterschutzprinzip als Fluchtpunkt der verfassungsrechtlichen Grenzen der Straftatbestände und ihrer Interpretation. In: Hefendehl R et al. (eds) Die Rechtsgutstheorie. Nomos, Baden-Baden, pp. 133–154.
Severino P (2014) Sicurezza dei mercati finanziari: Interessi tutelati e strumenti di tutela. Rivista italiana di diritto processuale penale 2: 672–683.
Silva Sánchez J M (2004) Sfide scientifiche e sfide politiche della scienza del diritto penale. In: Stortoni L, Foffani L (eds) Critica e giustificazione del diritto penale nel cambio di secolo. L'analisi critica della scuola di Francoforte. Giuffré, Milan, pp. 23–40.
Sotiriadis G (2010) Die Entwicklug der Gesetzgebung über Gewinnabschöpfung und Geldwäsche. Unter Berücksichtigung der jeweiligen kriminalpolitischen Tendenzen. Duncker & Humblot, Berlin.
Stratenwerth G (1998) Zum Begriff des „Rechtsgutes". In: Eser A (ed.) Festschrift für Theodor Leckner zum 70. Geburtstag. C H Beck, Munich, pp. 377–392.
Unger B, Ferwerda J, van den Broek M, Deleanu I (2014) The Economic And Legal Effectiveness Of The European Union's Anti-Money Laundering Policy. Edward Elgar Publishing Limited, Cheltenham.
Vest H (2001) Probleme des Herkunftsprinzips bei der Geldwäscherei. In: Ackermann J B (ed.) Wirtschaft und Strafrecht: Festschrift für Niklaus Schmid zum 65. Geburtstag. Schulthess, Zürich, pp. 417–436.
Voß M (1989) Symbolische Gesetzgebung. C H Beck, Munich.
Vogel J (1997) Geldwäsche - ein europaweit harmonisierter Straftatbestand? Zeitschrift für die gesamte Strafrechtswissenschaft (ZStW) 109 (2): 335–356.
Volk K (1985) Entkriminalisierung durch Strafwürdigkeitskriterien jenseits des Deliktsaufbaus. Zeitschrift für die gesamte Strafrechtswissenschaft 97(4): 871–918.
Von Hirsch (1996) Die Vermögensstrafe. Ein Beispiel für die unorganisierten Konsequenzen von gesetz-geberischen Anstrengungen zur Bekämpfung organisierter Kriminalität. ZStW 108: 333–353.
Von Hirsch A (2003) Extending the Harm Principle: "Remote" Harms and Fair Imputation. In: Aa Vv (eds) Harm and Culpability. Clarendon Press, Oxford, pp. 259–276.
Von Lampe K (1994) Der neue Tatbestand der Geldwaesche (para. 261 StGB). Juristen Zeitung (JZ) 3: 123–132.
Von Liszt (1882) Der Zweckgedanke im Strafrecht. Pfeil, Marburg.
Wallerstein S (2007) Criminalising remote harm and the case of anti-democratic activity. Cardozo Law Review 28 (6): 2697–2738.

Welzel H (1939) Studien zum System des Strafrechts. Zeitschrift für die gesamte Strafrechtswissenschaft (ZStW): 491–566.

Weschke E (1986) Netzstruktur-Kriminalität: Eine spezifische Form des Intensivitätsverhaltens. Kriminalstatistik 6: 297–317.

Wessels J, Hillenkamp T (2015) Strafrecht Besonderer Teil 2. 38 Auflage. C F Müller, Heidelberg.

Wohlers K (2001) Strafverteidigung vor den Schranken der Strafgerichtsbarkeit. Strafverteidiger (StV): 420–429.

Wohlers W (2000) Deliktstypen des Präventionsstrafrechts-zur Dogmatik "moderner" Gefährdungsdelikte. Duncker & Humblot, Berlin.

Zoppei V (2015) Money Laundering: A New Perspective in Assessing the Effectiveness of the AML Regime. The European Review of Organised Crime 2 (1): 130–148.

Part IV
The Implementation of the Anti-Money Laundering Regime: Between Law in Action and Law Inaction

Now all the criminals in their coats and their ties
Are free to drink martinis and watch the sun rise
While Rubin sits like Buddha in a ten-foot cell
An innocent man in a living hell.

Bob Dylan, Hurricane

Chapter 6
Data on the Implementation of the Anti-Money Laundering Regime

Abstract This chapter looks at the implementation of the criminal policy by observing the activity of law enforcement agencies and the judiciary. The effectiveness of these two organs of state is referred to as efficiency, which is measured in relation to their primary functions through criminal statistics on the number of (preliminary) investigations, proceedings, convictions, and types of punishments imposed. In order to disclose what impact that the money-laundering offence has had over the past years of its being in force, as compared to the above-mentioned highlighted intentions of the legislature, this part deals with the implementation of the law, which was identified in Part I as an empirical measure of the effectiveness of a law. The part looks both at the effects of criminalising money laundering and at the application of the Anti-Money Laundering Act. It does this by analysing official statistics and looking at the way the law is implemented, from the point of view of the authorities who provide the statistics. This data is not only representative of the implementation outcomes but expresses also the level of efficiency from the perspective of the different criminal justice authorities. Given the abundant literature that summarises and analyses the data and thanks to the results of an empirical research conducted shortly after the introduction of the anti-money laundering policy, this study, by now, approaches the statistics with an already critical perspective.

Keywords Financial intelligence unit · Suspicious transactions reports · Money-laundering investigations · Money-laundering convictions · Cost-benefit analysis

Contents

V. Zoppei, *Anti-Money Laundering Law: Socio-Legal Perspectives on the Effectiveness of German Practices*, International Criminal Justice Series 12,
DOI 10.1007/978-94-6265-180-7_6

The illicit side of globalisation operates in the gap between the authority to create laws and the ability to enforce such laws.[1] The police gauge efficiency by the number of cases resolved. From the point of view of the prosecution service, efficiency is measured by the number of indictments brought, and from the perspective of the judiciary what counts is the number of convictions for a certain offence. However, statistics alone say nothing about the reasons that trigger the actions of law enforcement bodies. In view of the fact that, as could be said of the application of the law in general, that those who implement the law might be biased, the outcome of law enforcement action is not always neutral. Therefore, the selectivity of the criminal justice system cannot be assumed as primarily neutral, although it should be. The part does not aim at assessing either the phenomenon of money laundering or the effectiveness of norms based on official figures, for this would imply that the effectiveness of a law depends merely on its implementation, and that the implementation could be assessed through statistics on compliance, deviance and punished deviance. This study is instead based on the assumption that the (in)effectiveness of a norm may also depend on different factors and that, in order to assess the implementation of a law, it is necessary to look at all the effects of a law, including those not registered in the official statistics. Furthermore, this study takes the view that a high convictions rate is not a reflection of the high efficacy of criminal law. As is argued in Part I, while compliance might not suffice to fulfil the indirect purpose of a law,[2] a high degree of disobedience does not mean that the norm has no effect.[3] Moreover, in order to interpret statistics on the implementation of a law, it is fundamental to understand legal practices and to establish what actors in the law think about the law. Therefore, the findings made in this part will, together with considerations bearing on the interviews presented in the next part, constitute a basis for evaluating the official statistics critically in order to evaluate the overall effectiveness of the German anti-money laundering policies.

Given the numerous statistical reports on law enforcement, this study confines itself to arriving at qualitative understanding of the issues. This is necessitated by the fact that the aim of this study is not to collect primary data. The criminal justice statistics in respect of money laundering and its preventive legal regime emanate are those derived

[1] Andreas 2015, pp. 52–53.

[2] Full compliance with Article 261 of GCC might not impede the infiltration of illicit financial flows, as much as the law that imposes a driving speed limit is not effective if car accidents take place despite obedience. *See* Rottleuthner 1983, p. 90.

[3] Aubert 1974, p. 86.

from official sources, which is to say, the appropriate public authorities. However, the figures are an approximation. This is because, on the one hand, Germany is a federal state in which statistics collated by the individual states are rounded up at a federal level, and on the other hand, the various authorities use their own respective methods of collecting information. Nonetheless, both constitute a basis on which further qualitative reflections can be developed. The official statistics are analysed, using a qualitative approach, based on hypotheses constructed on the outcomes of previous studies and on the line of inquiry followed in the previous parts of this study. The aim is to understand both the causes and effects of the described outcomes.

The figures are scrutinised against the background of factors identified as relevant, such as the number of investigations initiated and the number of cases finalised, the number of convictions relative to different forms of conduct punishable by Article 261 of the GCC, the type of punishment imposed, the amount of assets effectively confiscated in relation to the convictions for money laundering, the nationality of the individuals concerned and the seat of registration of the headquarters of the companies reported. Furthermore, the typology of Suspicious Transactions Reports (STRs) filed will be also taken into consideration in order to show to which offences suspicious transactions are normally linked.

In 2010, the FATF evaluated the German anti-money laundering regime and it published a follow-up report in 2014.[4] Both reports are sources of relevant information that complement the analysis of the statistics presented in this part. A vast body of literature has focused on evaluating the effectiveness of anti-money laundering laws, using different methodologies.[5] This study draws on the findings of some of the studies, for example, of a cost-benefit analysis conducted on the specific provision concerning the disclosure of Beneficial Ownerships (BOs). Furthermore, the book draws attention to a cost-benefit analysis of the European anti-money laundering policy, which compares the burden imposed by the money-laundering regime and the outcomes insofar as it affects the prevention and suppression of money laundering. It makes also use of a recent study conducted by the on the risks of money laundering connected to the non-financial sector.[6] This part concludes with speculations on potential *effet pervers* caused by the implementation of the policy and with considerations on the probable reasons of the revealed hindrances.

[4] The implementation of the Recommendations is rigorously assessed through Mutual Evaluation processes, and through the assessments conducted by the International Monetary Fund (IMF) and the World Bank (WB). After such mutual evaluations are conducted, Mutual Evaluation Reports are compiled, and countries that are found to be non-compliant with the standards are called upon to address the deficiencies. A follow-up report is thereafter published, the idea being to keep the countries on their toes. Jurisdictions that are found to be clearly non-compliant could be sanctioned. *See* FATF 2010, and 2014.

[5] *See*, among others, FATF 2013; Ferwerda 2009; Geiger and Wuensch 2007; Global Witness 2012; IMF 2011; Levi 2002; Levi et al. 2004; Savona and Riccardi 2015; Unger et al. 2013; Kemal 2014.

[6] *See* Bussman 2015.

6.1 General Information on Statistics Provided by the Federal Statistical Office, the Police and the Financial Intelligence Unit (FIU)

This part makes use of statistics provided by the Federal Statistical Office, *statistisiches Bundesamt* (hereafter Destatis), the Federal Police (The Statistical Report of the Police), *polizeiliche Kriminalstatistik* (hereafter PKS), and the reports of the Financial Intelligence Unit (hereafter FIU). All statistics are official, as they are published annually by national institutions such as the Federal Criminal Police Office, *Bundeskriminalamt* (hereafter BKA) in Wiesbaden, the Ministry of the Interior and the BKA. The Statistical Report of the Police reflect the perspective of the police, by which is meant they are based solely on cases known to the police, which include attempted commissions of crimes and narcotics-related cases dealt with by customs.[7] In relation to the criminal cases, the outcomes are thus different from those contained in the statistical report of Destatis, which are based on cased processed by the courts. The figures are collated by the BKA and originate from the local police authorities, *Landeskriminalämter* (hereafter LKAs) in the 16 States.[8] PKS statistics also give the clearance rate, which shows the extent to which the criminal justice system has managed to solve the cases. The accuracy of the figures given are subject to the qualification that, in the field of crime, there is always a grey number, which cannot be encompassed by the statistics. Another limitation is that such numbers do not provide explanations for the reasons underlying the deviant behaviour. Therefore, not only do they not reflect the reality of the criminal world, but they also do not take account of the factors that might motivate criminal behaviour. Destatis statistics are based on the figures that spring out of the administration of criminal justice, which is to say, the practical disposal of cases by the criminal courts and the criminal conduct registered and evaluated by the criminal courts.[9] Even though this part undertakes a considered analysis of the most recent statistics, meaning the years 2013–2015, it compares them with analyses of some statistics from earlier years. This is done to afford an overview of the eventual differences and to leave room for a study on the causes of such differences. Statistics on the administration of justice have been available as of 2002. The FIU annual report contains very detailed information not only on the typologies of

[7] Tax crimes and financial crimes are, for example excluded by these surveys. *See* PKS 2015, p. 1.

[8] The PKS statistics give information on the volume of cases processed by the police in relation to every offence. The aim of these statistics is to acquire a general overview regarding criminality and a specific overview of the types of offences committed, the volume and the structure of the suspects, as well as the changes in criminal rates. They also have the function of acquiring knowledge for planning, organising and deciding about the prevention and repression of criminality. In addition, they may be used for criminological and sociological research and criminal policies. *See* PKS 2015, p. 1.

[9] Destatis statistics are generated mainly for use by law enforcement departments, policy makers, legal actors and scholars. The media and other disseminators of information may make use of these statistics too. Destatis, Series 10, volume 3, Oswald 1997, p. 6.

suspicious transactions reports (STRs) received and on the processed cases, but also on the feedbacks received by law enforcement agencies. The latter aspect is particularly relevant for assessing the effectiveness of the co-operation between the private sector and the criminal justice system through the mediation of the FIU.[10] Nevertheless, such cases are not representative of all cases dealt with by the prosecutors, since the information contained in the FIU's report is based on only those cases that prosecutors send to the FIU.[11] A comparative analysis of FIU reports for the period between 2002 and 2014 shows that there are some trends discernible with respect to the filing of STRs and the elaboration of such information by the law enforcement agencies.

6.2 *Oswald*'s Research of 1996: A Starting Point for a Further Theorisation

Statistics on the implementation of the anti-money laundering policy in the unified Germany have been available from the year 2000. Therefore, data on the first years of the law enforcement derive from an empirical study conducted between 1994 and 1996 by *Oswald* at the Max Planck Institute of Freiburg, as part of her doctoral research.[12] The research aimed at analysing the implementation and thus the practical application and the execution of Article 261 of the GCC in conjunction with the Anti-Money Laundering Act a few years after the regulations entered into force.[13] The study focused specifically on the co-operation between the private

[10] However, in its 2013 Annual Report, the FIU lamented the fact that follow-up responses did not contain sufficient qualified information to enable a typological evaluation. The report stated that 'in many reports, the predicate offences are often the triggering factor for filing a suspicious transactions report, whereas mostly no information is provided on the actual money-laundering activities'. *See* FIU 2013, pp. 26, 33.

[11] Money-laundering cases can be differentiated between independent and integrated investigations. The former are commenced based on a suspicion of money laundering. A typical example would be where a suspicious transaction report is filed, according to Articles 11 and 13 of the Anti-Money-Laundering Act. The latter, i.e. the integrated investigations, are initiated in the context of another case relating to another offence and relating information are not communicated to the FIU.

[12] Oswald 1997.

[13] The empirical research consisted of a combination of three sources: an analysis of 380 law enforcement acts, oral interviews with 16 public prosecutors, and written questionnaires submitted to 75 financial institutions. For purposes of understanding how the system of STRs and the subsequent investigations function, criminal records were analysed in order to compile a profile of the transactions reported and the subsequent law enforcement activities. Oswald aimed at shedding light on the link between the criminalisation of money-laundering and the co-operation with the private sector and therefore focused her research on investigations commenced on the basis of a filed suspicious transaction, without taking into consideration cases where allegations of money-laundering were triggered by a previous investigation into the commission of a predicate offence. Due to the then limited quantity of statistics on the implementation, the research was

sector and law enforcement authorities, since this nexus represented a novelty at that time. The outcomes of *Oswald*'s study offer an important starting point for the present study. The author opted for an implementation-focused type of research, which observes the process of application of a law, rather than an evaluation type of study that instead assesses the effectiveness and the outcome of a policy, because the law was then very new.[14] The main outcomes of the *Oswald*'s study are summarised later, but only insofar, as they are relevant for the current study. It is particularly interesting to establish whether the cumbersome issues that cropped up in the first years of implementation have in the meantime been resolved or whether they still obstruct effective implementation. This will be verified by comparing *Oswald*'s outcomes with the implementation of the anti-money laundering policy in recent years. Most of the information gathered by *Oswald* is included in the official reports published by the FIU, the BKA, the FIU and the Federal Statistical Office.

The empirical research was based on eight hypotheses,[15] which were confirmed or proved wrong by the empirical research.[16] The outcomes of Oswald's study will be compared to the current state of affairs in the light of the analysis of the criminal statistics.

(1) Due to the vagueness of the wording of what the law considers a suspicious transaction, the filing of STRs may be influenced by discretionary and biased elements such as the social class or nationality of the customer. This was confirmed by the analysis of the 380 records of relevant money-laundering proceedings, where almost two-thirds of the suspected individuals reported were non-German nationals, and 80% were non-regular customers or relatively unknown new customers. A relatively high number of transactions that were filed were related to large amounts of money transacted by asylum seekers or involved transactions with countries in conflict or countries with a high incidence of organised crime, or unexplainable deposits of unknown foreign currencies from African states.[17]

(Footnote 13 continued)

conducted through extensive interviews with experts, the idea being not only to determine their opinions and attitudes towards the law, but also to compile surveys on the legal practice. Written questionnaires were submitted to financial institutions to find out what impact the Anti-Money-Laundering Act has had with respect to the burden imposed. Oswald was especially interested in revealing problems encountered in applying the law and in co-operating with the law enforcement agencies. She adopted this method not only because it was convenient in terms of the time and costs saved, but also to assure the anonymity of the respondents. Oswald 1997, pp. 120, 164.

[14] Oswald 1997, p. 110.

[15] The hypotheses are to be found in Oswald 1997, pp. 113–119.

[16] For the results of the interviews with public prosecutors that are discussed here, *see* Oswald 1997, pp. 147–162. For the results of the questionnaires submitted to credit institutions, *see* Oswald 1997, pp. 163–210. For the results of the analysis of criminal records, *see* Oswald 1997, pp. 267–268.

[17] Oswald 1997, p. 195.

(2) On account of the threat that Article 261(5) poses for professions and businesses, and their desire to avoid being incriminated, the number of STRs filed should be very high. Oswald found that bank employees could not differentiate easily between legal and illegal transactions. They could not discern, for instance, a 'mere' tax evasion operation from a money-laundering one.[18] As regards the wording of the Anti-Money Laundering Act, the interviewees lamented the difficulty faced by employees without a legal education in understanding the Anti-Money Laundering Act provisions. Due to this lack of understanding and to the threat posed by Article 261(5), many employees had been red flagging routinely. For example, the 67 interviewed credit institutions conducted an internal examination of 2,697 and found that only 857 deserved to be filed as suspicious transactions.

(3) The burden imposed on the private sector to prevent money-laundering transactions may be too high in proportion to the effectiveness of the mechanism. According to the 1994 government statistics, a total of 3,282 STRs were filed in 1994. Information on customers was recorded in 3.3 billion cases, but in only 0.001% of the cases did public prosecutors require the recorded information.[19] Given this state of affairs, the Central Credit Monitoring Authority refused the proposal of the SPD to lower the reporting threshold from 30,000 DM to 15,000 DM.[20] The rationale for the refusal was that a higher reporting threshold would diminish bureaucratic duties by 50% without lessening the effectiveness and efficiency of the regulation.[21]

(4) In view of the vagueness of the concept 'deriving', criminalising every act related to the object that is the proceed of a predicate offence, the offence may have a too broad scope, despite the restrictive interpretation of Article 261 of the GCC. Instead of causing a widespread criminalisation of money laundering, it results in a very low conviction rate. According to *Oswald*'s e empirical examination of the criminal records, of the 379 criminal proceedings, in 87% of the cases it was not possible to proceed with an indictment for money laundering. In 3.4% of the cases the closed proceedings were continued, pursuant to Article 11(6) Anti-Money Laundering Act.[22] The 66 prosecutors interviewed confirmed these statistics, according to whom in 1994 of the 1,203 money-laundering cases they had dealt with 88.5% were closed and in none of the cases did the proceeding result in a conviction for money laundering.[23] However, the reason was not the quality of the STRs filed, but rather the impossibility of proving the link between one of the predicate offences listed in the catalogue and the assets. Despite having a high suspicion that the assets had

---

[18] Ibid., p. 287.

[19] FIU 2002, p. 27; and Oswald 1997, pp. 286–287.

[20] BT-Drucksache 12/6784, p. 7.

[21] Oswald 1997, p. 288.

[22] Ibid.

[23] Ibid.

an illegal origin, the prosecutors could not adduce sufficient evidence to prove the derivation from one of the antecedent acts.[24] The '*doppelter Anfangsverdacht*'[25] was considered too high for the purposes of indictment pursuant to Article 152(2) of the German Code of Criminal Procedure.[26] As a solution, the prosecutors suggested that the catalogue of the predicate offences broadened and that criminal liability be extended to the perpetrators of predicate offences. However, a reversal of the burden of proof was not advocated, as it would not pass constitutional muster, according to the respondents. According to Oswald, the effectiveness of the inversion of the burden of proof, as adopted in the US, was overestimated.[27]

(5) Article 11(1) of the Anti-Money Laundering Act, which allows suspicious transactions to be nevertheless completed in order to facilitate money-laundering investigations, might have opened a legal loophole. However, neither *Oswald*'s study nor the present empirical investigation have proven this a valid assumption.

(6) The rules contained in the Anti-Money Laundering Act might not be welcomed by the banking sector, since they are too complicated and do not justify the burden they imposed. *Oswald* is of the view that particularly private sector employees, with no legal background, may find it very difficult to recognise a money-laundering operation. A further difficulty arises when banks have to explain to their customers about the money-laundering preventive regulations, their obligation to collect information about their customers and to report suspicious transactions. More than one-third of the 50 credit institutions that responded to the questionnaire highlighted the fact that the anti-money laundering laws had caused insecurity and customers losing confidence in the banks, which confirms *Oswald*'s third hypothesis.[28] It was especially the

[24] Ibid., p. 289.

[25] The '*doppel Anfangsverdacht*', double initial evidence was required in relation to both the laundering of proceeds of crimes and predicate offence.

[26] In a meeting held in 1994, the prosecutors, accordingly, agreed to link the possibility of opening an investigation where it is suspected that the asset derives from one of the designated predicate offences, according to the criminological practice. But the standard of proof required by Article 111 b–f of the German Code of Criminal Procedure, for the purpose of seizing criminal assets in relation to Article 261 of the GCC, namely the necessity of proving the origin of the assets from one of the listed predicate offences, was considered still too high to fulfil the goal of confiscating criminal assets. Also, the introduction of the extended confiscation regulated by Article 73d German Code of Criminal Procedure was not considered effective in practice, because even when prosecutors suspected t the illegal provenance of the goods but the accused was able to prove, at least, that he had some legitimate income, this would have been enough to discharge the suspicion. Oswald 1997, p. 155.

[27] FATF 2010, p. 50.

[28] Oswald 1997, p. 179.

regular customers who did not easily accept the obligation to divulge so much personal information. Customers were generally concerned about the recording of private information by the institutions.[29] But credit institutions generally accepted the duties imposed by the new regulations, and despite being of the opinion that some of them were not practicable, the majority agreed that such provisions were necessary.

(7) The lack of existence of a central authority that receives the STRs (the current FIU) may result in chaos where information is scattered. One of the main problems raised by the financial sector with respect to the co-operation with the law enforcement agencies was the lack of feedback on what the filing of STRs had effected. The respondents complained about the discretion prosecutors have in the handling of reported cases and lack of personnel devoted to following up on the suspicious transactions reported. In addition, they bemoaned the unclear division of duties within the different law enforcement authorities.[30] However, according to the opinion of the respondents, the level of co-operation between public prosecutors' offices and credit institutions was considered adequate, despite some problems of communication, identified mainly in the first months of introducing the new rules.

(8) The last hypothesis is that law enforcement authorities will predictably draw attention to the failure in co-operation with other states, especially offshore centres, when it comes to prosecuting transnational money-laundering cases. Investigators, indeed, claimed that the transnational nature of organised crime and the limited availability of instruments to investigate abroad hindered the successful prosecution of money laundering. The eighth hypothesis was thus verified.

Oswald's research focused also on the sanctions imposed in money-laundering cases, particularly concerning the volume of confiscated assets. Of the 380 cases researched, none of them resulted in a conviction for money laundering. Not a single Deutschmark was confiscated. In three cases, assets were seized but the seizure order was subsequently annulled. A total of 87% of the proceedings were dismissed in terms of Article 170(2) of the German Code of Criminal Procedure, mostly because of the impossibility of proving the origin of the asset from one of the listed predicate offences. Only 3.4% of the proceedings were dismissed and continued for another offence.[31]

---

[29] Ibid., p. 179.

[30] On two extreme cases, the private institutions observed a lack of interest and indifference from the offices, which did not reply to written requests or to arranged telephone calls for investigative purposes. Oswald 1997, p. 182.

[31] Ibid.

6.3 (Preliminary) Investigations, Type of Charges, Convictions and Penalties[32]

The following paragraphs describe the application of the laws and the effects of their implementation in more recent years. The depiction is seen of through the lenses of both law enforcement agencies and the FIU. The focus is particularly on the issues already raised by *Oswald* in 1997 and on the eventual emerging challenges. Convictions for money laundering do not occur often, if one compares the rates of other offences. The number of convictions for illicit possession of narcotics, pursuant to Article 29(1) 1, 3 of the Narcotics Act (*Betäubungsmittelgesetz*) is, for example, much higher (22,702 in 2013) than the number of convictions under Article 261 of the GCC (828 in 2013).[33]

The matter does not concern only the absolute number of convictions, the Destatis statistics classify the number of convictions according to the four different modes of conduct criminalised by Article 261 of the GCC, namely, the 'concealing offence' under para 1, 'the isolation conduct' under para 2, aggravated conduct under para 4, and finally, the reckless liability punishment contained in para 5. In 2013, out of a total of 828 individuals convicted for money laundering, a large majority (510 individuals) was convicted under Article 261(5) of the GCC, which corresponds to 61% of total convictions for money laundering. Very few persons were convicted under paras 2 and 4 (31 and 33, respectively), while the rest were convicted under Article 261(1) of the GCC, namely 30.6% of the total convictions for money laundering. This trend became noticeable from 2005 onwards. Between 2002 and 2004, most of the convictions were pursuant to Article 261(1). Since 2005 the number of persons convicted under Article 261(5) of the GCC increased consistently and kept on increasing in the following years to the point that, by 2007, the number of convicted persons under Article 261(5) of the GCC was higher than the number convicted under Article 261(1). The number increased from 14 cases in 2002 to 512 cases in 2012, with a small decrease in 2013 (510 cases). The number of convictions under para 2 has always been much lower in comparison to the convictions for para 1. However, it bears noting that there has been a growing trend since 2006. By looking at the total number of sentences passed and at the number of individuals convicted pursuant to Article 261 of the GCC, one cannot escape the observation that there was a general increase between 2002 and 2013.

The FATF assessors also registered this trend in 2010.[34] However, it is impossible to establish the reasons that led to this development. It might be related to a national increase in the incidence of money laundering, or to an improvement in law enforcement techniques. According to the FATF Report of 2010, the general

[32] Figures are provided by Destatis, Series 10 on the administration of justice, volume 3, from the year 2002 to 2013. The year 2003 is missing because there are no statistics available for that year.

[33] Destatis, Series 10, volume 3, 2013, pp. 37, 51.

[34] FATF 2010, p. 61.

increase in money laundering cases from the year 2006 can be partly ascribed to a technical factor, namely, to the fact that all Bundesländer compiled statistics only as of 2006, whereas previously the statistics denoted the situation in West Germany, including greater Berlin, prior to reunification.[35] But the German authorities did not offer any explanations to the FATF assessors why there had been an increase. The increase is especially evident in the case of convictions relating to the reckless conduct. In recent years, Article 261 of the GCC has been applied mostly against persons who act with recklessness. Consequently, if para 5 had not been added, a large part of the convictions for Article of 261 GCC would not have taken place.

Article 261 has been used rather rarely to punish organised crime groups or activities committed on a commercial basis. In fact, only 33 of the 828 criminal convictions in 2013 were related to para 4. Between 2002 and 2012, 229 persons were found guilty of aggravated conduct, while a total of 2,373 were found guilty under Article 261(5) of the GCC. Out of the 124,842 completed proceedings in the field of money laundering, tax crimes and economic crimes recorded by the offices of public prosecutors in 2013, a total of 2,163 (1.7%) were categorised as organised crime proceedings.[36] According to the same source, only 18% of the proceedings involved more than one person. The BKA statistics show the number of criminal cases involving an economic element and these are included under the technical definition of 'organised crime'.[37] What is striking is that in 2015 the BKA registered 566 ongoing cases of organised crime, of which 36.7% included money-laundering activities, but in only 2.1% of the cases money laundering was the main conduct.[38] These figures permit the hypothesis that Article 261(4) of the GCC is not used often to prosecute money laundering committed by organised crime groups. However, the outcome might be interpreted also as a symptom of the effective deterrent effect of the law. In addition, individuals convicted under Article 261(4) might not be visible in the official statistics due to a cumulative conviction for an offence with a higher punishment. According to the 2010 FATF, German criminal justice authorities prosecuted profit-making crimes under other offences. In fact, the authorities interviewed said that the offence of money laundering, due to various factors, is not used for this purpose. First, the impossibility of charging the offender of the predicate offence results in less allegations for money laundering

---

[35] In particular, the report specifies that data for the entire Federal Republic, i.e. including the Länder of Brandenburg, Mecklenburg-Western Pomerania, Saxony, Saxony-Anhalt and Thuringia, these data have only been recorded since 2007. *See* FATF 2010, p. 61.

[36] Destatis, Series 10 on the administration of justice by the state's prosecution, volume 2.6, 2013, p. 96.

[37] According to this definition, organised crime is 'the planned violation of the law for profit or to acquire power, which offences are each, or together, of major significance, and are carried out by more than two participants who co-operate within a division of labour for a long or undetermined time span using (a) commercial or commercial-like structures, or (b) violence or other means of intimidation, or (c) influence on politics, media, public administration, justice and the legitimate economy', *see* Levi 1998, pp. 335, 336.

[38] BKA 2015, pp. 6, 7.

and indictments for the predicate offence. In addition, the weak range of punishments available for money laundering and the chances of suspended sentence being imposed, cause public prosecutors to decide to substitute the charge with one that is visited with a more stringent penalty.[39] Moreover, acts of money laundering would be prosecuted as participation in the predicate offence, in the event that the perpetrator is not the same person who commits the predicate offence. This is due to the fast that predicate offences are usually easier to prove and carry a higher punishment than the sanctions envisaged for money laundering.[40]

Another relevant index concerns criminal records of individuals convicted pursuant to Article 216 of the GCC. Assuming that pre-trial custody is ordered for quite dangerous offenders, one can infer that persons convicted of money laundering are less dangerous, given that only a small number (45) of them have been held in pre-trial custody, as provided for by Article 112 of the German Code of Criminal Procedure. Another factor highlighted by the *Destatis* statistics is whether convicted persons had been punished before, and if so, with which penalty. What is noticeable with regard to Article 261(1) of the GCC is that the number of persons with previous convictions is almost equal to those without previous convictions (109 without, and 105 with). A total of 41 out of the 105 with previous convictions had been convicted five or more times, but most of them (49) received monetary fines. For convictions under Article 261(5) of the GCC, though, only a minority was subject to previous convictions before (171 out of 497).[41] Given that habitual offenders might be considered more dangerous, it can be inferred that individuals convicted pursuant to Article 261(5) are not considered socially dangerous. The situation described from the point of view of law enforcement agencies seems negate the notion that money launderers constitute a threat to the security of society as a whole. Detected money launderers do not correspond, in fact, with the description of habitual offenders who pose a risk to the integrity of the social fabric.

As regards the penalties imposed, in the vast majority of cases, the sentence is a *Geldstrafe*, a monetary fine (about 81% of the total). This is not the case for sentences under Article 261(4) of the GCC, which, indeed, prescribes a higher punishment.[42] However, given the low-end range of penalties, the fact that the majority of sanctions imposed do not involve prison sentences and in view of the fact that the vast majority of sanctions involving prison sentences are suspended, the FATF assessors concluded in 2010 that Article 261(1) of the GCC is bereft of effective, proportionate and dissuasive sanctions.[43] In its 2014 follow-up report the FATF stated that German authorities responded to this criticism by underlining that the range of punishments of imprisonment (from 3 months to 5 years) is broader than the average period of imprisonment (up to 5 years or fine) for similar offences

[39] FATF 2010, p. 63.

[40] Ibid., p. 64.

[41] Destatis, Series 10 on the administration of justice, volume 3, 2013, pp. 1438–1439.

[42] Ibid., pp. 214–215.

[43] FATF 2010, p. 60.

such as 'fraud' (Article 263 of the GCC), 'theft' (Article 242 of the GCC), 'receiving stolen goods' (Article 259 of the GCC) and 'accessory after the fact' (Article 257 of the GCC). According to the authorities, the implementation of sanctions under Article 261 of the GCC is also higher than the average. While the portion of sentences imposed for money laundering and involving a term of imprisonment is 19.6% the average is 17.64%. However, the FATF assessors replied that the share of sentences involving a term of imprisonment of more than 1 year was lower than the average: 4% for money laundering against 9% the average share. Very few convictions concern attempts to commit the crime.[44] This may question the deterrent effect of the law and its capacity to prevent money laundering. However, the low number might be explained with reference to Article 1(1) second sentence of the Anti-Money Laundering Act, which states that specific transactions shall not be reported when the reporting hinders the prosecution of money laundering. A positive element is the fact that most convictions (387 out of 764) under Articles 261(1) and (5) concern crimes committed a year prior to the conviction. This may mean that the co-operation between the private sector and law enforcement agencies could ensure prompt suppression. However, this has not been the case for acts listed under paras 2 and 4, which happened prior to the previous year. An explanation for this difference may lie in the difficulty of tendering enough evidence to prove the commercial basis or the perpetration of the crime by a gang or the modes conduct of third persons listed under para 2.

Another relevant factor that can be inferred from the criminal justice system's statistics is the comparison between the number of preliminary investigations and the number of convictions. The 2013 statistics show that, for example, public prosecutors, including federal and state prosecutors, completed 24,624 investigations into money-laundering cases.[45] This number is high compared to the total number of money-laundering cases in which a sentence was handed down (935, according to the 2013 *Destatis* statistics). Between the years 2004 and 2008[46] a total of 45,462 preliminary investigations were conducted, but only 2006 charges were laid.[47] In fact, the vast majority of investigations into money laundering are either suspended or discontinued and new proceedings are initiated for the predicate offence.[48] These figures confirm the fact that, while the number of STRs filed with law enforcement authorities is very high, and therefore the cases dealt with by prosecutors, few of the suspicions are confirmed in the preliminary investigations. However, as previously noted, the statistics do not provide figures on all convictions for money laundering. What is more, from the viewpoint of the authorities

---

[44] Destatis, Series 10 on the administration of justice, volume 3, 2013, pp. 136, 137.

[45] Ibid., volume 2.6, 2013, p. 22.

[46] The figures for the period 2004–2007 refer to the entire area of the Federal Republic of Germany. However, the year 2004 does not include figures for Schleswig-Holstein.

[47] Figures derived from the Destatis, Series 10 on the administration of justice by the state's prosecution service, volume 2.6, 2005–2008.

[48] FATF 2010, p. 60.

these outcomes are not a sign of inefficiency. On the contrary, they are considered consistent with the aim of resolving cases. As already mentioned, money-laundering cases might have been finally charged for other offences. Therefore, according to the police, cases have been cleared, even without a conviction pursuant to Article 261 of the GCC. The clearance rate for money-laundering cases provided by the police is, indeed, very high.[49] However, one can also argue that Article 261 of the GCC seems to serve more the purpose of facilitating investigations than convicting criminals. On the one hand, it appears that Article 261 of the GCC helps investigators to initiate criminal proceedings and to collect information, thanks to the access to the records kept by reporting entities, as ordained by the Anti-Money Laundering Act. On the other hand, prosecutors substitute charges under with other charges, which attract higher penalties but a lower burden of proof. Article 261 may thus have a procedural rather than a substantive function. In the minority of the cases, when investigators discover enough evidence to proceed with an indictment and a trial for money laundering does take place, the percentage of acquittals is very low. Between 2004 and 2008, the percentage was not more than 6%.[50] This may be an indicator that the type of evidence acquired by the prosecutors is of high quality, meaning that the case often ends with a conviction.

With regard to the nationality of the convicted individuals, the majority of persons convicted under paras 1, 2 and 5 were German nationals, whereas 57% of those convicted for the aggravated conduct held foreign citizenship.

6.4 The Co-operation Between FIU and Law Enforcement Agencies

The FIU reports contain, in part, statistics on the typologies of money-laundering convictions.[51] However, the FIU can provide statistics only with regard to the proceedings about which they receive information from the prosecutors' offices, through the follow-up reports mechanism. In 2015, the FIU received 29,108 STRs and 17,749 follow-up reactions from public prosecutors (in 2014 they amounted to 15,789). Of the total follow-up responses, only 321 (in 2014 the number was 414) referred to judgments, penalty orders or indictments, which corresponds to nearly 2%.[52] The main outcome is, however, the number of dismissal orders received by the FIU among the total of follow-up responses. They amounted to 94% of the total

[49] In 2015, it amounted to 92.6% and in 2013 it amounted to 92.6%. *See* PKS 2015, p. 97.

[50] *See* Destatis, Series 10 on the administration of justice, volume 3, from 2004 to 2008.

[51] Figures are provided by FIU, 2002–2015 reports on Germany. Reports are available both in German and English languages, however, the reports quoted here are the English versions, whereas the 2014 report available at the time of writing is in German.

[52] FIU, 2013 Report, p. 11.

(in 2014 to 91%). From the point of view of public prosecutors, in 2013, out of 124,842 court trials that were carried to the end in the field of money laundering, tax crimes and economic crimes, 39,322 were terminated due to insufficient reasons to prosecute, pursuant to Article 170(2) German Code of Criminal Procedure, namely, one-third of the total.[53] According to the 2013 FIU Report, 'the large number of dismissals is an indication that the threshold of suspicion for filing a report is very low and the suspicion of an offence—compared to the large number of reports—can be verified in a few cases only'.[54] This conclusion reflects and confirms the doctrinal debate and *Oswald*'s research outcomes about the standard of proof required by the wording of Article 261 of the GCC. Although the wording of the offence may cover a very broad range of conducts, it is ultimately very hard to adduce the evidence required for the indictment to stand. At the same time, the number of follow-up reports sent by the office of public prosecutors offices also increased. Despite the increasing amounts of information collected, the percentage of dismissals rose, thus reversing what looked like a positive trend in co-operation between the reporting entities and the law enforcement agencies. In 2005, 77% of the follow-up reports resulted in dismissals, whereas in 2012 the percentage increased to 89%, and in 2013 to almost 91%. There has been only a slight increase in the number of judgments, penal orders or indictments deriving from STRs, for example, from 4.9% in 2007 to, 5.9% in 2012. As a preliminary conclusion, it can be said that STRs filed with law enforcement agencies did not result in a number of court decisions sufficient to justify the existence of the whole reporting apparatus. However, STRs filed to the FIU may trigger several convictions. Moreover, proceedings for money laundering might take long, with the result that a STR filed might result in a conviction only some years later. Convictions registered in the same year might depend on STRs filed the previous years. In addition, it should not be overlooked that STRs filed in Germany might trigger criminal proceedings in another country, thanks to the international co-operation among FIUs. Convictions in Germany can be likewise triggered by offence notices gathered abroad.

As already mentioned, the FIU reports provide partial information on criminal proceedings initiated by the filing of a STR. The 2015 FIU report shows that 2,690 STRs filed related to the so-called 'financial agents' phenomenon. This phenomenon is not new to the FIU, which is why the report refers to the 'so called financial agents' phenomenon', meaning money-laundering transactions performed by individuals recruited by criminals, who tempt clients interested in investment opportunities. According to the FIU, such facilitators might be recruited by using professional job offers. 'When designing such job offers, the perpetrators attempt to prevent critical analysis by the potential financial agents through numerous variations'.[55] The 'financial agents' phenomenon has been registered since 2006. Most

[53] Destatis, Series 10 on the administration of justice by the state's prosecution, volume 2.6, 2013, p. 96.

[54] FIU, 2013 Report, p. 26.

[55] Ibid., p. 29.

STRs have been filed in 2015 due to suspicions connected to cash transactions (around 54%). An emerging phenomenon registered by the FIU in 2015 are STRs linked to transactions made by asylum seekers (94). In addition, the FIU highlights that terrorist attacks in Europe might have led to the increase in the number of STRs filed connected to terrorist financing and political motivated transactions, which have doubled since last year.[56]

6.5 Typologies of STRs Filed to the FIU

Statistics provided by the FIU reports are also relevant for assessing how Article 261 of the GCC is applied in conjunction with the Anti-Money Laundering Act. The statistics show, for example, from where the STRs emanate and hence what the attitude of designated businesses and professions is towards preventive reporting procedures. Since 1995, there has been an increase in the number of STRs filed. Whereas 2,759 STRs were filed in 1995, in 2012 the number shot up to 14,361. The upward trend incline even more in 2013 when 19,095 STRs were filed, and by 2015, the number had rocketed to 24,045.[57] Most of the STRs were filed by credit institutions that, in 2013 and 2014, filed 87% of the total of STRs received. STRs coming from the non-financial sector comprised only a tiny fraction of the total, meaning approximately 1%. And this has been the trend since 2013. According to the FIU, the number of reports filed by the non-financial sector is too small compared to STRs coming from the large number of designated business and professions, which play a significant role in the economy. Persons engaged in commercial trade of goods filed only 116 STRs, and real estate agents filed only 34 STRs, despite the awareness-raising initiatives undertaken by the competent local supervisory authorities. There is an overwhelming number of STRs coming from credit institutions, including banks. The financial sector has never contributed less than 79.5% of the total STRs, according statistics dating from 2002.[58] Whereas credit institutions and banks cannot be said to be withholding their co-operation with the authorities in respect of filing STRs, the same cannot be said of attorneys, who have shown a reluctance to file STRs. Their STRs constitute only 29 of the total number of STRs filed. Between 2004 and 2015, for instance, a total of 155 lawyers filed STRs.[59]

The FIU report provides some information also on the nationalities of individuals and on headquarters of the company reported. Interestingly, a high number of Arab nationals, particularly from Lebanon, Iran, Pakistan and Afghanistan, were reported in 2002. This might have been induced by fears of terroristic attacks

---

[56] FIU, 2015 Report, p. 29.

[57] Data are provided by FIU, 2002–2015 reports.

[58] Data referred to the previous years are provided by the FIU, 2002–2015 Reports.

[59] Data are provided by the FIU, 2002–2015 Reports.

connected to the 9/11 attacks. Another interesting piece of information mentioned in the 2013 FIU Report with regard to the typology of involved individuals, is that 101 STRs involved fraud perpetrated on senior citizens. Most of the indices showing senior citizens as victims of money launderers have been included in recent FIU reports. However, the FIU assumes that there remains a high incidence of unreported and unrecorded crime perpetrated on the elderly. For this reason, the reports do not state exactly what *modi operandi* resort to in perpetrating their fraudulent acts. Instead, the reports show that between 2004 and 2005a high number of low-income individuals were reported. They include students, pensioners, the unemployed and housewives who, together, constituted 19% of the people reported in 2005 and 17% in 2004. However, no explanations were provided for this trend.

A total of 5,867 (5,7679 in 2014) companies were subjects of STRs in 2015 and in almost half of the cases their respective headquarters were mentioned. Around 70% of the companies whose headquarters were mentioned were based in Germany), 118 (136 in 2014) in the UK, 83 (195 in 2014) in Cyprus, 77 (81 in 2014) in Switzerland, and 66 (75 in 2013) in the British Virgin Islands.[60] During the period under focus, the companies that were the subject of STRs were mostly headquartered in Germany. Only in 2009 were the headquarters of the majority of the companies abroad. The most recurrent headquarters have been the United Kingdom, Cyprus, Switzerland, Russia and the Virgin Islands. These figures could be interpreted as a symptom of the fact that it is easier to launder money through tax havens and offshore centres, such as the British Virgin Islands or Cyprus, or through jurisdictions with strong bank secrecy laws, such as Switzerland, or through countries with lax company laws—listed by the tax justice network as a secrecy jurisdictions—such as the UK.[61]

6.6 Critical Issues

The FATF considered the volume of transactions reported too low for an economy with a highly developed financial services sector, which ensures near-universal access to such services for its resident population.[62] In addition, only a few cases compared to the high number of STRs filed lead to an indictment, judicial verdict or a sentence. The percentage of such cases shows a decline over the years, with most cases being dismissed for lack of sufficient evidence to commence a criminal trial.[63]In addition, reports are filed mostly from one type of designated businesses and professions, namely, banks and financial services providers. The majority of

[60] FIU, 2015 Report, p. 13; FIU, 2014 Report, p. 15.

[61] Tax Justice Network 2015.

[62] FATF 2010, p. 170.

[63] FIU, 2013 Report, p. 46.

suspicions relate to one category of activity, namely, 'phishing' and the use of financial agents. According to the 2013 FIU Report, in 211 cases contracting parties did not disclose the fact that they were acting on behalf of beneficial owners.[64] In fact, there was suspicion that the contracting parties had not complied with their disclosure obligations when arranging a business relationship or a transaction. This issue cropped up already in 2012, but the number of cases more than doubled in 2013. Another noted grey area is considered the groups of the legal advisors and of the persons trading in goods. Here the suspicion of a large number of unreported or unrecorded cases arises because of the very small volume of STRs filed by such categories. According to the FIU, the non-financial sector is 'definitely in a position to recognise and report money-laundering activities'. Therefore, the lack of specific know-how or expertise of these groups would not be an excuse.[65] The high potential of these groups being used for money-laundering purposes on the one hand and the very low reporting rate on the other hand, are considered one of the two main challenges faced by the FIU in the prevention of money laundering. The BKA published a report in 2012 on the real estate sector and its role in (preventing) money laundering.[66] The necessity of compiling such a report was triggered by the assumption that the real estate sector was not much aware of the money-laundering risks in its field of operation and did not show much interest in complying with the Anti-Money Laundering Act regulations. in contrast to the volume of real estate transactions in 2011, which amounted to 22 billion euros, only 292 STRs were filed with the FIU by this sector, which represented a mere 2.6% of the total of the STRs filed. These figures justified the inference that there was a huge grey number of unreported money-laundering transactions, which was attributable to the low level of awareness throughout the sector. This assumption was confirmed by the outcomes of the research conducted by the BKA. In fact, only 94 out of 2,410 of those replied to the questionnaire in full, meaning 3.9% of the total.[67] Respondents had different perceptions about the threats posed by money laundering and the role of the Anti-Money Laundering Act. The general perception was that there was a lack of knowledge and of awareness about the issue and the related anti-money laundering policies. Most of the respondents did not recognise the specific risk existing in the real estate sector. In addition, the predicate crimes were often confused with the offence of money laundering, and the latter was mostly identified with cash transactions. A general prejudice against the category of real estate agents was registered by the questionnaires, while, according to the FIU, also other categories were used for the purpose of money-laundering operations. On the contrary, according to the FATF report of 2010, real estate agents were generally considered to be unlikely involved in suspicious transactions, since they do not accept client payments and because notaries and banks would be involved in any

[64] Ibid., p. 31.

[65] Ibid., p. 33.

[66] BKA 2012.

[67] Ibid., p. 4.

transaction. For this reason they would not be expected to perform regular due diligence on their clients.[68] As regards the content of the regulations, the FATF report pointed to the lack of co-operation, with law enforcement agencies not sending follow-up reports on the STRs filed. The FATF report strongly recommended that the legislature introduce the principle of reversal of the burden of proof, which means it should impose a duty on the suspect to show evidence of the legitimate source of assets which are strongly suspected to be of unlawful origin. It was furthermore suggested that a central register on real estate properties be introduced in order to facilitate the exchange of information and to increase transparency in the sector. Finally, the questionnaires highlighted the necessity of adapting the Anti-Money Laundering Act regulations to the peculiarities of the real estate sector. According to the FATF report, real estate agents were aware that they had to abide by the Anti-Money Laundering Act regulations, but they did do not appear to be taking systematic steps to do so. This was due both to the fact that the requirements did not fit within their customary business practices and to the fact that supervisory arrangements to promote compliance were underdeveloped.[69] From the FATF assessors' point of view, it was especially real estate agents who fell short of complying with the FATF standards.[70]

6.7 The Volume of the Phenomenon of Money Laundering in Germany: Economic Estimates

The most useful indicator to evaluate the effectiveness of the anti-money laundering policy to obstruct the infiltration of illicit financial flows into the German economy would be the volume of such flows. Although the volume of illicit assets may show how effective or ineffective the law is, it would reveal at least whether or not the efforts invested have been worth the burden they impose. Unfortunately, as at present, no statistics on this phenomenon are available, but only estimates by different international organisations. According to the 2010 FATF Report, proceeds of crime generated in the country are estimated to be between 43 and 57 billion euros, inclusive of tax evasion which is annually equivalent to between 1.2 and 1.6% of the annual national GDP. Given that Germany's GDP is one of the highest in the world from the percentages mentioned can easily be deduced that the value of assets involved exceeds the GDP of numerous countries and that it constitutes a huge part of the global illicit financial flows. However, the German authorities could not confirm these estimates.[71] According to the International Narcotics Control Strategy Report of 2009 of the US Government, Germany is a major

[68] FATF 2010, p. 213.
[69] Ibid., p. 221.
[70] Ibid., p. 213.
[71] Ibid., p. 24.

money-laundering country.[72] Figures provided by the Federal Criminal Police Office are significantly lower. The 2007 Situation Report on Economic Crime in the Federal Republic of Germany, for example, reported that the total loss or damage to the economy resulting was approximately 4.12 billion euros. The same office publishes reports regularly on organised crime activities in Germany, and according to the 2008 report, the profits of organised crime amounted to 0.66 billion euros. According to the FATF assessors, these figures seem relatively low. They concluded that this might be because such statistics do not address the amount of proceeds generated from evasion of taxes and excise duties.[73] As claimed by a very recent report on organised crime in Europe, the magnitude of criminal revenues from a selected number of illicit markets[74] amount, at least, to approximately 110 billion euros per year. The approximation corresponds on average to 0.9% of the GDP of European countries in 2010.[75] As for Germany, the amount of criminal revenue that could potentially be laundered is estimated to be approximately 17 billion euros, which, in turn, corresponds to 0.7% of the national GDP.[76] A study commissioned by the European Commission in 2013 estimated the revenue laundered in Germany amounted to 29,381 million euros, which is equivalent to 1.27% of the total GDP.[77] A dark-area study on money-laundering activities in the non-financial sector in Germany estimated the volume of dark area STRs to be between 20 and 30 billion euros in that sector. The study concludes that the amount of money laundered in the non-financial sector can be estimated to be 50 billion euros and thus the whole volume of money laundering in the country could reach even 100 billion euros.[78]

---

[72] A U.S. statute defines a major money-laundering country as one 'whose financial institutions engage in currency transactions involving significant amounts of proceeds from international narcotics trafficking.' However, the complex nature of money-laundering transactions nowadays makes it difficult in many cases to distinguish the proceeds of narcotics trafficking from the proceeds of other serious crime. Moreover, financial institutions that engage in transactions involving significant amounts of proceeds of other serious crime are vulnerable to narcotics-related money laundering. *See* Bureau for International Narcotics and Law Enforcement Affairs 2009.

[73] FATF 2010, p. 22.

[74] The selected illicit markets deal in the following: heroin, cocaine, cannabis, ecstasy, amphetamines, illicit trade in tobacco products, counterfeiting, missing trader intra-community fraud and cargo theft. The overall figures on illicit revenues may be very conservative. Some important illicit markets, such as trafficking in human beings, both for sexual and labour exploitation purposes, or extortion, illegal gambling and other types of fraud different from missing trader intra-community fraud, lack estimates for most of the 28 EU member states, and thus are not included in this calculation, *see* Savona and Riccardi 2015, p. 35.

[75] Savona and Riccardi 2015, p. 35.

[76] The estimates include the following illicit markets: heroin, cocaine, cannabis, amphetamines, ecstasy, illicit trade in tobacco products, counterfeiting, missing trader intra-community frauds, and organised cargo theft. *See* Savona and Riccardi 2015, pp. 36, 160.

[77] Unger et al. 2013, p. 39.

[78] See Bussman 2015. See also a critical text on the outcomes of this study: Schneider 2016.

Against background of estimates on the volume of money laundered in Germany, it bears noting that recent statistics do not show the exact value of the assets confiscated, nor are there any exact figures on the amounts of assets seized and confiscated in respect of each of the offences listed. The FIU estimates that for the offence of money laundering a net value of approximately 21 million euros was seized in 2014. The figure is arrived at by subtracting the volume of cancellation of seizure from the total seizure of cash, movable property, claims, titles, and immovable property seized in the context of proceedings resulting directly or indirectly from information obtained by the law enforcement authorities through suspicious transaction reports pursuant to the Anti-Money Laundering Act[79] As reported by the FATF in 2010, the total volume of assets forfeited or confiscated in 2007 in relation to Article 261 of the GCC amounted to 15,074,378 €, in 2004 to 23,710,160 €, in 2003 to 65,453,313 € and in 2002 to 32,948,160 €.[80] There is no information that permits an interpretation of the fluctuating trend. The BKA, too, gives only estimates of the volume of the proceeds of crime and the value of the assets seized and confiscated in Germany. The total amount of loss deriving from organised crime in 2015 was estimated by the BKA at 539 million euros, and the proceeds of crime generated and proved amounted to 230 million euros. Assets were provisionally forfeited in 24.2% of the ongoing cases, representing a total amount of temporarily forfeited assets of 65 million euros.[81]

6.8 Cost-Benefit Analyses

The effectiveness of the anti-money laundering policy has been assessed through cost-benefits analyses. The results of two of these analyses are presented here in summary.[82] The research institute 'Transcrime'[83] conducted a quantitative research on the costs and benefits of the disclosure system of beneficial owners (BOs) in the context of the prevention of money laundering.[84] The beneficial ownership

[79] FIU 2013, p. 22.

[80] FATF 2010, p. 82.

[81] BKA 2015, p. 6.

[82] The European Parliament commissioned a study on the impact of organised crime in Europe. However, money laundering was excluded, despite the fact that it was considered an important enabler, because its costs would have doubled the costs already counted for the predicate crimes, since it was assumed that the offence of money laundering itself did not generate costs for victims. Statistics on the costs of organised crime in Europe are measured on the basis of the financial and welfare impact organised crime has on European victims and on Europeans who are indirect victims. The costs are not measured based on the benefits that accrue to criminal offenders in Europe, nor do costs entail the value of the assets realised in consequence of the confiscation of criminal assets. Levi et al. 2013, pp. 15, 20.

[83] Transcrime is a Joint Research Centre on Transnational Crime, Università di Trento/Università Cattolica del Sacro Cuore di Milano (Italy).

[84] Savona et al. 2007, pp. 13, 153.

disclosure is the process of revealing externally information about a company's beneficial owner. The process implies collecting, verifying, analysing and elaborating this information and then communicating it. The aim of the study was to compare two beneficial ownership disclosure systems in terms of the costs and benefits that may arise from their implementation in the 27 EU countries. The outcome of both types of measuring methods utilised for assessing the cost-benefit effectiveness of the German system of BOs disclosure was negative. However, in both cases the indirect net benefits were positive.[85] From this, the inference may be drawn that the system has significant effects in the long term rather than in the short term. However, since it is a cost-intense process, long-term effects might not convince policy makers of the utility of the system.

In 2014, a European study, the Ecolef study,[86] on the economic and legal effectiveness of the European anti-money laundering policy in the Member States aimed at evaluating the effectiveness of the anti-money laundering regimes by comparing the implementation of policies with the purpose of identifying best practices.[87] The authors explained as follows why such an assessment was particularly needed at the time, after two Conventions and three Directives had already been enacted: 'Many actors have been involved, many efforts have been made and much money has been invested in this policy area. It seems time to stand still for a moment and to investigate whether all these efforts achieved their intended goals. And has the investment in police, public prosecution, reporting system and supervision had a positive impact on combating laundering and terrorist financing?'[88] For the purpose of the Ecolef study, the effectiveness is measured by means of different legal and economic factors, such as the level of international co-operation, the number of STRs filed, the incidence of prosecutions and convictions, the structure and the definition of the anti-money laundering policy, and the authorities involved.[89] The particular policy to achieve is economic effectiveness, by which is meant the reduction and prevention of money laundering or of crime in general. Legal effectiveness, in comparison, is measured by looking to see

---

[85] *See* Savona et al. 2007, p. 13.

[86] *See* Unger et al. 2013.

[87] One consideration needs to be made on the premises of the ECOLEF project. In order to assess the threat of money laundering, the authors have assumed that 'money launderers are economic actors, and [...] they follow the law of economics, which dictates that they should maximise profits and minimise risks'. This has been shown not to hold true for the Italian Mafia. For example, mafia bosses may decide to invest and launder their money in a low-profit business to establish their hegemony over a territory. Also, were it the case that maximisation of profits and the reducing of risks were the prime aim of money launderers, there would be much less drug-related criminality, given the high incidence of imprisonment that attends those who are involved in this field. This would lower the economic gain resulting from the crime. Unger et al. 2013, p. 12.

[88] Unger et al. 2014, p. vii.

[89] The study starts from a money-laundering threat-analysis and carries on by looking at the legal implementation of the policies, at the execution of such policies, at the enforcement and international co-operation, and it ends with a final evaluation of the effectiveness, which is the result of a cost-benefit analysis. Unger et al. 2014, p. 2.

whether the norms for achieving the policy goal make sense and whether they are obeyed and applied. Furthermore, with legal effectiveness, the authors of the study meant to establish whether there are legal hindrances, such as horizontal or vertical conflicts between norms or loopholes, or other factors, such as insufficient resources or awareness, that negatively influence the application of the law.[90] Ecolef is the result of a combination of technical assessments, carried out using quantitative data, and of a qualitative evaluation of the 'law in action', conducted through interviews in the Member States. As far as Germany in concerned, quantitative data are sourced mainly from the FIU annual reports and the FATF Mutual Evaluation Report of 2010. The European research is based on the assumption that the (in)-effectiveness of a policy depends on how it is implemented and it assumes that the policy's goal is the reduction or prevention of money laundering or other crimes, without contemplating eventual latent or symbolic functions of the law. The Ecolef study takes a neutral approach, directed at evaluating objectively the implementation of policies through a cost-benefit analysis. With specific regard to the assessment of the effectiveness of criminal law, this book takes the view that a criminal justice system is effective if punishment is visited on deviant criminal behaviour for the sake of deterring future deviance.[91] The results of the European study that are pertinent to this research are summarised below. According to the Ecolef report, Germany scored lowest when it came to estimating the threat posed to the national economy by money laundering. Expressed as a percentage of GDP, in 2009 the threat to Germany was 4.7%, whereas for Estonia the estimation was 207, 7%.[92] The study score countries on their suppression ability, based on the assumptions that effective suppression ensures sufficiently high and frequent sanctioning.[93] The suggested equation is calculated using of the incidence detected deviance in relation to the incidence. If the expected punishment is higher than the benefits yielded by the commission of money laundering, the assumption is that people will probably not commit the crime. Based on this calculation, Germany has a medium-high score of effective repression. The economic and legal effectiveness is calculated based on some indicators, which are identified in the FATF compliance score, the legal effectiveness of preventing money laundering, the third EU money-laundering implementation timelines, the international co-operation score,

[90] Unger et al. 2014, p. 6.

[91] Ibid., p. 125. The European study differs from the present study in the approach it takes. This study measures the effectiveness of a criminal justice system by the limited utilisation of criminal law, having regard to the principles of proportionality and subsidiarity. In addition, this book takes account of the possibility that ineffective criminalisation creates de facto impunity and that this 'process of decriminalisation' might have been a latent intent or at least an acceptable consequence. Furthermore, this book postulates that a high rate of conviction might not be a symptom of effectiveness. The fact that an increase in the rate of convictions may be attributed to an increase in the incidence of money laundering and not to the effectiveness of the criminal justice system is discussed elsewhere in this book. *See* Unger et al. 2014, p. 170.

[92] See Unger et al. 2013.

[93] Unger et al. 2014, p. 140.

the information flow score, the number of money-laundering convictions and the FIU policy response.[94] According to these indicators, the German policy scores a standard level of effectiveness compared to the other Member States, without being considered under-proportional for any of the elements.[95] The cost-benefit analysis is based on factors identified as costs of the policy and benefits of the policy response. The analysis is calculated based on which costs a hypothetical country that has standard scores among the EU Member States would save without a money-laundering policy in action, and what benefits it would lose consequently.[96] The total costs of anti-money laundering policy for the EU have been estimated at two billion euros, with an undetermined reduction of privacy and social inefficiency.[97] Unfortunately, it has been possible 'to estimate most of the costs, but hardly any of the benefits'.[98] However, the study produced an estimate of the costs and of benefits for every country: Germany scored higher, with 378,177,540 € of estimated costs and 4,063254 € in estimated benefits.[99] It concludes that 'the cost-benefit dilemma for AML [Anti-Money Laundering] policy is reduced to the question: are we willing to spend almost 44 million euros, with a reduction in privacy and efficiency costs for unknown benefits?'[100] The question could be answered with another question, namely: Are we willing to give up on the fight against money laundering? *Whitehouse* has answered this dilemma by stating that 'it would be a brave person who steps up to say that it is too high price to pay for countering terrorism and serious crime'.[101] The securitisation rhetoric has so far supported the extreme importance of such measures, and anti-money laundering policy has been growing. Nevertheless, the question could be inverted: Do we really want to fight money laundering and, by doing so, are we willing to threaten the financial system, as we know it today? A certain amount of illicit financial flows may be considered an acceptable price to pay for a market where free mobility of capital is guaranteed.

---

[94] The indicators are explained in Unger et al. 2014, pp. 188–199.

[95] Results are shown by means of a table, *see* Unger et al. 2014, pp. 202–203.

[96] Costs are considered on-going policymaking, sanction costs, FIU, supervision, law enforcement and court trials, duties of the private sector, reduction in privacy, efficiency costs for society and the financial system. Benefits components taken into consideration are fines, confiscated proceeds, reduction for money-laundering and predicate offences, reduction in the damages to the real economy and the risks to the financial sector. Unger et al. 2014; p. 207.

[97] Unger et al. 2014, p. 235.

[98] Ibid., p. 218.

[99] Ibid., p. 220.

[100] Ibid., p. 218.

[101] Whitehouse 2003, p. 140.

6.9 Considerations

The results exposed in the previous paragraphs about the effects of the implementation of the anti-money laundering policy are summarised here for subsequent discussion. The eight hypotheses set by Oswald in 1997 are compared to the outcomes emerging from the present empirical study.

(1) The hypothesised relevance of nationality or social class of the persons, whose transactions are reported as suspicious, has been partly confirmed by the recent FIU reports. 57% of those convicted for the aggravated money laundering have been non-German nationals. In Berlin, for instance, a study has revealed that refugees are often turned down when they wish to open a bank account because they have no identification documents, which translates into discriminatory access to financial services based on nationality.[102] In addition, the FIU draws attention on asylum seekers reported in 2015 and on the high number of low income individuals reported, namely, students, pensioners, the jobless and housewives, who in sum constituted a 19% of the population for the reported year 2005 and 17% in 2004. However, no reasons were given for this trend.
(2) The most recent situation described by the FIU reports has confirmed the high number of STRs filed with the FIU, yet the FATF assessors claimed that the number was not sufficient when compared to the volume of the national economic sector.[103]
(3) According to two cost-benefit analyses conducted recently by a private researcher, the costs of implementation of the current anti-money laundering policy, and in particular of the mechanisms used to disclose beneficial ownerships, were too high when measured against the estimated benefits.[104] The introduction of a national register could therefore represent a solution to lower private sectors costs of compliance.
(4) Prosecutors interviewed by the FATF assessors in Germany in 2010 explained that in practice, while it may not be a statutory requirement, it is easier to prosecute and convict a person for money-laundering under Article 261 of the GCC when there is a prior conviction for the predicate offence, as prosecutors always need to establish a 'link' or 'connection' between the money-laundering conduct and the predicate offence involved (i.e. the court must be convinced of the existence of the predicate offence). This means that the prosecutor will have to prove the specifics of the predicate offence, for example, that the conduct amounted to a designated offence, the perpetrator, and the types of assets that

[102] *See*, for example a study conducted in Berlin by an NGO: Antidiskriminierungsberatung Brandenburg 2013. Killias and Nunes conducted similar research that led to parallel conclusions in Switzerland. The authors repudiate the notion that anti-money-laundering regulations led to the discrimination of foreign citizens because they are not allowed to open bank accounts; *see* Killias and Nunes 2012.

[103] FATF 2010, p. 170.

[104] For more details on the cost-benefit assessments, *see* Sect. 4.9.

originated from the predicate offence, which is a rather high standard of proof.'[105] In practice, therefore, a reply has been given to the question regarding the standard of proof required to start a money-laundering case. Interviews conducted by the FATF assessors in 2010 have confirmed that proceedings are closed because of the impossibility of bringing concrete evidence of the commission of a predicate offence. Therefore, the standard of proof is one of the main obstacles for obtaining a conviction under 261 of the GCC in Germany.[106]

(5) *Oswald* hypothesised that Article 11(1) of the Anti-Money Laundering Act, which allowed suspicious transactions to be completed in order not to hinder the pursuing of beneficiaries of a money-laundering operation, would have opened a legal loophole. However, the present empirical study has not verified *Oswald*'s hypothesis.

(6) Until now, regulations for the designated financial and non-financial businesses and professions have increased and have become even more complicated from the time of *Oswald*'s study. However, one should not overlook the fact that some categories of designated businesses and professions are still reluctant to comply with anti-money laundering standards, because of their complexity and the costs of giving effect to them.

(7) In the meantime, a FIU has been established firstly at the Federal Criminal Police Office, and recently moved to the Customs. This receives all STRs and forwards them to the competent law enforcement units for investigations. The system of filing suspected transactions has thus been regulated and is no longer as chaotic as it was in the mid-1990s. The FIU reports show that a high number of follow-up reports are now filed with the FIU with information on the proceedings initiated based on STRs. The centralised system created in 2002 has indeed notably increased the communication between the two parties. This development seems to represent a solution to *Oswald*'s point, which criticised the lack of coordination with regard to filing and receiving STRs. However, the FIU in its 2013 annual report regretted the fact that the offices of public prosecutors provide very little information about the cases sent to them.[107]

(8) Difficulties deriving from international cooperation still represent an obstacle for money-laundering investigations. Despite the existing legal framework for international co-operation and the possibilities of requesting and providing mutual legal assistance, the complexity of financial operations, the involvement of offshore jurisdictions and the demolition of borders within the EU have not alleviated the difficulties encountered in co-operating in the fight against money laundering. This problem was confirmed by the answers to questions put to interviewees, which is the subject of the next part. In a globalised economy, as long as some jurisdictions do not commit themselves—or if so, only

[105] FATF 2010, p. 50.

[106] Ibid.

[107] *See* FIU, 2013 report, p. 46.

symbolically—to impeding the laundering of proceeds of crime, the effectiveness of other compliant legal systems will be frustrated. This is exemplified by the fact that, as stated in the FIU reports for the years between 2002 and 2015, the most frequent headquarters of companies reported have been tax havens or lax or secrecy jurisdictions. However, it would be simplistic to blame everything on the lack of international co-operation.

One of the most striking observations is that organised crime and 'gross money laundering' are not prosecuted by way of Article 261 of GCC. This fact can be inferred from the small number of convictions pursuant to Article 261(4), by the scarcity of money-laundering proceedings categorised as organised crime and by the rare investigations into money laundering, tax crimes and economic crimes recorded by public prosecutors offices in 2013, where more than one person was involved (18%). Yet, this does not mean that the criminal justice system does not act against them, but rather that it uses other tools to achieve the goal. While the low conviction rate for serious money-laundering cases could be also a symptom of a the legal provision's high deterrent capacity, it appears that law enforcement agencies use the money-laundering charge as a fall-back for authorities who are unable to gather sufficient evidence of the commission of a predicate crime and where other information is not accessible. The charge of money laundering allows investigators to access the vast amount of information recorded pursuant to the Anti-Money Laundering Act, which would not be otherwise accessible. Yet, after the investigative phase, prosecutors seem to prefer to modify the charge and opt instead to charge the suspect with a predicate offence. The law seems to be effective to the extent that it facilitates the initial investigations, while it does not serve directly the function of punishing money launderers. Besides being substantive in nature, the legal provisions seem like they serve procedural ends. This necessitates the inference that prosecutors are hard to put adducing evidence in money-laundering cases involving organised crime. The fact of the matter is that professional offenders do not leave traces, as already highlighted by *Oswald*'s findings. In view of the rare use of Article 261 of the GCC for tackling organised crime, one cannot escape the impression that the measure is not serving the purpose for which it was enacted. It could be assumed that other measures may well be more suitable for dealing with 'gross money laundering'. As early as 1997, *Oswald* positively considered the introduction of anti-money laundering to be a positive development. She acknowledged the positive effects triggered by the information provided by the designated business and professions to law enforcement agencies for conducting financial investigations.

Given the high number of STRs filed and the low number of money-laundering charges and of convictions deriving from the STRs since the introduction of the laws, it can be assumed that the system has nevertheless been maintained because it still provides some sort of benefits. Presumably, a benefit is seen for information placed at the disposal of the investigating authorities which for other causes in terms of Article 11(6) Anti-Money Laundering Act, even where the case is dismissed. The information obtained is helpful, not only to support further indictments, but also to enhance awareness among personnel about the ever-changing money-laundering techniques and schemes. Therefore, the law is used, as already revealed by the prosecutors interviewed by *Oswald*, to gather information rather than to confiscate criminal assets. Again, the effect of the 'law in action' differs in this respect to the declared intentions of the legislature, which justified the criminalisation of money laundering with the need to combat the economic power wielded by organised crime. By spelling out this purpose, the assessment on the effectiveness of the law, as a possible means of gathering information, can be positive. Yet, this effect could be considered a social cost rather than a benefit. On a theoretical side, many scholars see the recording of personal information by private actors as an infringement of the right to privacy.[108] On a more practical level, such a procedure involves considerable costs that have to be incurred by designated businesses and professions that are charged with collecting information.[109] When compared to the effective outcomes of the preventive regulations, seen in terms of the results of criminal investigations, the costs outweigh the benefits, as was shown in the studies cited. If one considers the advantages in terms of information collected, the policy may be considered worth the burden imposed. However, the fact that the laws would, in the long run, be effective in the fight against money laundering and organised crime may impart to them the attribute of having a diminished deterrent effect, because perpetrators would have the time to adapt to the new laws and find new ways of circumventing them. A side effect of the long-run effectiveness of the policy, theorised based on the outcomes of the research on the implementation, is the fact that perpetrators could take advantage of cases that have been initiated but not yet finalised, by acquainting themselves with the strategies used by law enforcement agencies and thus devising ways to elude them. On the contrary, it seems that the legislature is perpetually at pains to cope ever-changing schemes conceived by money launderers. In fact, specific new sectors are regulated whenever there is a risk that they may fall prey to money laundering. But by the time the regulations are in place, the money launderers might have already moved their laundering activities to another sector. This hypothesis will be further debated in the last part.

On the assumption that the inclusion of the reckless conduct would have the potential effect of making people incur criminal liability for ordinary, day-to-day activities, it was necessary to look at the number of convictions related to Article 261(5) to verify whom, in fact, was targeted by this provision of the GCC. Since the year 2005, a high number of convictions have been based on behaviour that was considered to amount to reckless money laundering. This shows that the offence is used to punish primarily 'petty money laundering'. This circumstance fact can also be inferred from the significant number of money-laundering cases that victimise senior citizens, as recent FIU reports have indicated. Also, the fact that a significant

[108] *See*, among others, the essay of Hassemer and Starzacher, who argue that data protection should be considered a fundamental right. Hassemer and Starzacher 1993, pp. 16 ss.

[109] The study puts the costs of the policy at 44 million euros. *See* Unger et al. 2014, p. 218.

number of STRs are filed in relation to the 'financial agents' phenomenon is a symptom that the preventive mechanism targets more the small fry rather than chiefs. Individuals convicted for reckless conduct may be even victims of a fraud perpetrated by criminal networks. However, the criminal network acting behind the offender remains undetected. The money-laundering offence was initially introduced to combat serious crimes. The observed effect, however, changes the function and the nature of the law, such that Article 261 of the GCC could be considered more of a blue-collar than a white-collar crime.

The spill over effect of preventive regulations has been confirmed by the FIU as well. An inference may be drawn from an analysis of the reports published from 2002 to 2015 with regard to the quality of STRs filed to the FIU, that certain designated professions and businesses are very reluctant to file STRs, even though they are markedly exposed to the risk of being used as conduits for money laundering. The list of designated professions and businesses has been expanded over the years, precisely because the crime of money laundering relocates itself from one are to another. Yet some professionals, such as lawyers, do not report suspicious schemes, despite their ability of their ability to spot unlawful conduct intuitively. The fact that some sectors make no effort to prevent money laundering, but instead let the proceeds of crime creep into the lawful economy, undermines the value of the anti-money laundering policy.

This part supports only partly the underlying hypotheses of a symbolic effectiveness and of an intended ineffectiveness of the money-laundering offence. In fact, it has shown that the law has the instrumental effect of punishing offenders and triggering co-operation between obligated entities and law enforcement agencies in the red flagging of suspicious transactions. However, some of the effects do not appear to meet what the legislature declared to be its goals. For example, the legislature has fallen short of its expectation that the law would collar the grey area and punish gatekeepers. Equally, the legislature fell short liquidating its main target, namely, serious and organised crime. Given the huge expenses incurred in implementing the law, as was brought to light in the cost-benefits analyses, the rather inconsequential outcomes hardly meet the legislature's expectations of what the law would accomplish in practice. Given that, without its harbouring latent purposes, it would be impossible to justify why a law was enacted and is still maintained,[110] it reasonable to conclude that the declared intentions of the lawmakers do not justify the reasons why Article 261 was introduced into the GCC. This gives good reason for postulating the hypothesis that Article 261 of the GCC is an example of symbolic legislation that has been passed as a compromise to appease impassioned parliamentary debate.

[110] Merton 1983, p. 201.

References

Andreas P (2015) Illicit Globalisation Myths and Misconceptions. In: Mitsilegas V et al. (eds.) Globalisation, Criminal Law and Criminal Justice: Theoretical, Comparative and Transnational Perspectives. Hart, Oxford.

Antidiskriminierungsberatung Brandenburg (2013) Geldinstitute verweigern Flüchtlingen die Eröffnung von Bankkonten. http://www.antidiskriminierungsberatung-brandenburg.de/sites/default/files/attachements/Hintergrundpapier%20Banken%20verweigern%20Konten_ADB%202013_1.pdf. Last accessed on 16 September 2016.

Aubert V (1974) The social functions of law. Archiv für Rechts- und Sozialphilosophie 8: 85–97.

BKA (2012) Managementfassung zur Fachstudie „Geldwäsche im Immobiliensektor in Deutschland". https://www.bka.de/SharedDocs/Downloads/DE/UnsereAufgaben/Deliktsbereiche/GeldwaescheFIU/fiuFachstudieGeldwaescheImmobiliensektor.html. Last accessed on 16 September 2016.

BKA (2015) Bundeslagebild Organisierte Kriminalität 2013. https://www.bka.de/SharedDocs/Downloads/DE/Publikationen/JahresberichteUndLagebilder/OrganisierteKriminalitaet/organisierteKriminalitaetBundeslagebild2015.html?nn=2798. Last accessed on 16 September 2016.

Bureau for International Narcotics and Law Enforcement Affairs (2009) Major Money Laundering Countries. http://www.state.gov/j/inl/rls/nrcrpt/2009/vol2/116550.htm. Last accessed on 16 September 2016.

Bussman K (2015) Dark figure study on the prevalence of money laundering in Germany and the risks of money laundering in individual economic sectors. http://wcms.itz.uni-halle.de/download.php?down=41244&elem=2937177. Last accessed on 16 September 2016.

Destatis (2002–2013) Rechtspflege Strafverfolgung (10) 3. https://www.destatis.de/DE/Publikationen/Thematisch/Rechtspflege/AlteAusgaben/StrafverfolgungAlt.html. Last accessed on 16 September 2016.

Destatis (2005–2008) Rechtspflege Staatsanwaltschaften. https://www.destatis.de/DE/Publikationen/Thematisch/Rechtspflege/AlteAusgaben/StaatsanwaltschaftenAlt.html. Last accessed on 16 September 2016.

Destatis (2013) Rechtspflege Strafverfolgung (10) 3. https://www.destatis.de/DE/Publikationen/Thematisch/Rechtspflege/StrafverfolgungVollzug/Strafverfolgung2100300137004.pdf?__blob=publicationFile. Last accessed on 16 September 2016.

Destatis (2013) Rechtspflege Staatsanwaltschaften (2) 6. https://www.destatis.de/DE/Publikationen/Thematisch/Rechtspflege/GerichtePersonal/Staatsanwaltschaften2100260147004.pdf?__blob=publicationFile. Last accessed on 16 September 2016.

FATF (2010) Mutual Evaluation Report of Germany. http://www.fatf-gafi.org/media/fatf/documents/reports/mer/MER%20Germany%20full.pdf. Last accessed on 16 September 2016.

FATF (2013) Methodology for assessing technical compliance with the FATF Recommendations and the effectiveness of AML/CFT systems. http://www.fatf-gafi.org/media/fatf/documents/methodology/FATF%20Methodology%2022%20Feb%202013.pdf. Last accessed on 16 September 2016.

FATF (2014) 3rd Follow-up Report of Germany. http://www.fatf-gafi.org/media/fatf/documents/reports/mer/FUR-Germany-2014.pdf. Last accessed on 16 September 2016.

Ferwerda J (2009) The Economics of Crime and Money Laundering: Does Anti-Money Laundering Reduce Crime? Review of Law and Economics 5: 903–929.

FIU (2002) Annual Report Germany. https://www.bka.de/SharedDocs/Downloads/EN/Publications/AnnualReportsAndSituationAssessments/FIU/fiuJahresbericht2002Englisch.html?nn=39788. Last accessed on 16 September 2016.

FIU (2002–2014) Annual Reports Germany. https://www.bka.de/EN/CurrentInformation/SituationAssessments/FinancialIntelligenceUnitGermany/financialintelligenceunitgermany_node.html. Last accessed on 16 September 2016.

Geiger H and Wuensch O (2007) The fight against money laundering: An economic analysis of a cost-benefit paradox. Journal of Money Laundering Control 10 (1): 91–106.

Global Witness (2012) How can FATF measure and promote an effective anti-money laundering system. https://www.globalwitness.org/sites/default/files/library/How%20FATF%20can%20measure%20and%20promote%20an%20effective%20anti-money%20laundering%20system.pdf. Last accessed on 16 September 2016.

Hassemer W, Starzacher K (1993) Organisierte Kriminalität - geschützt vom Datenschutz? Nomos Verlag, Baden-Baden.

IMF (2011) Anti-Money Laundering and Combating the Financing of Terrorism (AML/CFT). Report on the Review of the Effectiveness of the Program. http://www.imf.org/external/np/pp/eng/2011/051111.pdf. Last accessed on 16 September 2016.

Kemal M U (2014) Anti-money laundering regulations and its effectiveness. Journal of Money Laundering Control (17) 4: 416–427.

Killias M, Nunes A (2012) Diskriminierung. Nebeneffekte der Geldwäscherei-Bekämpfung. Neue Zürcher Zeitung, 21 May 2012. http://www.nzz.ch/meinung/debatte/nebeneffekte-der-geldwaescherei-bekaempfung-1.16973351. Last accessed on 16 September 2016.

Levi M (1998) Perspectives on 'Organised Crime': An Overview. The Howard Journal of Criminal Justice 37 (4): 335–345.

Levi M (2002) Money laundering and its regulation. Annals of the American Academy of Political and Social Science 582: 181–194.

Levi M et al. (eds) (2004) Reducing and Preventing Organised Crime: An Evidence-Based Critique. Crime, Law and Social Change 41(5): 397–469.

Levi M et al. (eds) (2013) The Economic, Financial & Social Impacts of Organised Crime in the EU. http://www.europarl.europa.eu/RegData/etudes/etudes/join/2013/493018/IPOL-JOIN_ET%282013%29493018_EN.pdf. Last accessed on 16 September 2016.

Merton R K (1983) Teoria e struttura sociale 1. Teoria sociologica e ricerca empirica. Il Mulino, Bologna.

Oswald K (1997) Die Implementation gesetzlicher Massnahmen zur Bekämpfung der Geldwäsche in der Bundesrepublik Deutschland: Eine empirische Untersuchung des § 261 StGB i.V.m. dem Geldwäsche. Max-Planck-Institut für ausländisches und internationales Strafrecht, Freiburg.

PKS (2015) Die Kriminalität in der Bundesrepublik Deutschland. Bericht 2015. https://www.bka.de/DE/AktuelleInformationen/StatistikenLagebilder/PolizeilicheKriminalstatistik/PKS2015/pks2015_node.html. Last accessed on 16 September 2016.

Rottleuthner H (1983) Teoria del diritto e sociologia del diritto. Il Mulino, Bologna.

Savona U et al. (eds.) (2007) Cost Benefit Analysis of Transparency Requirements in the Company/Corporate Field and Banking Sector Relevant for the Fight Against Money laundering and Other Financial Crime. http://www.transcrime.it/wp-content/uploads/2013/11/CBA-Study_Final_Report_revised_version.pdf. Last accessed on 16 September 2016.

Savona E, Riccardi M (eds) (2015) From illegal markets to legitimate businesses: the portfolio of organised crime in Europe. Final Report of Project OCP - Organised Crime Portfolio. http://www.transcrime.it/wp-content/uploads/2015/12/ocp.pdf. Last accessed on 16 September 2016.

Schneider F (2016) Der Umfang der Geldwäsche in Deutschland und weltweit: Einige Fakten und eine kritische Auseinandersetzung mit der Dunkelfeldstudie von Kai Bussmann. Friedrich Naumann Stiftung. http://stiftung-marktwirtschaft.de/fileadmin/user_upload/Tagungsunterlagen/21_09_Bargeld/Schneider_FNS-Studie_Geldwaesche_2016.pdf. Last accessed on 16 December 2016.

Tax Justice Network (2015) Financial Secrecy Index. http://www.financialsecrecyindex.com/introduction/fsi-2015-results. Last accessed on 16 September 2016.

Unger B, Addink H, Walker J, Ferwerda J, van den Broek M, Deleanu I (2013) ECOLEF final report. http://www2.econ.uu.nl/users/unger/ecolef_files/Final%20ECOLEF%20report%20(digital%20version).pdf. Last accessed on 16 September 2016.

Unger B, Ferwerda J, van den Broek M, Deleanu I (2014) The Economic And Legal Effectiveness Of The European Union's Anti-Money Laundering Policy. Edward Elgar Publishing Limited, Cheltenham.

Whitehouse A (2003) A brave new world: The impact of domestic and international regulation on money laundering prevention in the UK. Journal of Financial Regulation and Compliance 11 (2): 138–145.

Chapter 7
Opinions on the Anti-Money Laundering Regime. The Implementation of the Law from the Perspective of Legal Actors and Experts

Abstract This part concludes the qualitative assessment of the effectiveness of the money-laundering offence by looking at legal role-players' opinion and perception of the law. Issues that have emerged through the documental analysis are further discussed with experts and legal role-players. The interviews focus particularly on the size of the phenomenon of money laundering in Germany, on the legal framework's technical appropriateness, on the conflicting interests, and finally, on the interviewees' perceived (symbolic) effectiveness of the policy. Due to the fact that the enforcement of the money-laundering offence is strongly linked to other preventive and repressive measures, interviews consider also respondents' opinion and perception on related regulations. Given the transnational nature of money laundering and of the anti-money laundering regulations, this part, whilst focusing on a national legal system, re-opens the perspective onto the global level. Some of the challenges faced at this global level to tackle money laundering, in fact, have an impact on the domestic dimension. At the same time, issues that are raised in the national context can be further theorised in a wider context.

Keywords Anti-money laundering policy · Illicit financial flows · Dirty money · Capital flight · Effectiveness of the anti-money laundering policy

Contents

V. Zoppei, *Anti-Money Laundering Law: Socio-Legal Perspectives on the Effectiveness of German Practices*, International Criminal Justice Series 12,
DOI 10.1007/978-94-6265-180-7_7

7.1 Is Germany an Eldorado for Money Launderers?

As shown in the previous part, estimates on the volume of money laundered in Germany are not consistent. It is therefore unsurprising that individuals differ in the perceptions of the extent to which money laundering manifests itself in Germany. Between 2012 and 2013 the media recurrently reported that the country is a preferential place for money launderers.[1] This assumption was supported, among other factors, from the declaration of a notorious senior public prosecutor from Palermo (Italy), who said that 'if he was a money launderer he would have invested in Germany' ('*Wenn ich Mafiosi wäre, würde ich meine Gelder in Deutschland anlagen*').[2] In 2013, five non-profit organisations published a report that drew attention to the alarming estimates provided by the IMF about the volume of money laundered in Germany. This volume was said to be the equivalent of 1.3–1.7% of the German GDP.[3] On the basis of such estimates the authors defined Germany as a '*Schattenfinanzzentrum*' (an offshore financial centre). However, 'there is no evidence that in Germany more money is laundered than in Italy, France or the USA,

---

[1] Among others, *see* 'OECD: Deutschland ist Geldwäsche-Paradies' in Deutsche Wirtschafts Nachrichten, 18.01.13; Dick W, Germany, a safe haven for money laundering. Deutsche Welle, 30/10/2012; Rimpel K, Geldwäsche-Paradies Deutschland. Nummer acht unter den Steueroasen. Tz-online, 07/11/2013; Ramthum C, OECD: Deutschland versagt im Kampf gegen Geldwäsche. Wirtschaftswoche, 26/04/2014; Deutsche Presse Agentur, Steueroase Deutschland ist Eldorado für Geldwäsche. Handelsblatt, 07/11/2013; 'Deutschland ein "Eldorado für Geldwäsche"?' In Deutsche Welle, 07.11.2013; Netzwerk Steuergerechtigkeit, Deutschland ist ein Eldorado für Geldwäsche In Frankfurter Allgemein, 07.11.2013.

[2] The statement was recalled in various sources; among them a judges association in Hamburg (Hamburgerische Richterverein) invited the senior prosecutor to give a speech and quoted the statement in the report of the meeting. *See* Kaufmann 2011, p. 45.

[3] Henn et al. 2013, pp. 4–6.

therefore it would be incorrect to refer to Germany as 'the paradise for money launderers', say the respondents in the Justice Ministry.[4] Other respondents disagree as well with the statement of the FATF that Germany does too little to tackle money laundering.[5] 'In fact, even 'if this would be the case [that Germany is an Eldorado for money launderers], the reason would not be because of lax legislation, because Germany has the necessary laws to tackle money laundering'.[6] The detective chief superintendents from the financial investigations group of Berlin add that 'if one says that Germany is a paradise for money launderers it would mean that the criminal justice system does not function. Yet, this cannot be true because the financial investigations groups within the local detective unit (LKA) of the police have been in existence for 20 years.'[7] The representative of Land of Hesse, one of the states that have been most engaged in preventing money laundering, believes that 'thanks to public awareness and thanks to the involvement of non-financial institutions the laundering of proceeds of crime has recently become more difficult in Germany. Thus, Germany is on the right track to eliminate the existing problem of money laundering'.[8] The respondent thinks 'in the past, it was recognized on an international level, that the amount of money laundered in Germany was very high, but thanks to the intense commitment with a focus on the non-banking sector, it is likely to decline'. A respondent from the detective branch of the Berlin police, instead, confirms the possibility that 'Germany is a favoured country in Europe for the laundering of proceeds of crimes', but at the same time he considers 'the label 'Eldorado' exaggerated, because it does not acknowledge the efforts made to prevent money laundering, which have successfully diminished the phenomenon'.[9]

The problem can be effectively summarised in a respondent's answer: 'Nobody knows exactly how much money is washed'.[10] In reply to the question whether it is true that Germany is an Eldorado for money laundering, as described by the newspapers, one of the respondents says that 'this question clearly has a yes/no (*Jain*) answer. Nobody can tell the truth, because what we possess are only estimates'.[11] Given the lack of objective figures on the volume of money laundered that emerged in Part IV, the reader will not be surprised that almost all of the respondents share this opinion. The Ministries do not possess enough data to produce a correct estimate of the volume of money laundered since part of the data is handled by the *Länder*. The BMJV, too, acknowledged the impossibility of providing figures on the volume of money laundered due to the fact that 'it is the *Länder* that have the authority to deal with these issues and they are not obligated to report their work in

[4] Interview with author 2014.
[5] Ibid.
[6] Ibid.
[7] Ibid.
[8] Ibid.
[9] Ibid.
[10] Ibid.
[11] Ibid.

the field of anti-money laundering to the Ministry'.[12] Yet, according to local authorities, at the state level institutions also do not possess solid statistics about the amount of money laundered in Germany, 'therefore it is not possible to evaluate the phenomenon objectively'.[13] 'However, the fact that Germany is a federal state and therefore more complicated to co-ordinate, it is not only a matter that concerns money-laundering control', adds the civil servant. The BMF confirms that 'we do not possess reliable statistical data on the volume of money laundered, neither do we about the organised criminal activities. What we actually need is empirical research on the real amount of money laundered and reliable data of law enforcement activities in the states'.[14] There is thus a consensus among the representatives of the Ministries as regards the lack of reliable figures on the phenomenon of money laundering. The NGO 'WEED' interprets this lack of reliable data as a missed chance for the institutions to tackle the problem effectively, because 'the lack of reliable figures on money laundering hinders the effective fight against it. If there were statistics that objectively showed how much money is laundered in Germany, they would support the argument that there is a need to do more. Currently, there is not enough evidence of the volume of money laundered in Germany. Facts, statistics and numbers of clear-cut-cases are lacking, so the real amount could be much lower or much higher than the estimate that we have of 50 Billion Euros'.[15] Indeed, according to senior prosecutor, 'the dark number in this field [of money laundering] is much higher than in other fields. What emerges through the legal prevention and repression is only the tip of the iceberg'.[16] This is confirmed also by other police officers, who say 'organised criminal groups have been active in Germany even before the fall of the wall, however, their structures are not visible'. 'Even the estimates produced by the OECD [Organisation for Economic Cooperation and Development] on the amount of money laundered in Germany are biased because they are only based on cases dealt with in the country, while proceeds of crimes committed abroad can be also laundered here. For instance, with these estimates, they do not take into account the money invested by the Italian Mafia, because they would also need to compare Italian statistics. […] Even *Fiedler*,[17] who is an expert in the casino sector, did not provide evidence of the phenomenon based on reliable estimates or clear-cut cases. Also, in the context of derivatives, attempts have been made to measure the volume of money-laundering transactions but so far they have been unsuccessful. For the first time, the Ministry of Finance has recently commissioned a study to collect information about money laundering in the non-banking sector. However, from the author's point of view, the absence of reliable data and the fact that such a study has only just been commissioned are elements from which we

[12] Ibid.

[13] Ibid.

[14] Ibid.

[15] Ibid.

[16] Ibid.

[17] Fiedler is deputy head of the federation of German Police Officers.

can interpret that there has not been enough involvement. If even people in the Ministries, who have been working in the field for a very long time, cannot evaluate the estimates of the volume of money laundered in Germany, it seems that there is a lack of interest in providing such figures. However, the law is no longer young, for it has been in force for 20 years and it should show its results'.[18] The policy officer thinks that on the other hand 'the lack of statistics undermines the credibility of those who advocate for a more effective response from the State, based on the estimated threat of money laundering in the country'. In his opinion 'many authors argue that the regime is not effective, yet, the lack of reliable figures makes it hard to criticise the system. Even those who say that the anti-money laundering regime has not yet helped to tackle illicit financial flows do not possess data that objectively shows this failure, since the failure might have been triggered by other factors'. The lack of reliable figures, which has already emerged from the FATF [Financial Action task Force] assessment in 2010, was confirmed by the follow-up report in 2014.[19]

One respondent draws our attention to another relevant issue connected to the compilation of statistics. The Ministry of Interior interprets the phenomenon of money laundering and organised crime using the data provided by the 16 *Länder* (States), the *Bundeskriminalamt* (BKA, Federal Criminal Police Office) and the FIU (Financial Intelligence Unit) according to the BKA's definition of organised crime. Yet such a definition is perceived to be too restrictive and does not encompass the many activities that are typical of criminal networks.[20] According to a respondent, for example, 'the biggest problem linked to organised crime in Germany is corruption, but this is not included in the definition of organised crime provided by the BKA and therefore does not contribute to the statistics on organised crime in the country'. In addition 'the FIU focuses only on the offence of money laundering, and does not take into consideration the predicate offences, which means that the impression gained from a reading of FIU reports does not mirror the whole phenomenon of money laundering and of the actions to counteract it'.

---

[18] Interview with author 2014.

[19] FATF 2014, p. 25. This has prevented the assessors formulating a judgement on the implementation of specific provisions relating to money laundering. In particular, comprehensive annual statistics were missing or not available, or both, in relation to, for instance, sanctions imposed for convictions pursuant to Article 261 of the GCC to legal persons; the value of transactions associated with STRs; the provisional measures applied. Already in 2010, the FATF assessors observed that 'Nevertheless, given the high value of forfeitures and confiscations, assessors have no reason to doubt the authorities' claim that provisional measures were being applied in Germany. There is the possibility, however, that the use of provisional measures could be improved to help increase the level of assets confiscated and forfeited compared to the total claim made by the State for confiscation and forfeiture. FATF 2010, p. 85.

[20] Interview with author 2014. 'Organised crime is the planned violation of the law for profit or to acquire power, which offences are each, or together, of a major significance, and are carried out by more than two participants who co-operate within a division of labour for a long or undetermined time span using (a) commercial or commercial-like structures, or (b) violence or other means of intimidation, or (c) influence on politics, media, public administration, justice and the legitimate economy' BKA, 1999, translation of Levi 1998, p. 335.

The respondents point out that the media influences the social perception of the size of the phenomenon: 'the fact that the media has recently started reporting more about economic crimes can be related to the fact that the criminal justice system started dealing with crimes such as corruption and money laundering only 30 years ago, and currently there are very specialised agencies that are responsible for law enforcement in this field, therefore many more offences are detected and more information is provided to the public'.[21] According to the respondents from the Ministry of Justice, 'the media has an interest in presenting big scandals to the public, they prioritise hot topics and money laundering is a phenomenon that attracts public attention.[22] Actually, the fact that big money laundering cases are reported, can be also interpreted as a success of the criminal justice system, which proves the fact that law enforcement has detected and persecuted the crime. Moreover, showing the public how seriously these crimes are prosecuted has a deterrent effect'.[23] Yet 'the media, while drawing attention to the estimated volume of illicit financial flows in Germany, does not report the legal steps undertaken to tackle them, so the picture presented to the public is biased'.[24] The work of professional investigative journalists is considered a factor that has contributed in raising people's awareness, and 'public perception and politicians sensitivity to the topic are increasing, thanks to the public work of the law enforcement agencies that have in recent years drawn the attention of political institutions to these topics, and thanks to investigative journalists who have been reporting the huge increasing level of organised crime's infiltration into Germany'.[25] Yet, according to the respondent from the Ministry of Finance, the image of money laundering presented by the media is distorted: 'The media provides an image of money laundering as primarily connected to red light crime and criminal activities committed by foreigners and refugees. Journalists use secondary material and are therefore not able to provide a real picture of what money laundering is. This plays a big role in the inaccurate perception of this phenomenon in Germany'.[26]

7.1.1 What Is the Impact of Money Laundering?

The respondents were asked for their opinion on what the consequences of money laundering are on the German society and economy and thus why the state should

[21] Interview with author 2014.

[22] To use Dalla Chiesa's words, especially in recent times there has been a growing 'mythology' surrounding the economic side of organised crime, in relation to the volume of profits deriving from illegal businesses reinvested in the legal economic circle. *See* Dalla Chiesa 2012, p. 11. The author highlights the importance of discerning grounded studies on the economic dimension of the Mafia from exaggerated theories that emphasize the volume of the Mafia business.

[23] Interview with author 2014.

[24] Ibid.

[25] Ibid.

[26] Ibid.

block the infiltration of illicit money into the country. Practitioners and experts expressed similar opinions, the most recurrent answer being that it is in the interest of the state to prosecute money laundering given the threat it poses to both society and the economy'.[27] 'The biggest threat posed by money laundering in Germany is the infiltration of illegal structures into the legitimate economy'; yet even the report published by the BMF on the risks of money laundering to the financial sector, is based on assumptions and not on proven data, therefore I cannot assess the risk to the whole Germany'. The BMJV adds that 'within the FATF meetings, it has often been said that money laundering was one of the main causes of the financial crisis. However, nobody could explain to us how money laundering has played a role in the financial crises.[28] According to another respondent, money laundering negatively impacts economic competition: 'Entrepreneurs that launder and invest their ill-gotten money in the legal economic sector undermine economic competition, and through their economic power they can indirectly influence politics and thus undermine the whole democracy and civil society'.[29] Investigators perceive the fight against money laundering as a duty. Police forces confirm that 'all actors have an interest in combating money laundering, from the banks to the government, but among the police there is a particularly strict engagement in the fight against crime, because the police perceive the infiltration of any type of money deriving from a criminal action as a threat'.[30] They add that the interest in tackling money laundering generally relies in the goal of 'not letting the economy be distorted by illegal capital. Since market capitalism is the dominant economic structure, law-abiding individuals have an interest in not being put out of competition by those who are favoured through the infiltration of criminal assets. The legally protected interest is the interest of the law-abiding professionals, businesses and industries. Indirectly, this has also had an impact on the whole society, through the impact on the labour market, and especially on the employees whose life depends on those businesses, commercial and industrial activities that might be infiltrated or contaminated by the infiltration of illegal capital'.[31] It is indeed a common perception that 'money laundering can affect the real economy by distorting consumption, savings, investments, inflation, competition, trade and employment. [...] It can affect the financial sector with an increased risk of insolvency, liquidity, reputation and integrity of the sector'.[32] Yet, in the literature there is the idea that money laundering could also be good for the economy, for example because it increases profits and the availability of credit.[33]

[27] Ibid.

[28] Ibid.

[29] Ibid.

[30] Ibid.

[31] Ibid.

[32] Unger et al. 2014, pp. 217–218.

[33] Ibid.

7.1.2 *Economic Stability, Rule of Law: A Fertile or Hostile Environment for Money Launderers?*

Interestingly, some characteristics of the German legal, political and economic system were perceived by the respondents as both enabling and obstructing money laundering. In particular, some factors are considered to be connected, either as enablers or as obstacles, to the threat of money laundering. Among them, the most recurrent is the level of corruption, the rule of law, the transparency of the administrative apparatus, the integrity of public officials, and the soundness of the economic system. The respondents express differing opinions on these relations; again, the lack of empirical data on the matter impedes the reaching a univocal conclusion. According to one respondent, 'the fact that Germany has a secure banking sector and a strong financial centre attracts money launderers'. 'Due to its stable economy, Germany is a relevant country for the investment of illegal monies generated in thirds countries'.[34] 'In the report ['Schattenfinanzzentrum Deutschland'] we argue that the fact that Germany has a stable economic and political system, is an attracting factor for money launderers who are willing to invest their money'.[35] The report infers from the size of the financial centre, the volume of the banking sector, and from the high amount of cash transactions, that Germany is a preferential country for money launderers.[36] Also, the FATF report of 2010 identifies some factors making Germany a country susceptible to money laundering, and these are 'the large economy and financial centres, as well as the strategic location in Europe, the strong international links, the large informal sector (more than 400 billion euros), and the diffused use of cash'.[37] The link between the size of the economy and the amount of revenue from illicit markets is confirmed by a report dealing with illicit markets too.[38] In particular, drafters state 'it is not surprising that the four biggest European economies (Germany, Italy, France and the UK) are those that produce the highest revenues from illicit markets.[39] However, not all respondents share this assumption. In fact, according to interviewees from the BMJV 'the great dimension of the German financial centre might be connected to the volume of money laundered'. 'It is not only organised crime that invests a lot of money in the country; in fact German total tax revenue is very high. Since the whole volume of the financial sector, and thus of the legal economy,

[34] Interview with author 2014.

[35] Ibid.

[36] According to the authors, the fact that the big banking sector attracts money launderers was particularly evident after the Arab Spring, when it was revealed that almost all political leaders and/or their relatives have had financial relations with Germany. *See* Henn et al. 2013, pp. 5, 7.

[37] FATF 2010, p. 9.

[38] Savona and Riccardi 2015, p. 37.

[39] Ibid.

is big, the volume of the illegal sector is proportional to it'.[40] There are objective factors that favour criminals against law enforcement. These are, however, not peculiar to Germany, such as the speed of the financial system and the globalisation of the economic and financial structures.[41] Another factor facilitating money laundering is said to be the widespread use of cash, which is supposed to complicate the tracing of ill-gotten gains. Cash transactions are highly debated in Germany in relation to anti-money laundering prevention: 'People say that Germany has the highest number of 100 € notes circulating, and it is true that in Germany there is still a high number of cash transactions. […] Therefore, I would not agree with the statement that money launderers come to Germany because our legal system has loopholes that favour the laundering of money'.[42] In addition, 'Even though cash transactions hinder the tracing of dirty money, it is not enough to describe the country as a paradise for money launderers. It is true that in Germany organised criminal groups are active, especially foreign ones, but their activities are prosecuted by law enforcement; of course, there are some cases that remain unresolved but this happens in every legal system'.[43] The link between the size of the financial centre and the amount of illicit financial flows is contested too. 'If one makes the estimates in relation to the volume of the economy, since Germany has a big economy, the number would be high. Yet, even those who infer that Frankfurt is a big centre for money laundering because it is a big financial centre, they do not have the evidence to give credence to this relationship. On the other hand, Germany has a long-standing tradition of subscribing to the rule of law, which makes it more difficult to infiltrate proceeds of crime in the country'.[44] The strong rule of law and the transparent administration is a counter-argument also raised by another respondent.[45] The former senior policeman interpreted the low level of corruption as a deterrent factor: 'corruption is not deeply rooted in society and in the economy; it does not affect the daily life of citizens. There are often cases of corruption, but it is not in the nature of the people to procure themselves privileges through corruption; in fact, there is a massive repudiation of corruption practices amongst the population'.[46] Moreover, the legal and regulative frameworks provide 'firewalls', namely specific compliance departments that impede corruption and money laundering both in the private and in the public sector, the possibility of reporting corruption cases anonymously, and protection for whistle-blowers'. These assumptions have been used in the NGO report of 2013 too. The document states that the rule of law and the low level of corruption, inferred from the Transparency

---

[40] The respondent actually confirms in this way the theory that links the size of the legitimate economy to the size of the illegitimate economy. Interview with author 2014.

[41] Interview with author 2014.

[42] Ibid.

[43] Ibid.

[44] Ibid.

[45] Ibid.

[46] Ibid.

International Index,[47] are factors that make the laundering of proceeds of crime more difficult in Germany.[48] Also, the 2010 FATF report identifies the long-standing legal tradition of the rule of law, the political environment, and the integrity of the law enforcement personnel and of the judiciary as strength factors.[49] Another attorney holds a different opinion relating to the degree of corruption in Germany and on the impact of corruption on law enforcement activities: 'Germany is a very corrupt country, especially the state and the economic sector. The most corrupt state is Bavaria, therefore I do not believe that there will be any further investigation [with regard to the *Hoeneß* case[50]]. This would destabilise the equilibrium between the fans, the sponsors, like Siemens, and the whole community'.

7.1.3 Considerations

There are three issues on which the respondents agree. These are the lack of reliable statistics about the volume of money laundering in the country, the role played by the media in influencing public opinion and the fact that money laundering has, at least indirectly, a negative impact on society. These assumptions are, however, interpreted in different ways and thus cannot be used as independent variables. Some respondents are of the opinion that since estimates could also be much lower, lawmakers cannot rely on them in order to design new policies. Others interpret the fact that the responsible authorities have not yet found a way to provide more reliable figures as being due to a lack of commitment. The role of the media is perceived differently among the interviewees. While some accuse the media of providing a biased representation of money laundering, others believe that the media contribution has increased people's awareness. Finally, with respect to the impact of money laundering on German society, interviewees do not appear to have any doubts that the laundering of proceeds of crime through the legitimate economy distorts economic competition with a resultant negative impact on the whole

---

[47] Germany is listed the 10th position out of 168 countries assessed by the Transparency International. *See* Transparency International 2015.

[48] According to the authors, the fact that the big banking sector attracts money launderers was particularly evident after the Arab spring, when it was revealed that almost all political leaders and/or their relatives have had financial relations with Germany. Henn et al. 2013, pp. 5, 7.

[49] FATF, MER 2010, p. 9. The assessors report: 'the excellence of the prosecutors from the public prosecution offices of the German *Bundesländer*, of the judges at the courts and the lawyers within the Ministry of Justice, their remarkable knowledge of the law, and their dedication to the responsibility that they have been entrusted with, confirms the solid foundation upon which the German system is established'. FATF 2010, p. 115.

[50] Hoeneß, President of Bayern Munich football team, was convicted on 13 March 2014 for tax evasion committed on speculative business in Switzerland. Rehle M, Hoeneß spekulierte Mithilfe mehrerer Banken. Die Zeit online, 26/03/2014.

society.[51] However, given the lack of reliable figures on the real scale of money laundered in the country, even this element cannot be used as common ground to assess the policy's effectiveness.

7.2 Is the Current Policy Appropriate for Tackling Money Laundering? What Are the Legal Hindrances and Technical Strengths of the Policy?

The respondents are asked to highlight the strengths and weaknesses of the current policy. Some of the issues are specifically related to the wording of the provisions regulating and preventing money laundering. Other technical factors refer to the criminal justice system and thus cannot be ascribed only to the formulation of the anti-money-laundering legislation. The aim of the interviews on the perceived appropriateness is to highlight the existing differing perceptions in order to stress the complexity of the topic. The interviews are not directed at evaluating the effectiveness of the whole legislation on the basis of technical challenges and advantages.

7.2.1 Legal Hindrances

Issues already revealed in *Oswald*'s research, for instance, the steep **burden of proof** required by Article 261 of the GCC, are still perceived as hindering the capacity of prosecuting the crime money laundering. According to one defence lawyer, 'the high burden of proof lowers the ability of prosecutors to prosecute money-laundering cases successfully.' Also, three of the public prosecutors interviewed confirm that 'the burden of proof of the illegitimate origin of the assets is very high, which results in the fact that only a few charges are preferred, based on the information received through STRs'. In order to further facilitate the work of the prosecutors and to lower the burden of proof, what is under discussion at present is whether there is a need to **reverse the burden of proof**.[52] The criticism raised by the Italian senior prosecutor, *Scarpinato*, has had a significant impact on the national debate in Germany on this particular issue.[53] While according to one

[51] The literature on the 'bad' impact of money laundering is abundant, *see* for example *Masciandaro* 1999, 2000. Yet some respondents are sceptical, for example, about attributing the European financial crisis of 2008/2009 to money laundering. Interview with author 2014.

[52] In the meantime, on 23 March 2017 the German Parliament agreed on a law (*Drucksache* 18/9525) that introduces a non-conviction based type of confiscation measure (*selbständige Einziehung*) under article 76 a, para 4 of the GCC. The law allows a sort of reversal of the burden of proof in the context of organized crime and terrorism cases. *See* BT-Drucks 18/9525, pp. 14, 58.

[53] Interview with author 2014. Scarpinato has already been interviewed in 2011 and heard by different sources in Germany about the presence of organised crime and the consequent need for

respondent, 'this might be changed at some point, it is not very probable that Germany will ever enact a system similar to the Italian one [with regard to the reversal of the burden of proof], because of the specificities of our legal culture.[54] In addition, it could be argued that, despite the efficient asset recovery system, Italy has not yet managed to defeat the Mafia. This makes the effectiveness of reversal of the onus of proof debatable, but one can say that without having it, the situation would be much worse'. According to the public prosecutors interviewed, 'the reversal of the burden of proof would help us overcome these obstacles [of bringing evidence of the elements if the crime]. If we could infer the illegal origin of assets from circumstances and then require the accused to prove the contrary, this would contribute enormously to the successful prosecution of money-laundering cases'. Those who welcome the introduction of the reversal of the burden of proof in the field of money laundering, believe that 'this provision would play a significantly positive role'.[55] In order not to violate constitutional principles, the measure should be authorised by a judge and not by the police and should be limited to cases of serious criminality. Yet, such reform does not find the approval of all respondents. The chief superintendents are convinced that 'it will not be possible to introduce the reversal of the burden of proof in Germany because this concept goes against the fundamental principles of criminal law and against the rule of law. In Germany nobody is supposed to defend themselves—*nemo tenetur se detegere*—the accused has the right to remain silent in terms of Article 136(1) of the GCC'. In addition, the investigators claim that they are 'used to working without this instrument, so we would not feel comfortable introducing it in actual practice of criminal proceedings'. Were the respondents to place themselves in the position of a potential accused person, they 'would not like to be subject to this burden if I were to be prosecuted'.[56]

As regards the **exemption of punishment, which is** regulated by Article 261(9) of the GCC, the interviewees differ in their opinions as to whether this provision hinders an effective implementation of the law or not. At the time of the interviews, Article 261(9) still excluded from punishment the perpetrators of the predicate

---

(Footnote 53 continued)

legal reforms. The prosecutor advocated specifically for the introduction of the crime of participation in a criminal organisation, a broader use of telephone tapping instruments and the reversal of the burden of proof. *See* Bund Deutscher Kriminalbeamter, Interview mit Generalstaatsanwalt Roberto Scarpinato. Blickpunkt 4, Kölner Stadt Anzeiger, 11/10/2012; Meyer U, Mafia-Jäger warnt in Hamburg vor sizilianischen Verhältnissen. Hamburger Abendblatt, 27/09/2011; Lüke U, Tagung in Köln über das organisierte Verbrechen. General Anzeiger Bonn, 15/10/2012; Stoldt T-R, Wie stark ist die Mafia in Nordrhein-Westfalen? Die Welt, 20/10/2012; Kreikenbaum U, Die Mafia kann relativ frei arbeiten. Kölner-stadt Anzeiger, 10/09/2015.

[54] Judge Scarpinato is famous for having also stated, indeed: 'Es ist erstaunlich, dass in Deutschland die Angst vor dem Staat größer ist, als die vor der Mafia'. English translation: It is astonishing that in Germany the fear of the State is greater than the fear of the Mafia. *See* Kaufmann 2011, p. 45.

[55] Interview with author 2014.

[56] Ibid.

offence.[57] The exclusion was based on the constitutional principle of freedom from self-incrimination (*Selbstbelastungsfreiheit*).[58] Much has been written on this topic. The issue is controversial because on the one hand it obviously limits the liability of the accused, whilst on the other hand, this limitation is emphasised as a fundamental guarantee for the accused. According to an attorney, 'offenders should be punished only for perpetrating the predicate offences, not for money laundering as well, otherwise it would be a double punishment for the same conduct'.[59] The private sector does not distinguish whether the individual who carried out the suspicious transaction could have been the same person who committed the predicate offence'. The provision would violate the constitutional right not to incriminate oneself, which accordingly means that 'it would be inappropriate 'to hold the perpetrators of the predicate offence liable'.[60] One respondent does not consider the notion of making someone liable for 'self-money laundering under Article 261 of the GCC a viable option for enhancing the combating of money laundering'. The Ministry of Justice had even commissioned a study on the issue to argue against the criminalisation of self-money laundering. This initiative was triggered by the FATF's declaration that Germany should introduce the principle of self-money laundering.[61] One respondent, in particular believes that 'the introduction of a general self-money laundering offence could mean that even a thief who steals something and hides it would be liable for money laundering because of the act of hiding the proceeds of the theft, and this is not in line with the fundamental principles of our criminal legal system'.[62] According to a public prosecutor, 'self-money laundering should incur criminal liability under the criminal code and Article 261(9) should be scrapped'.[63] 'This is a legal loophole that should be filled. Even though this would

[57] The provision excludes criminal liability for those who participated in the predicate offences, out of the cases in which the offenders put in circulation the objects deriving from the offences, in order to conceal their illegitimate origin, under Article 261(9) 2 GCC. Article 1, BGBI. 2015 I, p. 2025.

[58] The principle derives from the application of Articles 1(1) and 2(1) of the German constitution (Grundgesetz, GG) on criminal proceedings. Article 1(1) GG states that *Die Würde des Menschen ist unantastbar. Sie zu achten und zu schützen ist Verpflichtung aller staatlichen Gewalt* (Human dignity shall be inviolable. To respect and protect it shall be the duty of all state authority); Article 2(1) GG declares that *Jeder hat das Recht auf die freie Entfaltung seiner Persönlichkeit, soweit er nicht die Rechte anderer verletzt und nicht gegen die verfassungsmäßige Ordnung oder das Sittengesetz verstößt* (Every person shall have the right to free development of his personality insofar as he does not violate the rights of others or offend the constitutional order or the moral law).

[59] Interview with author 2014.

[60] Ibid.

[61] 'The investigation reaches the conclusion that self-laundering must remain exempt from separate punishment. The text is based on an expert report, which was commissioned by the Federal Ministry of Justice of the Federal Republic of Germany. It was prompted mainly by the FATF's 'Mutual Evaluation Report on Germany of 19 February 2010'. *See* Schröder 2013.

[62] Interview with author 2014.

[63] Ibid.

not entirely solve the problem, at least it would not be wrong to have it in the criminal code, because otherwise it is not possible to prosecute someone for money laundering if it is suspected that he/she was also involved in the predicate offence. Parliament has, in fact, announced that this might be introduced in the near future'.[64] The Parliament was indeed obligated by the Fourth Anti-Money Laundering Directive to do away with Article 261(9) of the GCC.[65] This provision affects the filing of STRs, too, according to the BMF, and given the exemption of punishment as provided under Article 261(9)(2), there should be no requirement that STRs be filed in cases in which it is clear that the perpetrator of the main offence is the same person who launders the proceeds of his crime.[66]

The long-debated issue of the legally protected goods is here recalled. One of the problems with Article 261 of the GCC is 'that is not clear which are the legally protected goods.' The conflict that has emerged during the law-making process with regard to the interests protected by Article 261 has had an impact on the application of the norm. This is also recognised by the BMF, which declares that the determination of the *Rechtsgut* (legal interest), far from being a merely a doctrinal issue, impacts the practical implementation of the law. The BMF advocates a change of paradigm and for the identification of the *Rechtsgut* with the protection of the financial system in opposition to the protection of the administration of justice, since the latter is not considered by any of the EU Member States and does not reflect the nature of the offence. With respect to the identification of the interests protected by Article 261 of the GCC, a representative of the BMJV acknowledges that the BMF's approach that supports the idea that the law should protect the financial system and not the administration of justice. 'There has been a switch from the initial position which departed from the fact that the crime of money laundering was created to fight organised crime, to one where there is a tendency in Germany nowadays to consider it as a tool to protect the lawful economy from the infiltration of illegal money. In fact, whereas initially it was the Ministry of the Interior that was responsible for drafting the law, at the moment the duty lies in the hands of the Ministry of Finance'.[67]

Another issue that has emerged from the empirical research is the approach taken by Germany, from the beginning, with regard to the **catalogue of the predicate offences** for money laundering. International lawmakers did not impose any particular approach, which is why certain jurisdictions have opted for the 'all crimes approach', according to which all crimes are regarded as predicate crimes for money laundering. Other jurisdictions have limited the list to certain offences, hence adopting the 'threshold approach'.[68] Germany chose a combination of the

---

[64] Ibid.

[65] Ibid.

[66] The opinion of the Ministry of Finance in respect of the need to change § 261 of GCC and the deficits in legal practice with respect to the grounds excluding liability under § 261(9)(2) relating to self money laundering VII A 3-VK 5160/06/0002:005, 2013, p. 1 (unpublished).

[67] Interview with author 2014.

[68] The Fourth Anti-Money Laundering Directive under Article 3 lists a number of predicate crimes that have to be included by Member States.

'threshold approach' and the compilation of a catalogue of offences, which is continuously being expanded by the legislature. In the interview with a Ministry representative, the introduction of the 'all crimes approach' would be a necessary step in aiding prosecutors', 'thus improving the law's effectiveness. Specifically, 'the 'all crimes approach' might result in an advantage for the prosecution in the sense that prosecutors will need to adduce evidence of the money-laundering offence where without having to prove one of the predicate offences listed in the catalogue, but rather only the general criminal origin of the proceeds'.[69] This change might finally release prosecutors from the so-called "*doppel Anfangsverdacht*", namely, from the duty of providing evidence not only of the laundering conduct and of the illicit origin of the property, but also of the specific commission of an antecedent act.

Another issue pertaining to the German criminal justice system is the seizure of criminal assets. The problem is summarised in the words of two policemen who state that 'at the end of the proceedings, prosecutors manage to confiscate only the half of what they seized'.[70] The criminalisation of money laundering was directed at the confiscation of criminal assets to deprive drug traffickers of their ill-gotten gains in order to eliminate the incentive for engaging in crime and to undermine the financial power of organised crime. The opinions of the respondents regarding this issue partly describe it as a hindrance and an advantage and partly as not even corresponding to the policy's purpose. Confiscation can be a very useful preventive tool, yet the goal of law enforcement is not to confiscate the assets, but rather to imprison the offenders.[71] According to the one attorney interviewed, 'the law [regulating asset forfeiture] is quite reasonable and there are no serious hindrances'. One prosecutor expressed the opinion that 'the confiscation of criminal assets is a much more effective punishment for money launderers than 1 year of imprisonment'. The implementation of the law does not seem satisfactory. In fact, according to the NGO, asset recovery is not considered very effective and thus is not often used by law enforcement authorities: 'Authorities appear not to rely much on this tool and do not invest many resources in it. It is a very complicated system that requires specific knowledge and is time consuming. I believe that Germany is not very good at asset recovery because our system considers the convictions of individuals to be more effective. I know that, for instance, the Italian system has much higher figures on asset recovery compared to Germany.[72] The chief investigator explains that in Germany up to 10,000 € of confiscated assets can be kept by the prosecuting State. Usually, the confiscated assets are devolved to the victims. In the case of economic crimes, which are victimless, the assets go to the public

[69] Interview with author 2014.

[70] Opinion expressly stated by Parliament. Confiscation should have impeded the proceeds of crime constituting the 'operating capital' (*Betriebskapital*) for the commission of further offences. See BT-Drucks 12/2720, p. 2.

[71] Interview with author 2014.

[72] Ibid.

budget of the *Bundesland* and not to the federal state, nor to the police offices'.[73] There should be thus an interest to improve confiscation procedures at the state level in order to be able to face the costs of investigations, as also suggested by the draft bill, for example.[74] In order to confiscate the proceeds of crime effectively, without enabling perpetrators to invest them in legal enterprises that produce legitimate profit, or making it possible for them to sell goods to third parties in good faith, or to stash the money away in offshore jurisdictions, or to make the tracing of the ill-gotten gains complicated by resorting to complex schemes, prosecutors should be able to freeze the assets rapidly. According to the FATF report of 2010, the authorities noted that measures are generally taken as early as possible to seize the assets held by a party charged with a crime at the beginning of the criminal investigation procedures in order to prevent the assets from being removed unlawfully. However, some prosecutors also indicated that seizures were typically used to the extent that they can support the evidence in a criminal investigation and not as a means to prevent the dealing with, transfer or disposal of property subject to forfeiture or confiscation.[75]

7.2.2 Systematic Hindrances

One of the most discussed topics in the field of the prevention of money laundering is the disclosure of **beneficial ownerships**[76] through the establishment of a public

---

[73] Ibid.

[74] BT-Drucks 12/3533, 1992, p. 11.

[75] FATF 2010, p. 85.

[76] Under European law a beneficial owner is 'any natural person(s) who ultimately owns or controls the customer and/or the natural person(s) on whose behalf a transaction or activity is being conducted and includes at least' a series of natural persons. Article 3 of the Directive (EU) 2015/849 of the European Parliament and of the Council of 20 May 2015 on the prevention of the use of the financial system for the purposes of money laundering or terrorist financing, amending Regulation (EU) No 648/2012 of the European Parliament and of the Council, and repealing Directive 2005/60/EC of the European Parliament and of the Council and Commission Directive 2006/70/EC, OJ L 141, 5.6.2015, p. 73–117. (a) in the case of corporate entities: (i) the natural person(s) who ultimately owns or controls a legal entity through direct or indirect ownership of a sufficient percentage of the shares or voting rights or ownership interest in that entity, including through bearer shareholdings, or through control via other means, other than a company listed on a regulated market that is subject to disclosure requirements consistent with Union law or subject to equivalent international standards which ensure adequate transparency of ownership information. A shareholding of 25% plus one share or an ownership interest of more than 25% in the customer held by a natural person shall be an indication of direct ownership. A shareholding of 25% plus one share or an ownership interest of more than 25% in the customer held by a corporate entity, which is under the control of a natural person(s), or by multiple corporate entities, which are under the control of the same natural person(s), shall be an indication of indirect ownership. This applies without prejudice to the right of Member States to decide that a lower percentage may be an indication of ownership or control. Control through other means may be determined, inter alia,

register.[77] At the moment, there are 16 different state registers in Germany, which are not integrated on a federal level. With regard to this question, respondents' opinions differ. On the one hand, prosecutors and the BMJV advocate for the introduction of a federal beneficial owners' register as this would, in their opinions, hugely facilitate investigations. For example, according to one prosecutor, 'when criminals use relatives to launder their money, and the relatives have a legal source of income, it is difficult to provide evidence of the illegal origin of that specific asset, since money is neutral in nature. While it is easier to catch the nominees of dummy companies, it is much harder to catch those who act behind them, namely, the beneficial owners. Most often, indeed, nominees do not actually know who manages and profits from the business. Unfortunately, there are many individuals who are willing to act as nominees in exchange for some profit'.[78] The lack of transparency in the workings of companies lends itself to their being misused for money-laundering purposes, according to the NGOs report of 2013.[79] The authors believe that German companies are required to comply with transparency standards only partially. On the contrary, it is argued that law enforcement authorities can already access high quantities of information and that company registers are held at state level.[80] Therefore, there it is not necessary to introduce a federal register on beneficial owners. A respondent explains that 'the BMJV has published a report on the issue of beneficial owners which states that there is a need for a public national

(Footnote 76 continued)

in accordance with the criteria in Article 22(1)–(5) of Directive 2013/34/EU of the European Parliament and of the Council of 26 June 2013 on the annual financial statements, consolidated financial statements and related reports of certain types of undertakings, amending Directive 2006/43/EC of the European Parliament and of the Council and repealing Council Directives 78/660/EEC and 83/349/EEC Text with EEA relevance; (ii) if, after having exhausted all possible means and provided there are no grounds for suspicion, no person under point (i) is identified, or if there is any doubt that the person(s) identified are the beneficial owner(s), the natural person(s) who hold the position of senior managing official(s), the obliged entities shall keep records of the actions taken in order to identify the beneficial ownership under point (i) and this point; (b) in the case of trusts: (i) the settlor; (ii) the trustee(s); (iii) the protector, if any; (iv) the beneficiaries, or where the individuals benefiting from the legal arrangement or entity have yet to be determined, the class of persons in whose main interest the legal arrangement or entity is set up or operates; (v) any other natural person exercising ultimate control over the trust by means of direct or indirect ownership or by other means; (c) in the case of legal entities such as foundations, and legal arrangements similar to trusts, the natural person(s) holding equivalent or similar positions to those referred to in point (b).

[77] Given the most recent developments in European law, soon there will be a European central register of beneficial owners of companies. The details of this novelty are explained in Part II. On the current debate about the introduction of a public register, *see* among others Meinzer 2016.

[78] Interview with author 2014.

[79] Henn et al. 2013, pp. 33–40.

[80] A report commissioned by the EU Commission on the effectiveness of asset recovery mechanism states that the Federal Financial Services Supervisory Authority (BaFin) has access to a database for basic data of account details of naturalised persons and legal entities in Germany, which is made available on request to law enforcement authorities in the process of investigation. Irvin and Levi 2009, p. 51.

register of beneficial owners, not only for companies and legal entities, but also for boats and real estate and other types of properties, in order to improve the implementation of the anti-money laundering regime. 'Citizens, whose data is collected in a public registry would regard the creation of such a register as a danger'.[81] In the banking sector 'there is a significant focus on the disclosure of beneficial owners. However, this system is not effective. The legislature and also the FATF have assumed, for example, that Mafia bosses acting behind the nominees would actually provide their identity. In reality, money launderers lie and conceal their identity, so that even when one traces the beneficial owners of a company, it would be impossible to find out who they are. The burden is very heavy: companies need to provide data of the beneficial owners and we need to verify it. If the beneficial owner of a company is another legal person, it is required to trace back the beneficial owner of the latter, and this process can go back five or six layers. Yet, through this system it has never happened that a money launderer has actually provided his/her identity to the bank. Why would he/she? She/he would be weary of life or crazy if she/he were to say that she/he works for the Mafia. Nobody would do it, yet all believe this'.[82] Yet, there is quite a widespread consensus on the importance of disclosing beneficial owners of legal persons.[83] In 2010 the FATF assessors expressed particular concern about the issue of beneficial ownership of companies and other legal entities because German businesses and professions found non-compliant with the FATF requirements on the verification of beneficial ownership. Assessors found that the designated businesses and professionals differed in their understanding of the applicable law.[84] According to the report published by the NGOs in 2013, since 2005 every state has had a bank account register in which all banks are required to register all bank accounts, which law enforcement and revenue authorities have used often in the past few years for purposes of mutual

[81] Interview with author 2014.

[82] Ibid.

[83] For example, according to a report published by the Global Agenda Council on Organized Crime, the use of complex cross-border schemes of corporate vehicles with a 'Chinese box' structure to conceal identities and hide illegal proceeds is considered to be an 'enabler' of money laundering. Organised crime enablers include 'the individuals, mechanism and facilities used for primarily legal purposes that are adapted for criminal objectives. They play an important role in facilitating organized crime activities, whether intentionally or inadvertently, increasing its benefits and scale, and predominantly reducing its risks'. According to the report, the hiding of the offenders' identity behind the veil of beneficial ownerships, in particular, is essential for providing an appearance of legality and thus avoiding prosecution and confiscation. See Global Agenda Council on Organised Crime 2012, p. 15.

[84] FATF 2010, p. 146. Yet according to a study commissioned by the European Commission in 2009 approximately 15 Member States agreed that the European definition of beneficial owner is clear and not too wide. However, the definition is only clear in the case of simple corporate structures or companies; where multi-level holding structures are concerned, the notion is still vague. See Deloitte 2009, pp. 66–67.

legal assistance.[85] Yet, the report concludes that, given the cumbersome procedures required to access the registers for the purpose of sharing information with foreign authorities the practice might even diminish the effectiveness of several bilateral agreements between Germany and other countries in respect of the exchange of information. In addition, the document draws attention to the European law-making process and to the role played by the German government. The authors complain about the fact that Germany, together with other member countries, has blocked for long time the process of establishing a common European register.[86] Despite the blockage, the EU has recently gone through a paradigm change.[87] In fact, the Fourth Anti-Money Laundering Directive has introduced a public register of beneficial owners across Europe.[88] Yet further criticisms have been raised: 'with the introduction of the beneficial owner policy, the responsibility is put on the clients, who now have the duty to disclose information'.[89]

Another controversial matter concerning the preventive part of the anti-money laundering policy concerns the enhanced due diligence that obliged entities need to apply in case of dealing with **Politically Exposed Persons** (PEPs). This is a highly controversial topic, because it is very political and can potentially create diplomatic problems between countries. For example, as one respondent of the NGO WEED observes, 'if we look at the Arab Spring, and at the relations between Germany and Egypt, they were good until 2011, when Mubarak was delegitimised by his own people and by the international community. Only then, Mubarak was named as a dictator, however, at that point the preventive purpose of the anti-money laundering law was no longer fulfilled. What was, applied, however, was the asset recovery mechanism, which is indeed very effective. On the other hand, it would have been a highly political issue had German banks seized his assets while he was ruling the country. There is too much discretion in this area, which might be abused for political reasons. On the other hand, providing official lists of PEPs would still not be a solution. Such lists would always need to be updated, and they could potentially ignite diplomatic disputes between states. This has already been experienced on an international level, for instance, as regards tax havens. Blacklisting also raises many of human rights issues. The alternative to providing an index of potentially risky persons or countries would not solve the problem either, because in a legal context it is necessary to be able to differentiate between black and white, and not to have a gradual evaluation'. In addition, 'also, in this case the banking sector bears a heavy burden. About 60,000 € annually are spent buying the lists of PEPs. For every transaction it is required to verify whether the individuals involved are on the list. Yet, as long as the

[85] Henn et al. 2013, pp. 33–40. The register has been introduced pursuant to Article 24c of the Kredit Wirtschaft Gesetz (KWG). In 2012 there have been for example 114,364 requests. See BaFin 2012.

[86] Henn et al. 2013, pp. 33–40.

[87] Interview with author 2014.

[88] See Part II, Sect. 2.2.5

[89] Interview with author 2014.

PEP carries out only normal transactions it is not required to intervene. Interventions are required only when the transactions are suspicious, but such operations would emerge anyway through the normal monitoring system. This, again, seems to be not very effective' according to one attorney. It is advocated, at least, that such lists shall be public in order to reduce the burden for the private sector'.[90]

Currently, secrecy covers not only banking activities, but also a whole range of financial transactions. Regulations that provide secrecy include laws that allow a low degree of transparency in the establishment and accounting by corporate entities, the creation of trusts whose real beneficiaries remain anonymous, zero or low tax rates and minimal exchange of tax information with other tax jurisdictions, banking secrecy, and barriers for the exchange of information relating to criminal matters. Secrecy is a controversial topic. The right to privacy is a fundamental right of any individual,[91] and secrecy can, in fact, serve lawful and valid purposes.[92] Yet, secrecy can be exploited for unlawful purposes, such as for purposes of violating of national tax or anti-money laundering laws through the concealing of financial transactions. Banking secrecy has been used as a ground to refuse mutual legal assistance and co-operation in criminal matters, thus impeding or hindering criminal investigations or other legal proceedings.[93] In this scenario, professionals can misuse the absence of direct supervision to launder funds or act as intermediaries in helping others to launder. In addition, money launderers can be the beneficial owners of brokerages or firm of accountants and lawyers.[94] According to one attorney, there is a particular area in which secrecy has not yet been regulated, namely, bank deposit boxes. 'Preventive regulations that impose a duty to collect information about clients and to share it with law enforcement agencies on request are not applicable to deposit boxes. While prosecutors may receive information about a suspect's transactions carried out on a bank account in the last 2 years, they cannot access the same information on deposit boxes. For example, in the *Hoeneß* case, he might still even have millions of Euros hidden in thirty deposit boxes in Germany. Assets hidden in deposit boxes in the form of gold or security papers do not reflect in any bank accounts, and Germany has no central register for them, therefore investigators would never have access to this information. The Mafia

---

[90] Ibid.

[91] Article 12 of the United Nations Declaration on Human rights (1948): *No one shall be subjected to arbitrary interference with his privacy, family, home or correspondence, nor to attacks upon his honour and reputation. Everyone has the right to the protection of the law against such interference or attacks.*

[92] For example, politically persecuted individuals can use secrecy to secure their assets from being confiscated by authoritarian regimes. Secrecy can also be in the interest of the family. For instance, the original purpose of trusts (financial tools which provide secrecy) was to promote the protection of spouses who are unable to look after their own affairs.

[93] The veil of secrecy can be a bar to investigations, thus a guarantee of impunity. For example, secrecy has been used by corrupt dictators around the world to conceal stolen assets. See Baker 2005, p. 238.

[94] Global Agenda Council on Organised Crime 2012, p. 8.

could also have such deposit boxes in Germany and nobody would know. Why? Because the State has for years refused to create a specific central register. It would actually be very easy for the banks to communicate the required information because they collect it for internal purposes. Yet, the legislature has decided not to regulate this sector and I do not understand why. It could help investigator hugely. I actually believe that disclosing information about deposit boxes would help more than filing STRs; I would reduce the number of STRs and improve this other aspect. This would also reduce the burden for banks and would improve the effectiveness of the system'.[95]

Another issue raised by quite a number of interviewees is the lack of **knowledge**. The assumption was that the role-players were familiar with the content of the legislation, given the fact that they were selected on the basis of their expertise in the field. The empirical study was, therefore, not conducted to measure respondents' level of knowledge. However, this assumption has been proven wrong by empirical research. In fact, according to the interviewees, there is rather a low level of expertise. This can be blamed on the either the lack of specific legal training in the public and private sectors, or on the vague formulation of the law. A Ministry representative, for example, advocates that the wording of Article 261 should be formulated in a clearer way. According to an attorney, 'Many lawyers have not even read the provisions of the Anti-Money Laundering Act nor Article 261 of the GCC, and without sounding arrogant, if they were to do so, they would not understand the details straightaway after the first reading'.[96] Neither prosecutors nor judges seem to be familiar with the law. According to a senior prosecutor, 'prosecutors who do not work in this department have never even read it and there is no judge that has ever read the whole legislation, and this is the reason why most of them do not understand how the law is drafted'.[97] The prosecutor believes that the lack of knowledge is related not only to the unclear formulation, but also to the lack of proper training. 'The legal provision is not included in the law syllabus and is not part of the state exam for the legal profession in Berlin. Article 261 of the GCC is also not part of the university examinations. What students are taught is what would be a case of money laundering. Consequently, those who embark on a professional carrier in law have no expertise in this field. The lack of legal training leads to the fact that, often when someone is charged with money laundering, the courts are very surprised and do not know how to react'. 'There is a need to update legal training, as criminal law professors in Germany are still reluctant to engage with the legal provisions that regulate economic crimes. What is lacking is a profound and precise knowledge on this matter. The private sector, especially industries, fund huge segments of legal education, which results in even less critical thinking'.[98] According to one interviewee, the courts too have neither contributed to a better

[95] Interview with author 2014.

[96] Ibid.

[97] Ibid.

[98] Ibid.

interpretation of the law, nor has the jurisprudence emanating from them clarified the law. In fact 'decisions taken by the upper state courts or by the Supreme Court are confusing and do not set clear guidelines; despite the existence of a considerable amount of jurisprudence on this topic whether such jurisprudence could be applied usefully in a criminal matter is another matter. For example, recently published court decisions have not tackled fundamental issues; they instead deal with matters of a routine economic nature'.[99]

However, as regards the Berlin criminal investigators the situation is different as they are specifically knowledgeable in the field of financial investigations: 'Investigators working in this field receive special training that is conducted at a federal level, making it uniform for the whole country. Young professionals who are currently involved in financial investigations are experts and must keep on updating their knowledge. In Berlin there are 14 offices devoted exclusively to investigating money-laundering cases'.[100] This might, if it is true, speak for the state of Berlin, but does not appear to reflect the situation in the whole country. Within the supervisory authorities, too, 'there is a need for specific training in the field. In all areas of operation employees can receive specialized training and there should be soon be such opportunities also in the field of anti-money laundering law as well.[101] The public officials stress that 'the Anti-Money Laundering Act has been a frequently amended law, therefore it is an ongoing process of updating and improving. Individuals that start working in this field have to learn from the very basics what money laundering is. The anti-money laundering policy implies an ongoing learning process that requires professionals to always be up-to-date. One of the reasons why the process [of improvement of the policy] takes so long is because while applying new rules, issues and problems may arise. Sometimes, we can solve those issues by looking at some precedent examples, but in other cases, the challenges are completely new so that we need to figure out a solution on our own. Sometimes we pose questions to the State Ministry of Internal Affairs in Hesse, and if they do not have an answer then they direct our query to the Federal Ministry of Finance in Berlin'. An example of a problematic issue is the following: 'At what time should a real estate agent identify the client of a contract? Every particular profession and business has different problems when applying the Anti-Money Laundering Act and there are approximately 66,000 obligated businesses and individuals in our district that should be supervised, and we do not "know" them. There is no register that lists companies obliged to observe the Anti-Money Laundering Act rules. We do not have adequate knowledge of their professions, of their way of working or their special risks, but still we have to supervise them. It is therefore difficult for the authorities to provide answers in this context. Obviously we need to apply a "risk-based approach" that allows us to focus on those activities

[99] Ibid.

[100] Ibid.

[101] Ibid.

where the risk of money laundering is higher'.[102] However, thanks to the introduction of the Anti-Money Laundering Act, employees' awareness of the threats of money laundering in the private sector has increased. This has already been observed by credit institutions taking part in *Oswald*'s empirical research. The credit institutions that took part in the survey with regard to the suitability of the—at that time current—regulation to prevent and repress organised crime considered the law necessary because it helped employees to understand the risks of money laundering.[103] The law was hence considered suitable for the purpose of making the private sector aware of the risks of money laundering. This, in the long term, would have been a prerogative for the effective prevention of the infiltration of criminal assets through credit institutions. Important steps have been made also with regard to the exchange of information between the supervisory authorities at the state level. Given that anti-money laundering regulations have been in force for more than 20 years, one can expect that the law instigators are indeed sensitised to the issue. Indeed, according to a respondent there is currently a much higher perception of the problem than 15 years ago. In addition, in order to favour the exchange of information between local authorities, 'the Federal Ministry of Finance organizes a meeting several times a year where representatives of all the German states participate and exchange information, in order to co-ordinate actions at all levels. This does not work for all topics but it allows them to reach agreements on the most important issues'. The foundation stone for good co-operation has been laid: 'Since 2011,' adds the public official, 'I have been to the police academy each year to show and report our work as a supervisory authority. And the *Regierungspräsidium* Darmstadt invites representatives of police departments, the state office of criminal investigation (Landeskriminalamt), tax offices, the customs office, prosecution authorities and the German Financial Intelligence Unit (FIU) to our annual congress. So they receive information about our administrative responsibilities and sometimes we receive information in return'.[104]

'Even if there were to be only one jurisdiction that does not enforce anti-money laundering standards, the problem could not be solved completely'.[105] One of the cumbersome matters pointed out by prosecutors interviewed by *Oswald* was the fact that some countries had not yet implemented adequate rules and thus it was not possible to receive **mutual legal assistance**.[106] This is still perceived quite unanimously by respondents as one of the main factors hindering the effectiveness of money-laundering investigations and prosecutions. In particular, one respondent mentions the example of economic operations conducted by foreign criminal organisations: 'When money comes from a foreign country, first of all it is very difficult to prove the illegal origin; secondly there is not much interest in

[102] Ibid.

[103] Oswald 1997, p. 208.

[104] Interview with author 2014.

[105] Ibid.

[106] Oswald 1997, p. 149.

investigating these cases. For instance, it is quite well known that Russian and Italian criminal networks operate in Germany, but it is very difficult to prove the illegal origin of the money invested. Let us say if, for example, money invested in the real estate sector derives from an illegitimate privatisation in Russia committed in the last century, it would be very hard to provide evidence of such an illegal act. Information on the operation would be difficult to trace and it would be necessary to translate it and to verify whether the act constituted an offence in the country at the time of commission, since the high degree of suspicion is not enough, prosecutors have to prove the illegal provenance and the commission of the predicate offence'. According to public prosecutors 'international co-operation works very well at least on paper, because the law provides all the instruments. However, in practice, this mostly depends on the countries with which one wants to co-operate. The problem is that money laundering is a transnational phenomenon, so as soon as the money has crossed several countries, it becomes very difficult to trace back the paper trail and to conduct financial investigations which end in the confiscation of assets. In addition, offshore centres and secrecy jurisdictions, where companies with limited responsibility are registered, do not provide information on real and beneficial owners. When the money reaches Germany, it appears to be clean. Also, foreign banks, if they do not belong to the same group as a national one, are reluctant to provide help in money-laundering investigations. In such cases we are forced to deal with the public authorities of the foreign states, but they require a higher burden of proof to co-operate'.[107] Also international co-operation is cumbersome because 'there are still major differences among the 28 EU member states. There are countries that have a great interest in integrating dirty money in their economies, in order to foster their GDP. Therefore, the German authorities have limited possibilities of identifying and detecting money-laundering transactions undertaken in those jurisdictions'.[108] However, one prosecutor specifies that 'issues relating to mutual legal assistance and the possible problems deriving from the need to ensure that the predicate offence, if committed abroad, constitutes a crime under foreign law, do not even appear in practice. Frequently the cases do not even reach the investigation stage because of the lack of evidence to commence investigations'. With regard to international co-operation as a factor that influences the effectiveness of a law, European research conducted recently looks at whether Member States have signed, ratified and implemented the main international and European instruments dealing with money laundering.[109] The non-ratification or non-implementation of international measures, according to the research project, might negatively influence the effectiveness of the policy, particularly in the field of international co-operation.[110] Besides being a missed opportunity for international co-operation, the fact of not ratifying international instruments might also be interpreted as unwillingness on the part of the

[107] Interview with author 2014.

[108] Ibid.

[109] Unger et al. 2013, p. 21.

[110] Ibid.

legislature to comply with international standards, or it could be ascribed to the incompatibility between such standards and the domestic legal system. As regards Germany, the country has recently ratified the UN Convention Against Corruption[111] and the Council of Europe Convention on Laundering, Search, Seizure and Confiscation of the Proceeds from Crime of 2005.

A further problematic issue raised by the respondents is the inappropriateness of **resources** allocated to the prevention and repression of money laundering. Instruments available for financial investigations have been updated; yet the lack of resources attributable to the underfunding of law enforcement personnel is still perceived as one of the main issues impeding the effective combating of money laundering. 'Investigations on the structure of organised crime are too expensive and time consuming; they take 4–5 years and they require one person to be permanently devoted to those proceedings, with the risk that the process might not culminate in a satisfactory conclusion'. The police do not have enough resources in order to deal with all this information. The personnel in the police has even been reduced in the last years, therefore they are not able to cope with the workload imposed by the anti-money laundering policy'.[112] This is due to the resources constraints regarding money-laundering investigations, according to two police officers.[113] Another attorney agrees with this criticism and points out the fact that 'trials in the field of economic crimes that last between 3–5 years are absurd and very ineffective. Law enforcement authorities are not able to deal with offence notices in due course, due to the lack of personnel'. The defence attorney recalls the example of proceedings that have been closed pursuant to Article 170(2) of the German Code of Criminal Procedure[114] because prosecutors could not prove the elements of the offence. '[…] Sometimes attorneys can also allow proceedings to 'die' on their own. One can be sure that the longer a proceeding lasts, the harder it would be for investigators to provide evidence of the facts'. Trials of money-laundering cases are costly and time-consuming. In fact, according to the attorney 'the risk for prosecutors is very high where they prefer charges and seek a conviction; they have to face 20–30 hearings, up to 50 witnesses, and someone has to pay for it'. 'My clients', continues the attorney 'are interested in neither a conviction nor an acquittal. We aim to wind up the proceedings by paying a fine (*Bußgeld*) pursuant to Article 153a of the German Code of Criminal Procedure. The

[111] The German Parliament, after eleven years, ratified UNCAC, so that it came into force on 12 December 2014, see BGBI 2015 II, p. 140. A specific delay in implementing the Third Directive was encountered in many states; however, this was not linked to the quality of the directive but rather to internal matters. Unger et al. 2014, pp. 144–145.

[112] Interview with author 2014.

[113] Ibid.

[114] Article 170(2) Conclusion of the Investigation Proceedings of the German Code of Criminal procedure: In all other cases the public prosecution office shall terminate the proceedings. The public prosecutor shall notify the accused thereof if he was examined as such or a warrant of arrest was issued against him; the same shall apply if he requested such notice or if there is a particular interest in the notification.

longer the proceedings take, the higher the chance of the prosecution accepting such a deal'. In the last 20/30 years there has been a cut of public expenditure; for example in Berlin there were 90 tribunals, while nowadays there are only 35. When a judge retires, she/he will be not replaced, but rather her/his duties will be shared between the remaining colleagues. This is one of the causes of the long preliminary investigations and proceedings'.[115]

Whilst more resources for law enforcement are advocated, a respondent believes that 'this is an issue that can be questioned in every government, which must set priorities in respect of where to invest its resources. Therefore, firstly the state must assess the risk and the threat posed by the issue and secondly, it must verify which possibilities the existing legal framework offers to tackle the problem'.[116] In this context, two policemen confirm that 'the priority of investigative personnel since 2001 has been terrorism'. As to the question linking the effectiveness of the policy to the availability of resources, yet quantity does not mean quality, and qualified personnel are more effective than a high number of employees.[117]

7.2.3 Considerations

The reader will have noticed that some of the obstacles pointed out by the respondents are in the focus of critical legal scholarship, too, and have in fact already been dealt with in Part III. Given that the respondents did not always agree on those matters, one can infer that they have not yet been solved, and thus the discussion still remains open. In addition, certain challenges have already been mentioned in the *Oswald*' research. This shows that despite almost 20 years of enforcement since the research was conducted in 1996, practitioners face similar obstacles. Despite an analysis previous research findings, the fact that certain problems are still perceived as unresolved points to the fact that legislative amendments that have been effected in the meantime have not led to the effective improvement as far as such issues are concerned. However, it seems that finally some of the hindrances that have emerged through the interviews conducted will be tackled, by Parliament in the process of implementing the Fourth Anti-Money Laundering Directive. In particular, 'the most important changes that will be introduced concern the introduction of a constitutionally legitimate inversion of the burden of proof, as has already been mentioned in the *Koalitionsvertrag* (coalition agreement);[118] the adoption of the 'all serious-crimes approach', and the criminal

[115] Interview with author 2014.

[116] Ibid.

[117] Ibid.

[118] On the most recent developments, *see* Footnote 52.

liability of the perpetrator of the predicate offence', which has recently been introduced. In addition, the interviewee claim that 'there is currently a debate about the possibility of introducing a mechanism that interrupts the transfer of the legal property when the first object was procured from a criminal action'.[119] This would avoid interception by a third party in good faith, who buys an object that was procured through illegal money and then sells it on, interrupting the 'illegal derivation' of that object. Yet the directive, given the differences existing among member states with regard to the regulation of corporate liability, does not tackle one of the fundamental matters relating to money-laundering control. In Germany criminal liability is only attributed to natural persons. This 'is an important area in which Germany needs to make some progress. It is almost impossible to tackle economic crimes with the same legal tools used for addressing other crimes such as bodily injury, because economic crimes are often undertaken by legal entities and not by natural persons. Yet criminal liability for legal persons has not been recognised and no political party is really fighting for this'.[120]

7.3 Perceived Conflicting Interests

The critical approach in the analysis of the law discloses conflicting interests that have either existed since the introduction of the policy or that have emerged during the course of its application. As shown in Part II, an analysis of the legislative process has revealed that introduction of Article 261 of the GCC was accompanied by different expectations. The contrasting expectations and intents connected to the criminalisation of money laundering reveal the conflicting interests surrounding the genesis of the anti-money laundering policy. Expectations that were conflicting with each other had to be negotiated and were compromised through the formulation of a vague offence that allowed different interpretations. Yet, the implementation of the law has led to the emergence again of some of the conflicting situations. In addition, given that the policy regulates a complex and multifaceted issue, new conflicts have surfaced through its enforcement. The effects triggered by the legal provision can indeed be perceived positively or negatively by the different actors involved. Again, the analysis of the conflicts is aimed at highlighting the perspective of legal actors representing the different points of view of practitioners and experts representing the divergent views of institutions.

---

[119] The institute proposed would be similar to the one regulated by Article 935 BGB, *Bürgerliches Gesetzbuch*, which regulates the 'No good faith acquisition of lost property'. Interview with author 2014.

[120] Interview with author 2014.

7.3.1 The Law-Making Process

The poor formulation of Article 261 of the GCC has to do with the law-making process. 'The offence derives from a complex international and European law-making process that has been influenced especially by the US'. 'This holds true for the preventive regime too', explains one prosecutor: 'The introduction of the FIU for the collecting of information on suspicious transactions was based on the American system'.[121] External actors, as is also shown in Part II, influenced the way the offence was described under German law. This, according to some of the respondents, has negatively impacted the formulation of the law, and consequently, its implementation. This is confirmed also by other respondents who said that Germany introduced the offence in order to comply with international standards.[122] In particular, the formulation of the offence under international law was constructed on the basis of the Anglo-American system, where there is no obligation to prosecute, and so the law was formulated broadly to allow more cases to be dealt with. Actually, under the German criminal system, in which prosecutors are obligated to initiate an investigation once they are notified of the commission of any offence, such an indeterminate offence creates problems of interpretation. Prosecutors sometimes do not know whether a case can be subsumed under the money-laundering definition or not. In such cases, prosecutors usually prefer to charge another offence'.[123] He adds that 'if the law had been drafted without having to comply with the FATF Recommendations and with the EU Directives, it would have been formulated in a much clearer way, so that it would not have resulted in such lack of specificity'. Not only was the formulation of the provision influenced by external factors, but it was also, in the first place, meant as a measure to tackle drug trafficking.[124] The fact that money laundering was dealt with in the same way as the war on drugs, and was thus part of a prohibition policy, does not reflect the European approach, where more compelling issues are infiltration of illegal money from white collar crimes or corruption in the legal economy. Also, the subsequent expansion of the scope of the policy to deal with terrorist financing is criticised as not being perfectly in line with the European approach. In fact, 'the financing of terrorism is the opposite phenomenon, because it consists of taking money with a legitimate origin in order to use it for illicit purposes. Yet, the anti-money laundering regime deals with illicit financial flows and therefore the financing of terrorism is considered to be part of it'.[125] As a consequence of the ambiguous formulation, the criminal definition of money laundering differs radically among European states, with the only commonality among the different laws being the fact that the proceeds of crime should not remain with the perpetrators, and these

[121] Ibid.
[122] Ibid.
[123] Ibid.
[124] Ibid.
[125] Ibid.

differences hamper co-operation between law enforcement authorities.[126] On the other hand, 'despite the FATF played a very relevant role in the law-making process and thanks to the first round of the mutual evaluation process, and the fact that Germany was bound by the First European Directive to introduce the money-laundering offence, this was not an external imposition because Germany did take part in the European decision-making process and it had a strong interest in the fight against organised crime'.[127] A recent publication of the European anti-money laundering regime also contests the significance of the role played by the FATF in shaping anti-money laundering policy.[128] The authors advocate in particular that the ownership of the policy be taken back to the European level. The reason is to avoid the uncritical transposing of FATF standards into EU law, and to adopt more suitable approaches befitting the different European legal cultures. Otherwise, there would be the risk that countries would inflate their policy outcomes to appear compliant on paper, without actually putting the standards into practice.

7.3.2 *Dirty Money Versus Capital Flight*

In the early days of the policy, a question emerged as to whether money laundering should have been linked to tax crimes by adding tax-related offences as predicate offences for money laundering or as to whether the offences should have been restricted to combat only serious crimes, namely, those crimes that, in the common understanding were perceived as posing a serious harm to society. It is a trite fact that white collar crimes are perceived as less dangerous than other crimes, also because they are victimless offences since they cause only indirect harm to individuals.[129] In fact, the credit institutions interviewed by *Oswald* between 1993 and

[126] Ibid.

[127] Ibid.

[128] Unger et al. 2014, pp. 240–241.

[129] Proceeds of crime are usually considered properties deriving from the commission of a criminal offence; for example, money obtained from drug smuggling is ab initio criminal. Monies deriving from tax evasion, are, instead, lawfully earned, but may become tainted, for example, when not declared or when retained due to fraudulent tax deductions. This has raised criticism, on the basis that the proceeds of tax evasion are different in nature from profits of conventional criminality; yet, even though the underlying conduct which generates the proceeds may be legal, it is the retention of the money that should be paid over as tax which constitutes the criminal conduct. It might be argued that proceeds of crime are monies 'derived from or obtained, directly or indirectly, through the commission of an offence' (Article 2 of UNCAC), and therefore monies retained are not included. However, it is the evasion of taxes that generates the illicit profits. It can be, thus, argued that those profits derive from an offence. Another controversial issue is related to tax evasion committed abroad. The traditional approach is, in fact, that countries are not supposed to enforce other countries' revenue laws. Some jurisdictions, therefore, do not consider tax offences predicate crimes if committed abroad.

1996 were of the opinion that organised crime was more serious on account of its danger to human rights, while capital flight was perceived as less harmful.[130] In addition, the financial system is partially based on illicit flows of money deriving from the violations fiscal, currency or export laws, so that financial centres are not interested in excluding the revenues derived from such crimes from their business.[131] Yet, given the growing awareness of the negative effects of offshore jurisdiction and tax evasion, questions relating to money laundering and tax matters have yet again been linked together as of early 2000. The anti-money laundering regime was considered an effective measure to counteract tax offences.[132] However, this change is still considered controversial. Also the NGO WEED, indeed, has come across the topic of money laundering by dealing with the issue of illicit financial flows: 'We were trying to understand where the money goes that is stashed away through, for example, high corruption and capital flight in developing countries. Money laundering is part of the problem'.[133] The report published by the NGO in 2013, in fact, focuses on money laundering in the context of the grand-corruption of autocrats, tax evasion conducted by multinational companies, and misinvoicing.[134] Indeed, 'according to criminal statistics, money-laundering offences are committed mostly in relation to economic crimes (*Wirtschaftskriminalität*), such as fraud'; and that 'the field in which there is the highest volume of prominent white-collar crimes is highly likely to be the financial sector. Employees of banks have also been involved in tax evasion which is committed especially through missing trader fraud (*Umsatzsteuerkarussell*).[135] This opinion is not shared by all respondents. Others believe that the two phenomena should be tackled separately: 'there is a common misunderstanding between the concepts of money laundering and black money, meaning tax evasion. While tax evasion is a problem in Germany which is experienced in daily life, the same cannot be said for money laundering. 'Fiscal crimes are widespread in Germany, but this does not mean that there is a lot of money laundering either'.[136] Given that the money saved through tax evasion is intermingled with legitimately originated profits, and that tax evasion is a predicate crime for money laundering, and from a theoretical perspective too, there is the potential of broad contamination, and thus of widespread commission of money laundering. On the other hand, from an official point of view, the BMF supports the idea that tax-related crimes are offences

---

[130] This was, for instance, revealed through the questionnaires submitted to credit institutions by Oswald in which employees lamented the fact that they were not able to discern proceeds of predicate offences from money laundering from capital flight. See Oswald 1997, p. 144.

[131] Pieth 1993, pp. 102 ss.

[132] Alldridge 2001, p. 350. Serious tax crimes were thus introduced in the FATF Recommendations revised in February 2012 under the definition of predicate offences provided in the Glossary, see FATF 2012, p. 12.

[133] Interview with author 2014.

[134] Henn et al. 2013.

[135] Interview with author 2014.

[136] Ibid.

connected to money laundering, because this helps to overcome the fact that tax havens refuse requests for mutual legal assistance based on tax evasion offences, raising sovereignty issues, since such requests could be grounded on the basis of money laundering.

7.3.3 *Conducting Business Versus Persecuting and Preventing Crime*

From the interviews with the prosecutors and with the three respondents who are in contact with businesses and professionals obligated as accounting bodies by the Anti-Money Laundering Act, it emerges that there seems to be a conflict between the need to access information in order to investigate and prosecute money laundering and the need to protect the right to privacy. If on the one hand, as we have seen, one of the perceived advantages of the policy is the availability of information provided by the designated financial and non-financial businesses and professions to investigators, on the other hand, the collecting and recording of such a vast amount of information can be considered a limitation, if not a violation of the right to privacy. There seems therefore to be a perceived tension between the need for law enforcement agencies to gain access to personal information in the course of money-laundering investigations, and the right to have one's personal data protected. However, the interviewees do not relate the right of privacy to the protection of fundamental civil rights. Their perspective is rather that of the private sector, which is reluctant to file STRs and share information with law enforcement authorities as they perceive this to be interference in their relationships with private customers. In addition, subjects obliged by the Anti-Money Laundering Act are reluctant to assume policing duties, such as searches. In sum, whereas criminal justice authorities are for more transparency in the workings of companies and financial institutions, the latter two are concerned that this would hinder the way they do business or practise their professions. Investigators, on the other hand, welcome information provided in order to be able to support their work. A senior prosecutor for instance, believes that the state interest in tackling organised criminality should prevail over the interest of not violating the privacy of the suspects, the reason being not keeping a balance between interests, but rather a matter of practicality. If investigators had to distinguish between the private life of suspected members of organised criminal networks and their criminal activities they would not be able to conduct investigations: 'We cannot say that what concerns the private life of perpetrators is not relevant for the investigations.' Also, the prosecutors agree on the need for more transparency in the field of corporate and banking services; yet they do not consider banking secrecy an obstacle to financial investigations. Also, according to the two chief detective superintendents, 'the main advantages introduced by the Anti-Money Laundering Act are the possibility of requiring recorded information about customers from the private sector, and the possibility of exchanging information. This represents a great advantage in terms of the speed of the investigation and of availability of data'. On the other hand, 'lots of Designated Non-Financial Businesses and Professions (DNFBP) have difficulties with their clients in explaining why they need to collect and verify personal information about customers, also because of privacy issues'.[137] For this reason, the regional council of Darmstadt in Hesse has designed a flyer with explanations that companies can use and show to their clients. For instance, 'While banks have time to collect information about clients during the business relationship, this is not the case with many professions that have rather short relationships with their customers. Especially in these cases, the extensive system of anti-money laundering rules is often burdensome. The obligation to report a money-laundering suspicion is difficult to communicate especially to individuals and small firms, because they fear retaliation'.[138] Private actors, especially companies, are afraid of hampering their relationships with clients when reporting suspicious operations: 'From the criminal investigations it emerges who has filed the STRs, therefore, even if the criminal proceeding triggered by the filing of a STR ends with a closure, the relationship between the suspected client and the filing institution is spoilt'. For this reason, lawyers advise their corporate clients, when dealing with good customers, 'that it is necessary to evaluate the situation in order not to compromise the relations between the company and the customer'.[139] Accountants and auditors, too, according to the federal chamber, do not file many STRs (only twelve in the last 3 years), because they are not interested in investigating the criminal connections of their customers or related third parties.[140] From the perspective of professionals, the duties imposed by the law in order to monitor operations to detect money launderers are not appropriate. 'The businesses and professions to whom we relate, as a supervisory authority, are not investigators, they only aim to conduct their own business in a clear way. Many of them do not possess adequate knowledge of how to tackle the phenomenon of offshore finance and of shell companies. Therefore, it is very hard for normal businesses to even recognize such cases'.[141] According to the representatives of the chamber of accountants and auditors, the supervisory body that receives and checks the STRs from the financial auditors and certified general accountants and sends them to the BKA and to the public prosecutors offices, 'these professions take the obligations imposed by the Anti-Money Laundering Act very seriously. In particular, financial auditors and certified general accountants belong to the designated professions that are obligated, pursuant to Article 2(1)8 GwG, to subject themselves to the anti-money laundering prevention measures according to Article 3 Anti-Money Laundering Act. In fact, we do not know of any cases in which financial auditors and certified general accountants have violated their

---

[137] Ibid.

[138] Ibid.

[139] Ibid.

[140] Ibid.

[141] Ibid.

obligations to file STRs pursuant to Article 11 Anti-Money Laundering Act'.[142] However, the two respondents consider the obligations too complex for the sector. In fact, they believe that 'the [low] number of STRs received by the authority confirms the opinion that obligations imposed by the Anti-Money Laundering Act are problematic with regard to the professions, from a proportionality point of view. The uncovering of criminal schemes among clients or other third parties is not their main activity, neither is it of those professions nor of other business accountants, nor is it something that frequently recurs or that can easily be detected by those professions'. In sum, 'the duty to investigate the identity of those who conduct suspicious transactions should actually belong to the police.[143] Banks are also burdened with bureaucratic duties imposed by the anti-money laundering policy. Yet, when they file the STRs, after having conducted this research, the police cannot use the information collected by the private entity to start investigations; they need to conduct their own investigations. Therefore research conducted is totally useless'. According to a respondent, the burden imposed on the real estate is also too heavy: 'Agents, for example, need to ask for the identity of clients from the very beginning of the business relationship. This means that in cities where the real estate sector is booming, such as Munich, for a flat there might be a 100 interested buyers, and the agent needs to verify the identity of each of them, even though only one will be able to buy the flat'. Actually, the real estate sector has been identified by empirical studies as one of the sectors at highest risk of money laundering. One of the reasons why this type of business is particularly abused by money launderers is that agents are not conscious about money-laundering risks. Therefore, if on the one hand, the legitimate interest of conducting real estate business shall not be hampered, on the other hand, it is necessary that agents become more engage in the prevention of money laundering.[144]

7.3.4 Expanding Criminal Law Versus Ultima Ratio

This conflict can be summarised with the words of a respondent, who said that 'the problem is due to the fact that Article 261 is closely connected to the Anti-Money Laundering Act, and therefore, although it is a criminal law, it has been drafted by the Ministry of Finance. In Germany 'there has been a switch: if at the beginning the crime of money laundering was created to fight organised crime, lately there has been a tendency to consider it a tool to protect the lawful economy from the infiltration of illegal money. In fact, if in the beginning the Federal Ministry of the Interior was responsible for the anti-money laundering law, currently it is the

[142] Ibid.

[143] Ibid.

[144] See two reports on the role of money laundering in the real estate sector: BKA 2012; Bussman 2015.

Ministry of Finance that drafts the bills'.[145] The Ministry of Justice can only approve the drafted text. The entire money-laundering legislation is a matter of financial policy'.[146] The problem is obviously referred to by the respondent not as a pure matter of competence but rather as something affecting the true meaning of the policy. This is due to the fact that 'there was a trend in the whole of Europe, and in the globalised world, to deregulate the financial sector [...]. The State, however, needs to take a clear position and to persecute financial misbehaviours.[147] Within the German debate on anti-money laundering law, the two interests are represented by the Ministry of Finance, which advocates for a stricter control of economic violations through criminal law, and the Ministry of Justice, which tries to put the brakes on the continuous expansion of criminal law. 'There is a recent tendency in Germany, but not only here, to harden criminal law. In the 1970s, there was the idea that the resort to criminal law should be limited. It was a time of decriminalisation. Nowadays, public opinion finds it easier to resort to criminal law than to tackle social problems. Therefore, the duty of the BMJV is to slow down this tendency and to keep penal law as an *ultima ratio* tool, otherwise the whole society would be subject to the control of criminal law'.[148] In addition, 'hardening the law shall not be the only way of catching big, organised criminals, because they always find a way to overcome the new regulations'.[149] On the other hand, 'for a criminal lawyer to say that a criminal law is made to protect the economic sector is shocking, but economic crimes also need to be tackled by criminal law, since they affect the economy and thus society, especially as society does not have the proper instruments to protect itself, not more than criminals who deal in narcotics'.[150] The use of criminal law to punish money laundering for the purpose of protecting the soundness of the global financial system or of the European internal market respectively, corresponds to the FATF and to the EU approaches too. In fact, according to respondents from the BMJV, 'these bodies do not always adequately take into consideration the necessity of balancing the prosecution of money laundering, corruption and other related offences, with the need for the State to respect the principle of proportionality, the privacy of its citizens, the personal and civil rights. Sometimes it is only Germany that raises these issues when the bodies hold their meetings. The problem is that states often send to such meetings professionals from the anti-money laundering sector who are convinced of the need to fight crime, and who are less concerned about the need to balance this interest with the rule of law and the respect for fundamental rights. Some delegates think of the FATF as an instrument that pressurizes their respective governments to advance its expert agenda politically'. The interviewee adds that 'this approach is highly problematic, since it is important to

[145] Interview with author 2014.

[146] Ibid.

[147] Ibid.

[148] Ibid.

[149] Ibid.

[150] Ibid.

maintain the law within the limits of our basic legal principles, as for example, the proportionality principle and data protection'.[151] It is further argued that at FATF meetings, 'when one tries to raise these issues, the others immediately think that he/she does not want to fight money laundering and wants to protect organised crime'.[152] Yet, the peculiarity of economic crimes and the massive impact that these have on society, requires a new approach that might collide with the traditional principles of criminal law. 'If one looks at the formulation of Article 261 of the GCC one can see that it mirrors these two contrary approaches, namely, on one hand the expansion of criminal law and on the other hand, the resistance towards criminalizing too broadly. The legislative debate shows the difficulty of mediating between the need of formulating a law in accordance with the principle of the rule of law in Germany, constitutional rights and the necessity of protecting the financial and the economic system from the infiltration of ill-gotten gains. The problem does not concern only Germany, it is rather a general issue: 'the financial system needs to be protected from the infiltration of illegal money; however, criminal law should not be the only instrument to do this'. In fact, 'the prevention of money laundering is much more important than its repression. But it costs more. In addition, the Anti-Money Laundering Act, despite requiring strict compliance from banks and other financial institutions, does not manage to completely prevent the infiltration of illegal money'.[153] Those advocating for a reduced use of criminal law do not actually underestimate the fight against money laundering, neither do they support the abstention of state control in the economy. What they are asking, in a way, is that lawmakers should limit the expectations raised by the criminal law by itself cannot deal adequately with illicit financial flows, since money flows are per se not criminal'.[154] The debate might find a compromise in the idea of tackling financial misbehaviours within a separate part of the criminal code that imposes administrative sanctions, as suggested by one respondent.[155]

7.3.5 Is It Possible to Tackle Illicit Financial Flows Without Conflicting with the Interests of a Free Market?

According to one respondent, 'through the financial crisis we have learned that the deregulation and the 'laissez faire' strategy have caused many problems, because they let finance reach the point where everything is allowed. This is why we need a clear distinction between illegality and legality'.[156] Therefore, the criminalisation of

[151] Ibid.
[152] Ibid.
[153] Ibid.
[154] Ibid.
[155] Ibid.
[156] Ibid.

money laundering should serve the purpose of reducing those situations of illegality that have consequently emerged due to the deregulation of the financial sector. Yet, given that from the point of view of the banks the deposit of money deriving from a crime into a bank account does not harm the bank itself, a conflict emerges between the interests of stopping illicit financial flows and the interests of allowing flows of money; indeed, as everyone knows '*pecunia non olet*', money has a neutral nature, observes the interviewee.[157] In addition, there are jurisdictions that do not mind receiving dirty money, 'for example those countries whose economies are based on foreign investment do not differentiate between licit and illicit in-flows'.[158] By assuring secrecy, such jurisdictions attract international investments and thus foster their economies. The interviewee maintains that the interest of some jurisdictions in stopping these flows of ill-gotten gains contrasts with the interests of other countries in taking advantage of such flows. Developing the argument even further, the attorney contends that 'abolishing the capitalist system would help reduce money laundering, because the capitalist economy aggravates the impact of illicit financial flows'. The capitalist system, from the point of view of the respondent, is thus an environment that favours money laundering. This clash between the claim for regulation and the demand for deregulation has already been highlighted in Part II with regard to the European law-making process. The tension emerged in the wording of the First Anti-Money Laundering Directive, which states that 'the lack of Community action against money laundering could lead Member States, for the purpose of protecting their financial systems, to adopt measures which could be inconsistent with completion of the single market'. The European Community, before and after the Union, were particularly concerned about the issue of money launderers taking special advantage of the freedom of capital movement and of the freedom of supplying financial services in the single market. Yet, the Community was concerned with the possible tendency of Member States implementing too restrictive measures limiting the free movement of capital. Thus, the common anti-money laundering control policy was introduced by way of avoiding Member States, while taking action to protect their own national economies from money laundering, from adopting measures inconsistent with the completion of the Internal Market. The European legislator seemed to have found a compromise while drafting the anti-money laundering policies. However, in the perception of the respondents the tension seems not to have been solved yet.

7.3.6 Considerations

Five principal conflicting situations have surfaced from the interviews. The first issue is the role played by external actors in the law-making process and the

[157] Ibid.

[158] Ibid.

constant influence exercised by those actors in the process of updating the policy. The imposition of a US approach to money-laundering control through the role of the FATF has also been highlighted in Part II. Specifically, some scholars see the development of a global prohibition regime fostered by the US in the diffusion of anti-money laundering law. These scholars argue that the powerful state creates an international regime focused on achieving its own goals through global acceptance triggered by the securitisation rhetoric and compliance processes.[159] The second conflict that emanates from the words of the respondents is the demands placed on criminal law to combat financial misconduct and the need to limit the tendency to expand the ambit of criminal law against the of the danger of financial instability. Given the previous deregulation of the market, policy makers need to control and sanction economic abuse in order to protect fair competition and law-abiding individuals. On the other hand, the state needs to respect fundamental principles, such as the rule of law and the principle of *ultima ratio* that imposes a restriction of the use of criminal law in situations in which no other measures are suitable. This conflict has already been raised along the formulation of the money-laundering offence with regard to the question of the interests protected by the law in Part III. However, no solution could be found. In fact, the question concerning the suitability of criminal law for tackling illicit financial flows is considered by this study as still unsolved. The matter does not only concern money-laundering control. On the contrary, it is a fairly widespread issue that has recently emerged due to the tendency of toughening the sanctions for economic crimes on the basis of the threat they constitute to the maintaining of financial stability. The third conflict can be summarised as follows: On the one hand, the policy is required to interfere with the personal sphere of suspected money launderers; on the other hand, private institutions are interested in protecting their relations with loyal and trusted customers. Therefore, they are reluctant to afford law enforcement authorities the possibility to interfere too much in their business. The interest manifested by the private sector involved in the prevention of money laundering seems thus to collide with the legislative intent of preventing the infiltration of dirty money by way of preventing gate-keepers to help money launderers.[160] At the same time, the privatisation of crime control is questionable, also from a governance point of view. It seems, therefore, that the public interest in the prosecution of crimes, through having access to personal information from the private sector, only marginally collides with the interest of protecting the right to privacy. The issue was also addressed during the national Parliamentary debate with regard to the degree of *mens rea* required to incur liability for the crime of money laundering. While one party was advocating for the criminalisation of gross negligence, the other parties opposed this proposal on the basis of the assumption that punishing gross negligent economic misbehaviours would have been cumbersome for ordinary business and for

[159] See for example Andreas and Nadelmann 2006. For a more complete overview on the literature, see Part II.
[160] BT-Drucks 12/989, p. 21.

the movement of goods and capitals, thus violating the interests of a free economic system. Making everybody taking part in economic or financial activities be actively involved in monitoring the economic system under the threat of criminal liability for negligent money laundering was considered harmful for the business market. The same debate has been picked up by legal scholars, too.[161] Yet, it seems that, despite the law being the result of negotiations, the question is still open.

The fourth issue concerns discordant opinions on the opportunity of including tax evasion as a predicate offence for money laundering. On one hand there is the interest of tackling tax evasion through the anti-money laundering regime, on the other hand there is the concern of keeping the two phenomena distinct in order to avoid an overrating of money laundering. Since the genesis of the anti-money laundering policy, some actors taking part in the international law-making process opposed the labelling of 'black money', naming money deriving from tax violations, as 'dirty money', which refers to all proceeds of crime typically committed by organised crime. This distinction was based on the perception that tax-related offences were less serious and less harmful than capital flight, and was advocated by financial centres in order to maintain a good reputation, while still offering peculiar financial services, such as bank secrecy. This issue is a good example of the labelling theory, to the extent that it shows how a practice that was firstly not considered criminal enough to amount to a predicate offence for money laundering, has become part of the scope of the anti-money laundering regime on the basis of a political decision of labelling it as such. Respondents of the current research have different perceptions of the degree of the seriousness of tax laws violations and thus about the appropriateness and necessity of tackling them under the umbrella of the anti-money laundering policy. Again, the matter that seemed to have been resolved through negotiations on an international and European level is still being debated at national level. The last conflict reflects the previous two on a macro-economic level. The two contrasting interests are the necessity of regulating the flows of money and the free movements of capital in a neo-liberal economy. The question is intrinsic in the nature of money laundering, which is a phenomenon that happens at the interface between legality and illegality. Regulations that facilitate the lawful exchange of goods, capital and services also facilitate the flow of ill-gotten gains; there are thus conflicting interests between the public interest of prosecuting crime and the desire for less regulation in a free market economy.

A key aspect of the money-laundering control strategy that ought to obstruct the infiltration of ill-gotten gains into the economic and financial sector, is the co-operation between gatekeepers and investigative authorities. However, this study has shown that by also improving anti-money laundering preventive mechanisms entails dealing with conflicting interests between private entities, such as the banks, companies, other financial and non-financial institutions, and public bodies, namely, law enforcement agencies. The shifting boundary between private and public spheres and interests affects not only money-laundering control. In fact, the

[161] See Part II, Sect. 2.3

central paradox of the global financial system is that, while a sound and stable economic and financial system is a public asset, banking and finance have always been treated as a private sphere. In the period often described as the era of financial deregulation, major transformation has taken place, such as the liberalisation of financial capital and the growth of the financial sector and its profitability. This process has been accompanied by the development of offshore systems. These changes have been facilitated by formalised regulation of financial institutions. In this context finance has become less regulated by public rules and more regulated in form of private self-regulation, generated by and among market participants themselves. This switch has led to the fact that regulations have followed private interests rather than public ones. New regulatory institutions, which have emerged in response to regulatory failure to exercise control over the forces leading to financialisation and speculation, and thus have generated new forms of risk and instability.

7.4 Perspectives on the Effectiveness of the Law

The respondents are asked to assess the effectiveness of the policy aimed at combating money laundering and organised crime. The interviews aim at elicit the views of legal experts on the effectiveness of the anti-money laundering policy. The interviewees are accordingly given neither a pre-determined definition of effectiveness nor of symbolic effectiveness. Given that the anti-money laundering policy has been in force for more than 20 years, the respondents' assessment is not to be interpreted as the potential effectiveness of the policy, but rather as the actual demonstrated effectiveness of the laws.

7.4.1 Is the Anti-Money Laundering (Law) Effective?

Some interesting data that has emerged from the interviews is that, while defence attorneys dealing with economic crimes have rather few cases relating to Article 261 of the GCC, investigators, prosecutors and public officials working in the specialised units deal with this provision on a daily basis. For example, from the lawyers' perspective, very vague allegations of money laundering makes the offence difficult to prove, to the advantage of suspects. Also, the lengths of sentences imposed for the basic conduct are considered to be very low. On the other hand, one senior prosecutor directing a department in Berlin exclusively responsible for money-laundering investigations states that usually around twenty-five STRs are dealt with daily'.[162] The STRs that arrive simultaneously at the FIU and at the

[162] Interview with author 2014.

public prosecutor's office trigger a preliminary investigation that has to be brought to a first clearance. After these preliminary investigations, which in the case of legal persons consist of a search in the company register, the cases arrive on my desk and I distribute them to the competent prosecutors. If there is enough evidence that further investigations would reveal more information about the alleged offence, the case proceeds, if there is no evidence, the procedure is closed and the case is considered solved'. Whereas the offence occupies the criminal justice authorities the whole day, for defence lawyers this is an exceptional situation. This discrepancy, in turn, has an impact on how the different legal role-players perceive the effectiveness of the law, as shall be shown below.

Defence attorneys are of the opinion that Article 261 of the GCC is not effective.[163] One attorney cynically comments as follows. 'As a defence attorney I am not unhappy about it'. Professional criminals in particular devise subterfuges in order not to avoid being brought within the reach of the law's preventive regulations and from being prosecuted for violating Article 261 of the GCC. The ineffectiveness of Article 261 is attributed to the inability of the overloaded criminal justice system to investigate and prosecute complex cases. Despite many proceedings are initiated on the basis of money-laundering offence charges for petty crimes, such cases do not meet the indirect target of the anti-money laundering policy, which is to convict professional criminals involved in complex money-laundering schemes and not to prosecute. According to one respondent 'in this year, out of the 18,000 STRs filed, only five cases involved big organised criminal activities. This shows that the effectiveness of the policy to detect organised crime has not improved despite the growing volume of information collected. The rest of the cases concerned petty criminals, yet the goal of the policy was to detect serious criminality. On the other hand, I know that there is the tendency to not report a client where only a minor offence is suspected. However, investigations of a minor offence can lead prosecutors can detect bigger cases. Therefore, it is important that the law imposes the duty to file STRs, also in cases of lesser offences. I believe that a reduction in the filing of STRs and thus a reduction in the number of money-laundering cases would actually improve the effectiveness of the anti-money laundering policy'.[164] However, another interviewee adds that 'although there have only been a handful of trials involving money launderers in which the accused were bankers, the provision should not be deleted'.[165] 'As far as I can judge, STRs filed on the basis of suspected terroristic activities are mostly proved wrong', which makes the policy ineffective in combating the financing of terrorism'.[166] Given that under Article 261 of the GCC, only minor offences are investigated, one can say that the indirect purpose of the provision has not been

[163] Ibid.

[164] Ibid.

[165] Ibid.

[166] Ibid.

accomplished. The inference can thus be drawn that both attorneys measured the effectiveness of the policy on its ability to achieve its indirect goals.

Senior prosecutor considers Article 261 of the GCC as 'one of the most unfortunate offences that the legislature included in the criminal code'.[167] Yet, the respondent has never considered how Article 261 could be improved, and has rather concentrated understanding of the categorisation of the provision, in order to make the work of the prosecutor easier. In fact, despite the complexity of the provision, financial investigations conducted in the specialised department are considered to be very efficient. Prosecutors have been motivated and seem to have actually figured out how to cope with this odd piece of legislation. Therefore, the overall evaluation on the work conducted by the personnel in the department is rather positive. Indeed the number of indictments, which is a factor that prosecutors usually take into consideration when measuring the effectiveness of a legal measure, is high. Against a badly drafted law, practitioners have thus managed to develop a strategy in order to comply with the existing framework in their daily work. Most cases involve less serious offences, as also proven by the prosecutors, but 'most serious cases remain in the dark', which does fulfil indirect policy goals as maintained by the attorneys interviewed, is not inconsistent with the wording of the norm. Therefore, it legitimizes the positive perception of the prosecutors with respect to their role. By refraining from any judgment on the formulation of the policy, prosecutors can comply with the law so that Article 261 results in being effectively implemented with respect to its direct function.

A positive assessment of the law's effectiveness is provided by investigators of the police department of Berlin. According to the police, the effectiveness of a provision corresponds to the clearance rate, which, as Part IV has shown, is very high for the money-laundering offence. Therefore, 'the low number of convictions pursuant to Article 261 of the GCC is not a symptom of a bad functioning criminal justice system. On the contrary, offenders are convicted for other crimes. The type of conviction does not play any role, what is relevant is the fact that the case has been concluded and that the assets can be confiscated. The goal of the German criminal justice system is, from the point of view of the police, is to reach a high clearance rate (*Aufklärungsquote*), which is based on conviction for any offence and confiscation'.[168] The Federal Ministry of the Interior sees the situation from the point of view of the federal police. 'According to the police, effectiveness corresponds to giving effect to the law in practice in the best way possible. Even though individuals are convicted for another offence, maybe the predicate offence, instead of for money-laundering offence, the result does not change. The important thing is to solve the case, while the type of charge is irrelevant. The goal is sanctioning perpetrators'.[169] Yet, according to the BMF, the difficulties that prosecutors face in tendering evidence of money laundering, accentuated by the complexity of financial

[167] Ibid.

[168] Ibid.

[169] Ibid.

transactions and by the fact that prosecutors are supposed to track the money back to the antecedent act, have an impact on the effectiveness of the law enforcement activities.[170] Despite the fact that prosecutors frequently handle money-laundering cases and receive a high number of STRs, only a few investigations are conducted on the basis of the information contained in the STRs.[171] For example, according to the prosecutors 'the mere suspicion of the illegal provenance of a high sum of cash suddenly deposited in the bank account of a low-income person (e.g. *Hartz-IV-Empfänger*, i.e. social grant recipient), would not suffice to receive an order to search the person's premises. Even though we could carry out the search, it would be very difficult to find evidence of the commission of a predicate offence and of the link between that offence and the suspicious transaction'. Therefore, proceedings are closed without the investigation leading to a charge of money laundering. However, proceedings for predicate offences might be initiated on the basis of the information collected. Yet, one respondents argues that 'it is absurd that proceedings often start with a charge of money laundering, because it allows for the use of more investigative instruments, but afterwards the charge is dismissed and the suspect is convicted of the predicate crime, which usually provides a higher sanction. I wonder whether this is actually legal'.[172] The crime is considered paramount by another interviewee because 'from a law enforcement perspective the offence is absolutely necessary, since it allows the use of fundamental procedural tools in this field'.[173] 'Even though it does not seem a completely legitimate mechanism, it is indeed very efficient'.[174]

With specific regard to the assessment of the effectiveness of money-laundering policy, the approach can be summarised as follows: 'The police have a different idea of efficiency than of political effectiveness. The process of assessment of the effectiveness of the anti-money laundering regime goes from bottom up. Instead of making an assessment at the federal level, every state reports practical problems and proposes improvements. There is no evaluation process but rather a debate about possible improvements. The question is not whether the law is effective or whether the goals have been achieved; the question is rather how law enforcement can improve the implementation of the law and overcome the impeding issues'.[175] This approach assumes the correctness of the policy. This notion of effectiveness can be compared to the concept '*Zielunabhängige Effizienz*' (goal-independent efficiency)

[170] BMF 'Stellungnahme des BMF zum Änderungsbedarf bei § 261 GCC und Defiziten in der Rechtspraxis aufgrund des Strafausschließungsgrundes des § 261 Abs. 9 S. 2 GCC bei der Selbstgeldwäsche'. VII A 3-VK 5160/06/000:005, 2013, p. 3 (unpublished).

[171] Interview with author 2014.

[172] Ibid.

[173] Ibid.

[174] Ibid. If one assumes that the policy was enacted with the function of allowing also the starting of other proceedings, one can infer that the legislation is indeed effective in achieving this effect. The same effect has been studied in relation to criminal law provisions in the field of terrorism. See Hawickhorst 2011.

[175] Ibid.

which was developed by German scholars.[176] The point of view of the 16 states and of the Ministry implies that the policy is directed at its implementation, without verifying whether it has any indirect functions. It is, indeed, one of the duties of the policymakers to design a policy that, if correctly applied, would lead to the desired indirect consequences. It cannot be expected that law enforcement, and in particular police forces, would question the suitability of the law. Their task is completely fulfilled through compliance. This does not exclude the possibility of improving the way the policy is implemented, however, this is limited to technicalities. It is, therefore, an approach that reduces the question of effectiveness to a technical matter.

Yet, the question is not as simple as it looks. Indeed, as Part II has highlighted, the debate about the functions attributed to the policy was very clear, and from the reconstruction of the law-making process it could not be possible to establish with certainty which the indirect functions were. Most probably the policy has several indirect functions. One of them is to punish predicate offences. In the words of a respondent 'the fight against money laundering is not a self-fulfilling mission. Instead, it has an indirect function, which is to eliminate predicate offences'. This goal has actually been achieved through Article 261 of the GCC. Investigations are initiated on the basis of a suspicion of money laundering and are afterwards continued for the predicate offences, because of the reasons presented in the previous parts. This makes the anti-money laundering policy actually a great instrument for the purpose of persecuting predicate offences because it facilitates the initial phase of the investigations by providing access to a range of information that would otherwise not be available. The Berlin investigators share this approach, in particular 'the purpose of the introduction of Article 261 GCC and of the Anti-Money Laundering Act was to facilitate the clearing of the predicate offences listed in Article 261(1) of the GCC. Proceedings are triggered by STRs and start with an allegation of money laundering. However, during the investigations, the charge is modified, usually in favour of a charge of one of the predicate offences, because of the prohibition to prosecute self-money laundering and because penalties for the other offences are higher than those provided for by Article 261 of the GCC. In this way the purpose of the law is fulfilled: the money-laundering offence has triggered investigations, which, thanks to the "follow the money" strategy, have led prosecutors to clarify the predicate offences. The scheme is as follows: from the illegal money—signalled through STRs to law enforcement agencies—investigators follow the paper trail to finally prosecute the predicate offence'.[177]

The respondents express rather positive opinions with regard to the effectiveness of the preventive regulations. It seems that even in this case the implementers of the law have developed practices that help the application of a rather complex law. Again, those who are called to apply the law on a daily basis find ways of coping with it in order to reduce the haze of the regulations. Resultantly, they are

---

[176] For the definition of '*Zielunabhängige Effizienz*', see Part I, Sect. 1.3

[177] Interview with author 2014.

compliant. As a consequence, if one considers effectiveness equivalent to a high degree of compliance, the regulatory body would score a high level of effectiveness. The investigators give the following example 'in the beginning banks were afraid of reporting suspicious transactions, because they feared a loss of reputation. Currently, instead, they file many STRs, because they are afraid of becoming victims of a money-laundering scheme and thus of being accused by the media of not being compliant with anti-money laundering regulations.[178] The interest in protecting the reputation of banking institutions has come to coincide with the interest of the preventive anti-money laundering regulations, at as far as compliance is concerned. Also 'companies perceive the threat that the offence poses and are willing to prevent damage to their reputation. The result is the same, namely, the prevention of money laundering'.[179] Whether the private sector is interested in complying not only in order not to be labelled as non-compliant and thus undermine its reputation, or whether actually shares the legislature's intent to preventing the infiltration of ill-gotten gains in the economy remains an open question. As a matter of fact, medium and big financial institutions that are concerned about their prestige comply with the regulations. The policy has thus found a way of being effective, at least with regard to the fulfilment of its direct function, namely, compliance with the regulations. The conclusion reached by the respondent assumes that private actors implementing the provisions of the Anti-Money Laundering Act correctly achieve the goal of preventing money laundering. Yet this has not always been shown to be true. Absolute compliance does not assure the accomplishment of the indirect functions of the policy. However, it is a political matter to verify this correlation. The law is effective because it can adapt to situations. 'Even though the law is far too complex and imposes a high burden on the industrial sector, so that the requirements cannot be completely fulfilled [...], the supervisory authorities are aware of the difficulties encountered by this sector, therefore the monitoring process is less stringent'.[180] In this sense, the Anti-Money Laundering Act is perceived by the respondent as effective, because it is a compromise between the two opposing needs. Indeed, 'if the law were less demanding and controls were more rigorous, the system would not have a deterrent effect'. In the opinion of the lawyer, the policy is effective because it manages to foster compliance among professions and businesses involved, despite being perceived by the latter as a burden. In this sense, the law has managed to partly solve the clash between the private interest of conducting business and the public interest of detecting money-laundering activities through the private sector.

Yet, a too high level of compliance could even frustrate the functions of the policy. In particular, according to one respondent 'this year the BKA has received about 18,000 STRs and they would like to reach the figure of 30,000 STRs per year in order to implement the law effectively. Yet increasing the number of STRs would

---

[178] Ibid.

[179] Ibid.

[180] Ibid.

actually lead to the consequence that the police would not be able to focus on those STRs that contain relevant information, because they would have to deal with the rest of STRs.'[181]

The effectiveness of the legislation is also evaluated from a more general perspective, as a policy embedded in a broader system. By considering the anti-money laundering legislation as a policy that involves different elements and that develops with time, the respondents' assessment is measurable. Especially from a dynamic perspective, a law's degree of effectiveness may vary during the course of its application. In fact, 'the public does not perceive the dangers of money-laundering; people rather perceive anti-money laundering regulations as a burden and as a measure that creates distrust of cash payments, which are actually not forbidden or limited in Germany'.[182] In this context, policymakers play an important role in assessing and reviewing the policy. Yet the legislature does not have the duty to review the implementation of the policy. Indeed, once the states have identified areas in which they can pursue improvements, they need to undertake this process on their own, since there is no feedback from the federal level. The Ministries cannot say whether the anti-money laundering regime is effective or not, because they do not possess enough figures to assess the policy.[183] Also, according to the FATF report of 2010, the legislature does not review the implementation of the anti-money laundering regime, and there is no evidence that overall reviews of effectiveness of the anti-money laundering system have been undertaken.[184] The FATF assessors have found out that authorities have no duty to report anti-money laundering matters to the Parliament, and none of the main policy ministries reported these matters in their annual report. According to the FATF report and to the report commissioned by the EU Commission in 2009, the German review mechanism consists mainly of periodical meetings.[185] Meetings are held, for example, among the heads of the financial investigation offices and heads of the asset recovery offices.[186] For instance, there are meetings between the authorities and associations and representatives from chambers of commerce (*Verbände und Kammervertretungen*) to discuss the potential difficulties in applying existing legal provisions, which have led to improvements in procedures. There are also regular meetings of the German delegation to the FATF, which have also been heard on proposals to amend legislation on the subject of money laundering. These meetings have the purpose of discussing and sharing information about emerging trends, best practices, effective techniques and experiences about how to deal with the

[181] Ibid.

[182] Ibid.

[183] Ibid.

[184] FATF 2010, p. 265.

[185] Deloitte, European Commission Final Study on the Application of the Anti-Money Laundering Directive, Service Contract ETD/2009/IM/F2/90, 2009, p. 139.

[186] FATF 2010, p. 110.

requirements successfully.[187] In fact, Article 44(1) of the Fourth Anti-Money Laundering Directive requires Member States to 'ensure that they are able to review the effectiveness of their systems to combat money laundering […] by maintaining comprehensive statistics on matters relevant to the effectiveness of such systems'.[188] Yet, the directive does not define the concept of effectiveness. National legislation in general does not provide a definition either.[189]

If some respondents believe that the policy's effectiveness can be inferred from the fact that there are many different public authorities that are involved in the prevention and repression of money laundering and organised crime,[190] others think that setting the legal framework is not enough.[191] In fact, 'in the USA, where cases like the one of the HSBC bank, which was sentenced to pay a high fine, the policy seems to be very effective. It is not the first time that this bank has been sued, and these facts might have a deterrent effect in the long term. It could be that, for example, in the next 10 years drug cartels would no longer know where to launder their money' concludes one respondent.[192]

7.4.2 *Is the Policy Effective in Deterring Organised Crime?*

One of the purposes of criminalising money laundering has been, from the start, to fight organised crime by making the commission of serious crimes less attractive through the threat of confiscation. It is thus interesting to verify whether legal actors and privileged observers perceive the law as being able to fulfil this function. Answers were sometimes ambiguous with respect to the deterrent capacity of the anti-money laundering policy to tackle organised criminal activities. In the research conducted by *Oswald* between 1993 and 1996 both prosecutors and credit institutions questioned the potential suitability of the policy either to infiltrate the structure of organised criminal networks or to deprive them of economic power. None of these goals were considered achievable by the majority (97%) of the interviewees through the law. In particular, 56% of the respondents considered the law only marginally suitable to impede the infiltration of illicit money into the lawful economy, or to diminish the economic power of organised crime. A total of 38.7% of the respondents stated the law was completely ineffective for this purpose. Prosecutors even questioned the very actual suitability of the two instruments to

[187] Ibid.

[188] Council Directive EU/2015/849, OJ L 141/73-115.

[189] The BaFin regularly undergoes an assessment. If it is found that improper implementation is widespread and therefore reflects more systemic problems, this would be published in the BaFin annual report.

[190] Interview with author 2014.

[191] Ibid.

[192] Ibid.

fight organised crime by preventing the infiltration of ill-gotten gains into the economy, given that organised crime groups do not leave traces of their illicit activities. According to the interviewees, in fact, professional criminals did not leave incriminating material, so the investigations were very often in vain. Therefore, aiming to fight organised crime through the implementation of anti-money laundering measures was considered a theoretical failure. In only 15% of the 380 analysed proceedings, further investigations were undertaken in order to gather more information of the contextual elements, and thus on the eventual criminal network acting behind offenders of the main criminal acts.[193] Respondents in this study had diverging opinions on this issue. According to one 'since most complex cases that are filed as suspicious transactions with the FIU are subsequently dismissed and do not reach the conviction phase, means that Article 261 of the GCC is applied mainly in trials related to "dis-organised crime" and only in very low-level criminal cases'.[194] In reality, according to prosecutors, most money-laundering cases are connected to fraud and tax crimes. Typical examples of fraud cases are phishing, the "nephew fraud", the "Romeo scam", and the "Nigerian Connection". The first one consists of elderly people living in the USA or in Australia with Polish surnames, who are contacted by a fictitious nephew, who would ask for financial help through a pretext, and the amount of money would be received by a "financial agent", who would then transfer it to the beneficiary. The "Romeo scam" functions in a similar way, but the victim is contacted for a dating purpose. The "Nigerian Connection" consists of individuals who, for instance, pretend to be American soldiers in Afghanistan and have found a treasure or have an inheritance to share, and who would then ask that money be remitted to them as a fee in advance for purposes of enabling the remitter of the funds to receive a share of the alleged treasure or inheritance sum. Also in these cases the "fees" paid by the victims are received by "financial agents" or deposited in fake bank accounts. In all these cases, individuals who accept to make their bank accounts available are at the same time perpetrators and victims of a larger money-laundering scheme. However, the criminal proceedings are meant to punish reckless conduct, namely, those who knew or should have known the illegal origin of the money. Investigations do not succeed in revealing the whole organised network behind the scheme.' Public prosecutors warn that even though in their work organised crime cases do not occur often, 'there are money-laundering cases dealt with in other departments, such as the organised crime division of the prosecution service that deals with drug smuggling and trafficking, human trafficking, cigarette smuggling and tax evasion perpetrated through the sale of gold. Organised crime also often lurks behind missing trader frauds (*Steuerkarruselen*). This year, for instance, we have not had any case relating to Article 261(4) of the GCC, and last year we had only one', said one prosecutor.[195]

[193] Oswald 1997, p. 293.

[194] Interview with author 2014.

[195] Ibid.

'The combination of Article 261 of the GCC and the Anti-Money Laundering Act has introduced a great change in the practice of persecuting organised crime: Whereas before the introduction of the laws investigators would have started from the predicate offence in order to trace the money in order to confiscate it, at present investigations are initiated on the suspicion of money with an illegal origin and then traced back the predicate offences. This novelty has made the fight against organised crime more effective'.[196] 'The Anti-Money Laundering Act is one of many tools in the fight against organized crime. Its rules provide the investigating authorities with useful and important paper trails'.[197] However, the two investigators emphasised that Article 129 of the GCC, which criminalises criminal associations, is statistically applied in very few cases and it has never been applied with respect to a money-laundering case. According to them 'the BKA definition of organised crime is also too restrictive, and there is no interest in classifying cases under this notion'. Lawyers are rather sceptical about the deterrent effect of the law against organised crime; they believe that 'Nobody who acts in an organised criminal group would ever think of not committing a crime in order not to become liable for money laundering'.[198]

The little use made of the law to counter organised crime was of concern to the FATF assessors as well. According to the 2010 report 'authorities have generally indicated that not much emphasis is being placed on prosecuting serious money laundering as an effective tool to tackle serious organized crime'.[199] Consequently, the assessors concluded that 'more efforts need to be put on raising awareness of the opportunity that money-laundering investigations and convictions represent to the general fight against organized crime'.[200] One of the obstacles that identified in the report was the impossibility of using some of the more intrusive special techniques of investigation on the grounds that the offence was categorised as a 'less serious offence.[201] In addition, the report confirms that there are relatively 'few investigations conducted on more complex structures, where professional money launderers may be acting separately from the people involved in the commission of the predicate offence, which is often the *modus operandi* for organized crime'.[202]

According to two respondents, the fact that Article 261 is not used to tackle organised crime is not a problem. In fact, 'the fight against organised crime is not a priority, therefore the law should not serve the purpose of tackling organised crime or drug criminality. These were priorities of other countries, such the USA. In Europe, however, anti-money laundering provisions are primarily directed at protecting the financial and economic system and its lawfully acting market

[196] Ibid.
[197] Ibid.
[198] Ibid.
[199] FATF 2010, p. 64.
[200] Ibid.
[201] Ibid., p. 116.
[202] Ibid., p. 115.

participants. In this context, fighting organised crime with repressive instruments fulfils this task only partially. German civil society is at the moment not severely threatened by organised crime related to drug trafficking or trafficking in human beings. These aspects of economic crime distort the public discussion about the real dimensions of money laundering and organised crime that impact on the economy'.[203] According to a respondent, most of the time money laundering is not committed by criminal groups, money-laundering offences are mostly committed in relation to economic crimes (*Wirtschaftskriminalität*), such as fraud, in which the perpetrators act either alone or constitute a few individuals and not organised criminal groups in the traditional understanding of the phenomenon 'organised crime'.[204]

7.4.3 Is Article 261 of the German Criminal Code (GCC) an Example of Symbolic Legislation?

The respondents are asked to express an opinion about the hypothesis that labels the anti-money laundering policy as a symbolic piece of legislation. Again, perceptions differ in relation to which functions respondents attribute to the policy. Also, while the answers provided were sometimes univocal (yes or no), the arguments show that the interviewees have rather nuanced opinions. The concept of symbolic legislation is understood by all respondents in a negative sense, which meant that a positive answer would accordingly have expressed a negative assessment of the policy.

Two respondents strongly oppose the idea that the policy is symbolic legislation by arguing that its importance consists in demarcating lawful and unlawful conduct. Therefore, 'it would be a catastrophe to delete Article 261, because it is very useful, at least, to describe what is legal and what is not, what people are allowed to do and what they are not'.[205] Also the Anti-Money Laundering Act is fundamental, because 'it defines clear red lines between legal and illegal economic activities'.[206] According to another respondent, 'the law is not symbolic because it is a boundary between lawful and unlawful activities; the question about the symbolic nature of the policy is a purely rhetorical scientific question, whereas Article 261 is an important and necessary landmark for the purpose of tackling money laundering'.[207] Especially because 'the motor of organised crime, which is the maximisation of profit by illegal means is not much different from what drives any profit-orientated company, Article 261 draws an indispensable clear distinction

[203] Interview with author 2014.

[204] Ibid.

[205] Ibid.

[206] Ibid.

[207] Ibid.

between illegality and legality.[208] The respondent grounds his arguments by pointing out the fact that the law creates a new paradigm that is supposed to prevent economic and financial activities conducted by non-criminal actors through subterfuges similar to those adopted by money launderers, which pose a danger to the economic system and thus to society. This is supported by the previously mentioned consideration of the need to avoid the increase of illegality within the financial sector which has been made possible by the process of market deregulation undertaken in the last 30 years. Concluded in summary the law has a deterrent function that cannot be defined as symbolic.

A second counter-argument raised by several respondents was that the anti-money laundering policy has triggered substantial activities in the realm of creating expertise and specialised authorities and routines, both within the public and private sectors. In the view of the respondents, this argument shows that the policy has had a strong instrumental impact and thus cannot be defined as symbolic. From a criminal justice system perspective, great efforts are made by law enforcement authorities to detect, investigate and prosecute money-laundering cases.[209] A whole new legal apparatus has been created to comply with the policy. The police department of Berlin, for instance, has deployed great expertise in this field and among practitioners who work on a daily basis with the anti-money laundering policy. This exercise cannot be simply symbolic. The same can be said of role-players involved in preventing money laundering as ordained by the Anti-Money Laundering Law. A Ministry representative emphasised in particular that the Anti-Money Laundering Law has had considerable effects in the sense that 'the whole preventive regulation that requires financial institutions to comply has a great impact on business. Banks have been convicted and have had to pay very high fines, and this cannot be called symbolic politics, because the law has practical consequences'. Hence, the burden placed on credit institutions to comply with anti-money laundering regulations is perceived as an instrumental effect of the policy. In addition, 'sanctions, too, imposed on non-compliant institutions in case of violations of the regulations are instrumental'. The policy does not have mere symbolic effectiveness, neither the 'other anti-money laundering measures, for example, the sophisticated rules of the Banking Act, the Insurance Supervision Act etc. have an impact on the entire economic and financial sector, and are therefore far from being symbolic laws'.[210] The commitment of those who are obliged by the Anti-Money Laundering Law to take part actively participate in the prevention of money laundering and in the work of the local supervisory authorities cannot be called symbolic.[211]

The creation of specialised units and of new expertise in order to comply with the money-laundering control standards was, however, seen differently by

---

[208] Ibid.

[209] Ibid.

[210] Ibid.

[211] Ibid.

respondents. The representative of the Ministry of Finance thought that 'the prevention of money laundering has become a business sector in itself. Companies and financial institutions have specific departments that undergo due diligence, and there is, therefore, a new professionalism that has been created'. The creation of a new professionalism was an aspect mentioned by the respondents in *Oswald*'s interviews. This was seen, at the dawn of the new policy, as a positive development which would strengthen the ability of law enforcement agencies to 'follow the paper trail'. A defence attorney is more critical of the creation of an exclusive apparatus and the development of specialist anti-money laundering personnel, arguing that this was an indicator of symbolic legislation. The attorneys believe that the anti-money laundering policy, and especially the FATF, has created opportunities for nurturing a new brand of remunerative professionalism and job positions. Scholars too have interpreted this proclaimed effect of the policy as an attempt to give the appearance that something has been achieved, while the practical declared effects have not.

Police forces disagree with the hypothesis of a symbolic piece of legislation by saying that 'the efforts that have been undertaken so far to prevent and repress money laundering cannot be defined as symbolic, because Article 261 makes it easier to investigate predicate offences. Therefore, the law is not symbolic; it has, at least, the instrumental function of facilitating investigations.[212] Given that one of the legislature's intentions was to reduce the number of predicate offences, respondents had a point in stating that the law leads to instrumental desired effects. Other respondents adopt this viewpoint as well. In fact, according to them, the anti-money laundering policy is primarily directed at reducing predicate crimes. This idea has already been presented above with regard to the perceptions on the policy's effectiveness. Yet, the function of facilitating the detection of predicate offences does not seem to explain fully the burden imposed by the policy, as noted above. In addition, attributing investigative functions to a substantive provision of criminal law does not seem a plausible, as acknowledged by *Henn* and legal scholars.[213]

Respondents from Ministry of Justice believe that the law was the result of a compromise in a positive sense, as results of a functioning democracy. 'It is the result of political compromise, as much as, for example, another criminal law provision, namely, Article 100a of the Code of Criminal Procedure that regulates telephone tapping'.[214] For this reason 'the law might not be 100% coherent. It

[212] Ibid.

[213] See the hypothesis on the potential use of Article 261 of the GCC for investigative purposes described in Part IV.

[214] Interview with author 2014. Article 100 of the German Code of Criminal Procedure has given rise to lively debate in Germany because investigations conducted by way of telephone tapping are considered to be too invasive of the personal sphere and thus violate the right to privacy of the individuals.

might even be a bit contradictory and may have some loopholes that make its application difficult 'but only because it was the result of a parliamentary compromise, yet it cannot be would called symbolic'.[215] This is thus an example of a democratic exercise.

The 2010 FATF report identified the FIU as a specific anti-money laundering authority with symbolic effectiveness. The assessors were of the opinion that it seems as the FIU was established to carry out kinds of symbolic functions of an analytical nature, elaborating the guidelines and publishing reports. The report further stated that the FIU makes only a modest contribution to the substantiation of suspicions of money laundering'.[216] The announced reform, which will move the FIU from the BKA to the customs might lead to more effective action.

7.4.4 Considerations

Given the fact that the anti-money laundering enactment prompts many preliminary investigations, investigators have to deal with it on a daily basis. This, in turn, influences the positive views of respondents regarding how the law was being implemented. The common ground on which respondents asserted their positive view was that it was that although it is not easy to implement the anti-money laundering law, those entrusted with applying the law in practice have devised means of making it workable. Defence lawyers specialised in the area of economic crimes, on the other hand, tended to have a negative perception of the effectiveness of the anti-money laundering law, also because they saw the law as being unable to achieve its indirect goals.

Diverse notions of effectiveness found in disciplines close to the sociology of law, and the different definitions of effectiveness given by sociologists of law, which were illustrated in Part I, turn out to be useful here. Particularly the notions of 'efficiency' and of 'efficiency regardless of the goals' prove to be very useful in interpreting the respondents' opinions. Efficiency is, from an administrative law point of departure, the optimal relation between the goals achieved and the instruments used. A sub-category of this concept is the efficiency measured by way of a cost-effectiveness analysis, some examples of which were given in Part IV, according to which efficiency is defined as the functioning of a legal order without evaluating the goals achieved. This type of analysis focuses on the correctness of the operating system since the purpose of the system is its own existence. It refers to a whole legal order rather than to a specific single provision. Given that the anti-money laundering policy constitutes a legal order, due to the diverse regulations involved and the competent authorities created in order to achieve the goals of the policy, this notion can be applied. In the field of administrative legal theories,

[215] Interview with author 2014.

[216] FATF 2010, pp. 105–106.

Part I has focussed on the approach that makes the (in)effectiveness of a law dependent on its (failing) enforcement. In fact, a high degree of compliance with the anti-money laundering legislation might correspond to a high level of effectiveness of the policy with respect to its direct function, but at the same time to a rather low level of effectiveness with regards to its indirect purposes. The way to evaluate the degree of effectiveness is therefore also different. While compliance with legal provisions is calculated through a quantitative assessment of the processes in force and of the functioning of the system, the achievement of the indirect functions is measured by evaluating the impact of the policy. Respondents had different perceptions about the indirect functions of the law as well. This shows once again that the anti-money laundering law was a result of a compromise between different expectations and that the legislature was not able to limit the scope of its application to a particular goal. The different expectations and intents, which already emerged in the doctrinal debate about the legally protected interests, appear again in the different perceptions of the interviewees. The respondents were asked about the legislation's effectiveness with regard to one of the indirect functions, namely, the capacity to deter organised crime. The legislature enacted the money-laundering offence in the context of the fight against drug trafficking and other forms of organised crime, thus the declared rationale underpinning Article 261 of the GCC is the prevention and repression of organised crime.

Respondents were finally asked whether or not the anti-money laundering provisions have a latent symbolic function, apart from the declared function of preventing and repressing money laundering. Their attitudes varied, with some agreeing that the law has merely a symbolic function and others strongly negating this hypothesis. The latter argued instead that the law is instrumentally effective in respect of their daily work, which cannot be defined as purely symbolic. According to most respondents, the law cannot be defined as symbolic, because it has led to instrumental effects. Firstly, information gathered, thanks to the Anti-Money Laundering Act, is used to start preliminary investigations under Article 261 of the GCC. Secondly, the organs created to give effect to the anti-money laundering policy are real and visible and their existence cannot be denied. Thirdly, the law is considered necessary because it labels a deviant behaviour. In particular, despite the fact that investigations do not lead to a conviction for money laundering, they allow investigators to collect information in support of criminal cases for the predicate offences or to start a preliminary investigation into the alleged commission of a predicate offence. In this sense, the function of the 'law in action', despite being questionable, is objectively instrumental. However, the fact that the law serves the purpose of tackling predicate offences through the support of investigations does not exclude the hypothesis that the law was enacted to pursue latent functions too. It is not necessary that the latent goal is the only one that plays a role, but it is necessary that the other purposes would not explain the analysed phenomenon completely.[217] Indeed, those who said that the law does not have a symbolic function also said that the results achieved through compliance do not

[217] Merton 1983, p. 201.

legitimate the burden imposed by the legislation. In other words, it seems that they recognise that the purpose of compliance cannot completely explain the policy makers' motivation, which re-opens the doors for the hypothesis of the existence of latent functions. In fact, such a demanding policy cannot be accepted for the sole purpose of re-enforcing the action of the criminal justice system in tackling predicate offences. On the other hand, compliance with the policy in terms of building of an organisational structure and of expertise does not automatically mean fulfilling the policy's purpose. Particularly the creation of new professionalism has been interpreted by scholars as an indicator to the public that the policy has produced certain effects. Finally, arguments stressing the fact that the law is a necessary landmark demarcating what is lawful and what is not can be interpreted also as supporting the hypothesis of a symbolic piece of legislation by attaching a positive connotation to the concept. According to this perspective, constitutional laws, for example, can have a strong positive symbolic effectiveness by laying down values and principles. However, in order for such principles to be put into effect and to enhance the rights of people in reality, they need to be validated in practice, otherwise they will remain empty promises; therefore, regulations that implement principles should have a more instrumental effectiveness.

7.5 General Considerations

Given the abundant literature on the ineffectiveness of the anti-money laundering regime to in achieving its goal, hypothesis undergirding this study was that especially the money-laundering offence, as drafted by the German legislature, was a purely symbolic provision, the function of which was to reach a compromise among political parties, to publicly declare the laundering of proceeds of crime as wrong, and to impart to the public the impression that something was being done. The hypothesis derived from an analysis socio-legal theories on the symbolic effectiveness of the law, and on the literature criticising the current anti-money laundering system. The socio-legal concept of symbolic legislation was especially adopted to explain why the law might not be an adequate tool to block the infiltration of illicit financial flows, despite its having amended and improved so often.

The discovery process, which started from the assumption that anti-money laundering legislation is necessary to protect fair competition in the economy, also revealed that whether money laundering is good or bad depends on the perspective of those who evaluate it. The diverse opinions on the phenomenon influence the functions attributed to the measures adopted to deter and punish money laundering. In other words, social actors have different expectations of the anti-money laundering provisions, both in regard to their introduction and implementation. Moreover, some hindrances deriving from the formulation of the offence, which does not explicitly specify the legal interests it seeks to protect. It is way too broadly worded and wide in scope, and which do not harmonise well with the existing legal framework. All these factors actually obstruct a complete acceptance of the new provision by legal scholars and role-players in the law, thus hindering its effective application. In particular, given the diverse and sometime conflicting opinions expressed manifestly or latently by lawmakers discussed in Part II, it has been hypothesised that the legislation was the result of many compromises. Due to the strong pressure placed on national legislatures by international, transnational and European legal instruments to implement them at national level, and against the background national parliaments enacting emergency criminal laws in recent years, especially with regard to combating organised crime, it was hypothesised that the money-laundering offence was formulated with urgency and to play a more symbolic function. In addition, given the securitisation rhetoric surrounding money laundering, which depicts grim scenarios and the most daunting challenges confronting financial systems and economies across the world, this book assumed that the criminalisation of such conduct could have served other policy goals of international governance.

Yet the case study has proven the initial hypothesis wrong. In fact, the German anti-money laundering law, besides having a symbolic function, does in fact have an instrumental effect in practice. The qualitative analysis of criminal statistics and economic figures, in particular, shows that Article 261 of the GCC has been applied quite often in criminal cases and thus cannot be described as having a purely symbolic effectiveness. From the interviews it emerged that the provision has a massive impact on the daily work of some actors in the field of law, and that there are instrumental effects that cannot be overlooked. An example here is the facilitated collection of information for the purpose of commencing preliminary criminal investigations. In addition, the combination of the offence with the preventive regulations may display a deterrent effect and thus positively impact the effectiveness of the criminal provision too. In the perception of respondents, the existence of a complex apparatus to prevent money laundering is a sign that the legislation is not purely symbolic and that it is actually efficient. Given the extreme complexity of the standards, once compliance is achieved, the perception of actors involved is that the goal is fulfilled. Thus, compliance becomes the goal. The question is not about the effectiveness of the regulations but rather about the efficiency of the structure. The goal of the structure becomes its existence. The ultimate purpose is not to impede the laundering of proceeds of crime, but rather to make any suspicious transaction (customer) traceable and thus kept under control. Even though investigations do not manage to reveal the networks or the single perpetrators operating behind those who are caught as money launderers, suspects are identified, charged and convicted. Cases are indeed resolved. What is more, information gathered through the anti-money laundering regime is used in other criminal proceedings as well. This further supports the idea that the law triggers instrumental effects. However, as long as the offence is used to prosecute '*Bauernopfer*' (sacrificial lambs)[218] it does not seem to be able to fulfil its indirect purpose.

[218] Term used by Münch to describe the phenomenon of innocent private persons' bank accounts used by offenders to launder money through 'financial agents'. See Münch T, Bauernopfer. Wie Privatleute zur Geldwäsche missbraucht werden. Sächsische Zeitung, 20/02/2016.

Given that the conduct was not considered a crime before the 1970s, one can infer that there was indeed a need to outlaw the further use of assets with a criminal provenance. According to the respondents, the anti-money laundering law has introduced a novel way of dealing with those profits from crime. It is not only directed at punishing criminals pumping dirty money into the lawful economy, but also at combating the growth of unlawful practices in the economy which been spawned by deregulation of economies over the past 30 years. The interviewees pointed out especially that, while companies operate to make profit, they do not behave dissimilarly to criminals. But the offence of money laundering relies on what has been already labelled by the criminal justice system as unlawful. In fact, the provision punishes actions related to the proceeds of unlawful acts, namely, acts that are already listed as offences under the German criminal law. Article 261 of the GCC does not regulate the process of making profits; it blocks unlawfully made profits from entering the legitimate economy in order to generate more unlawful profits. Therefore, it does not introduce a criminal label for certain ways in which profits are made immorally or unfairly. Hence, the goal of reducing illegality in the financial sector is limited to the boundaries of acts already labelled under the German law as deviant. An example would be a company that adopts an aggressive tax avoidance policy to the point of not to pay taxes despite having made huge profits. While the conduct sounds immoral, it does not amount to a crime given that tax avoidance is not unlawful. In this context the anti-money laundering policy cannot intervene, because it cannot create new types of criminal behaviour.[219] The scope of action of the offence is thus limited to what national governments already labelled as unlawful.

Thus, the policy has generated compliance in the 23 years of implementation, and has therefore fulfilled its direct function. However, it has not impeded the infiltration of illicit financial flows in the country, and therefore it has not achieved its indirect purpose. The impossibility of eliminating the infiltration of illegal capital in the licit economy might have been caused by factors other than the ineffective of the law. It can be hypothesised that those who designed the law knew from the start that would be impossible stop the flow of ill-gotten gains into the country completely by criminalising money laundering. Having said this, the purpose of protecting the soundness of the global financial system appears to be too ambitious.

[219] The example is described in a report published by Action Aid on 'aggressive tax avoidance' carried out by the second biggest brewery in the world, SAB Miller. The multinational corporation, through a system of misinvoicing managed not to pay taxes on the profits made in Ghana, by declaring a profit equivalent to zero. This was shown not to be true by the report that revealed that, while the company based in Ghana registered no profit, the sister companies based in tax havens did. Actually, the Ghanaian company managed to move almost all of its profits to those countries through misinvoicing. This scheme is about tax avoidance and not evasion. Yet, while being perfectly legal, it does not seem very fair. See Action Aid 2012.

References

Action Aid (2012) Calling Time. https://www.actionaid.org.uk/sites/default/files/doc_lib/calling_time_on_tax_avoidance.pdf. Last accessed on 16 September 2016.

Alldridge P (2001) Are Tax Offences Predicate Offences for Money-Laundering Offences? Journal of Money Laundering Control 4 (4): 350–359.

Andreas P, Nadelmann E (2006) Policing the Globe: Criminalization and Crime Control in International Relations. University Press, Oxford.

BaFin (2012) BaFin: Jahresbericht 2012. www.bafin.de/SharedDocs/Downloads/DE/Jahresbericht/dl_jb_2012.pdf?__blob=publicationFile&v=5. Last accessed on 16 September 2016.

Baker R W (2005) Capitalism's Achilles heel. Dirty money and how to renew the free market system. John Wiley & Sons, New Jersey.

BKA (2012) Managementfassung zur Fachstudie „Geldwäsche im Immobiliensektor in Deutschland". https://www.bka.de/SharedDocs/Downloads/DE/UnsereAufgaben/Deliktsbereiche/GeldwaescheFIU/fiuFachstudieGeldwaescheImmobiliensektor.html. Last accessed on 16 September 2016.

BMF (2013) Stellungnahme des BMF zum Änderungsbedarf bei § 261 GCC und Defiziten in der Rechtspraxis aufgrund des Strafausschließungsgrundes des § 261 Abs. 9 S. 2 GCC bei der Selbstgeldwäsche. VII A 3-VK 5160/06/000:005 (unpublished).

Bussman K (2015) Dark figure study on the prevalence of money laundering in Germany and the risks of money laundering in individual economic sectors. http://wcms.itz.uni-halle.de/download.php?down=41244&elem=2937177. Last accessed on 16 September 2016.

Dalla Chiesa F (2012) L'impresa mafiosa. Tra capitalismo violento e controllo sociale. Cavallotti University Press, Milan.

Deloitte (2009) European Commission Final Study on the Application of the Anti-Money Laundering Directive. Deloitte (2009) European Commission Final Study on the Application of the Anti-Money Laundering Directive, Service Contract ETD/2009/IM/F2/90. Last accessed on 16 September 2016.

FATF (2010) Mutual Evaluation Report of Germany. http://www.fatf-gafi.org/media/fatf/documents/reports/mer/MER%20Germany%20full.pdf. Last accessed on 16 September 2016.

FATF (2012) International standards on combating money laundering and the financing of terrorism & proliferation. FATF Recommendations. http://www.fatf-gafi.org/media/fatf/documents/recommendations/pdfs/FATF_Recommendations.pdf. Last accessed on 16 September 2016.

FATF (2014) 3rd Follow-up Report of Germany. http://www.fatf-gafi.org/media/fatf/documents/reports/mer/FUR-Germany-2014.pdf. Last accessed on 16 September 2016.

Global Agenda Council on Organised Crime (2012) Enablers of organised crime. http://reports.weforum.org/organized-crime-enablers-2012/#chapter-enablers-of-money-laundering. Last accessed on 16 September 2016.

Hawickhorst K (2011) § 129a StGB-ein feindstrafrechtlicher Irrweg zur Terrorismusbekämpfung: Kritische Analyse einer prozessualen Schlüsselnorm im materiellen Recht. Duncker & Humblot, Berlin.

Henn et al. (2013) Schattenfinanzzentrum Deutschland. Deutschlands Rolle bei globaler Geldwäsche, Kapitalflucht und Steuervermeidung, available at http://www2.weed-online.org/uploads/schattenfinanzzentrum_deutschland.pdf. Last accessed on 16 September 2016.

Implementation Review Group of the United Nations Convention against Corruption (2011).

Irvin B, Levi M (eds) (2009) Assessing the effectiveness of EU Member States' practices in the identification, tracing, freezing and confiscation of criminal assets. European Commission, Final Report. http://ec.europa.eu/dgs/home-affairs/what-is-w/news/pdf/final_asset_recovery_report_june_2009_en.pdf. Last accessed on 16 September 2016.

Levi M (1998) Perspectives on 'Organised Crime': An Overview. The Howard Journal of Criminal Justice 37 (4): 335–345.

Kaufmann J (2011) Mafia, Ein Parasit befällt Europa. Mitteilungen des Hamburgischen Richtervereins 4: 45.

Masciandaro D (1999) Money Laundering: The economics of regulation. European Journal of Law and Economics 7: 2–38.

Masciandaro D (2000) The illegal sector, Money Laundering and the legal economy: A macroeconomic analysis. Journal of Financial Crime 8 (2): 103–112.

Meinzer M (2016) Macht hoch die Tür für anonyme Firmen? Deutsche Richterzeitung 94: 5–175.

Merton R K (1983) Teoria e struttura sociale 1. Teoria sociologica e ricerca empirica. Il Mulino, Bologna.

Oswald K (1997) Die Implementation gesetzlicher Massnahmen zur Bekämpfung der Geldwäsche in der Bundesrepublik Deutschland: Eine empirische Untersuchung des § 261 StGB i.V.m. dem Geldwäsche. Max-Planck-Institut für ausländisches und internationales Strafrecht, Freiburg.

Pieth M (1993) "Symbolische Gesetzgebung" gegen Geldwäscherei und organisiertes Verbrechen? Vortrag am 17. Deutschen Strafverteidigertag, Münster, 7. - 9.5.1993. In: Strafverteidiger-vereinigungen, Organisationsbüro der Strafverteidigervereinigungen (ed.) Rechtsstaatliche Antworten auf neue Kriminalitätsformen. Der Andere Buchladen, Cologne, pp. 99–106.

Savona E, Riccardi M (eds) (2015) From illegal markets to legitimate businesses: the portfolio of organised crime in Europe. Final Report of Project OCP - Organised Crime Portfolio. http://www.transcrime.it/wp-content/uploads/2015/12/ocp.pdf. Last accessed on 16 September 2016.

Schröder C (2013) Warum die Selbstgeldwäsche straffrei bleiben muss. Berliner Wissenschaft Verlag, Berlin. English translation: Schröder C (2013) Why self-money laundering must remain exempt from punishment. Berliner Wissenschaft Verlag, Berlin.

Unger B, Addink H, Walker J, Ferwerda J, van den Broek M, Deleanu I (2013) ECOLEF final report, available at http://www2.econ.uu.nl/users/unger/ecolef_files/Final%20ECOLEF%20report%20(digital%20version).pdf. Last accessed on 16 September 2016.

Unger B, Ferwerda J, van den Broek M, Deleanu I (2014) The Economic And Legal Effectiveness Of The European Union's Anti-Money Laundering Policy. Edward Elgar Publishing Limited, Cheltenham.

Part V
Conclusions

Prima arrivano i loro soldi,
poi arrivano loro con i loro metodi.[1]
Falcone 1991, p. 18

[1]Own translation: First their monies *-the Mafiosi's-* come, then they arrive with their methods.

Chapter 8
Conclusions

Your businessman is my money launderer.

The empirical research has revealed that while some of the declared goals underlying the 'follow the money' strategy have not been completely fulfilled, which leads to the inference that the law is ineffective, its existence can be justified in the light of its latent functions.

The findings of this study lead to the conclusion that describing the money-laundering offence as a law with pure symbolical effectiveness does not reflect the complexity of the matter, for the anti-money laundering law does in fact instrumental effects. In fact, some see the law as being actually effective.

There are different interpretations about what purposes the law should serve. The assessment of effectiveness varies depending on whether the outcomes are the indirect elimination of illicit financial flows and protection of the integrity of the financial system, or whether they are the attainment of the direct goal of achieving compliance in the implementation of the law.

However, some declared functions attributed to it were too ambitious, for instance stopping the proceeds of crime from infiltrating the so-called 'legitimate economy'. From the very beginning controversy has surrounded the determining of the boundary between an areas defined as 'criminal' and those defined as spaces of 'legality'. In fact, money has a neutral nature: *pecunia non olet*. The protection of a free market is a very strong interest for both private and public entities, which sometimes collides with the one of eliminating illicit financial flows. In contemporary industrialised economies, there is a complicated and sometimes shifting boundary between legal and illegal transactions. This is particularly exacerbated in the context of financial capitalism, which 'subordinates the capitalist productive process to the circulation of money and monetary assets and hence to the accumulation of money profits'. The offshore financial system owes much to the tolerance, collusion and support of regulatory authorities in the leading countries, while some countries at the margins of the global economy have market niches in laundering and sheltering illicit financial flows. While one can assume that the current financial system is just and acceptable, and that money laundering is harmful because it interferes with the existing economic order, one can also assume

V. Zoppei, *Anti-Money Laundering Law: Socio-Legal Perspectives on the Effectiveness of German Practices*, International Criminal Justice Series 12,
DOI 10.1007/978-94-6265-180-7_8

that the capitalist system leads inherently to injustice and inequality, and that money laundering is actually embedded in this profit-oriented system and just represents the darker side of the capitalist economy. To use Hetzer's words: 'In einer Gesellschaft deren Selbstverständnis sich in der Gewinnmaximierung erschöpft, ist die Organisierte Kriminalität mindestens latent'.[1] A compromise viewpoint is the one that describes money laundering as an accepted collateral effect of the capitalist system, that is to say, 'a certain amount of illicit financial flows may be considered an acceptable price to pay for a market where free mobility of capital is guaranteed'. By this is meant a financial system in which the free circulation of capital is guaranteed, and in which financial systems compete with one another in attracting new investments and making profit. This activity, which often consists of a 'race to the bottom' with regard to regulations, is a perfect environment for money launderers. In other words, money laundering is at least exacerbated by the capitalist system.

Given that tightening and expanding domestic laws may just move criminality to less regulated sectors or geographical areas, regulations in the field of money-laundering control have been enacted through transnational policy-making processes. However, transnational anti-money laundering policy is an example of a regime that has been imposed across the world through an ad hoc body whose binding capacity has showed itself to be stronger than that of other international institutions, but whose democratic legitimation is rather controversial. Indeed, the established framework mirrors current controversial patterns of transnational soft law-making processes: In the international system, there has been a shift from formal law to 'quasi-legal forms', which are typically referred to as 'soft law', as opposed to 'hard law'. The research has indeed highlighted that, through the use of 'soft law', the anti-money laundering regime has been used to impose priorities on the international political agenda, and is bolstered by governments belonging to the 'club of rich countries'. In this way, the most powerful states typically determine which financial flows are illicit and which of the illicit flows are at the top of the political agenda. Money laundering and the policies to tackle it thus reflect broader power asymmetries in the international system.

In order to stop the 'race to the bottom' by harmonising regulations within the Union, the EU has adopted common policies in the field of money laundering. However, the growth of the EU in the post-World War II era is often seen as a result of co-operation aimed at achieving social solidarity, but contrary to such expectations, the European effort has focused more on 'economic unity'. In fact, while aiming at harmonising anti-money laundering legislation within the Union, European lawmakers have made sure that such legislation would have not been cumbersome for the creation of the free Single Market. If it is true that 'there are certainly inherent limits to how much states can deter and forbid illegal cross-border economic activities, especially if they wish to maintain open borders and societies',

[1] Hetzer 2001, p. 38. Own translation: In a society in which the maximisation of profit is seen as self-evident, organised crime is at least latent.

it is also true that today borders have been closed for natural persons while capital and legal persons can cross national borders freely.

This study has highlighted the technical hindrances that might soon be removed through legal reforms, also in response to the debate triggered by the recent global investigation known as the Panama papers. However, the findings on the inherent political, economic and financial conflicting interests that hamper a higher level of effectiveness and that require policymakers to adopt a different approach towards illicit financial flows, can assist prospective researchers further in interpreting future changes in the law. This book serves as an instrument with which to interpret critically forthcoming developments through the methodological definition set for the empirical analysis.

References

Falcone G (1991) Cose di Cosa Nostra. Rizzoli, Milan.

Hetzer W (2001) Organisierte Kriminalität und Korruption. Schattenseiten der Globalisierung. Aus Politik und Zeitgeschichte B 32-33/2001. http://www.bpb.de/apuz/26102/organisierte-kriminalitaet-und-korruption?p=all. Last accessed on 16 September 2016.

Index

V. Zoppei, *Anti-Money Laundering Law: Socio-Legal Perspectives on the Effectiveness of German Practices*, International Criminal Justice Series 12,
DOI 10.1007/978-94-6265-180-7

MIX
Papier aus verantwortungsvollen Quellen
Paper from responsible sources
FSC® C105338

If you have any concerns about our products,
you can contact us on
ProductSafety@springernature.com

In case Publisher is established outside the EU,
the EU authorized representative is:
Springer Nature Customer Service Center GmbH
Europaplatz 3, 69115 Heidelberg, Germany

Printed by Libri Plureos GmbH
in Hamburg, Germany